Beyond the Numbers

Making Data Work for Teachers & School Leaders

Additional Praise

In any data-driven culture, early warning indicators of student performance are critical in order for timely, corrective action to be taken so that desired results are achieved. Dr. White's "canaries in a coal mine" strategies for acquiring this information should be in every school's repertoire of practice.

Dr. Karen Gould
Assistant Superintendent
Metropolitan District of Wayne Township
Wayne Township, Indiana

Dr. White has written a book that contains numerous common-sense approaches to improving the education of children. Through examples and work activities, the readers will not only expand their knowledge but will have practiced the steps needed for educational reform.

Change in education will only come if the stakeholders are informed about how change can occur. This book gives the reader a variety of options through which change can be implemented.

Gary Meers, Ed.D.
University of Nebraska-Lincoln
Lincoln, Nebraska

Beyond the Numbers

Making Data Work for Teachers & School Leaders

Stephen H. White

LEAD+
LEARN
PRESS

Lead + Learn Press

317 Inverness Way South, Suite 150

Englewood, Colorado 80112

Phone +1.866.399.6019 ■ Fax 303.504.9417

www.LeadandLearnPress.com

Library of Congress Cataloging-in-Publication Data:

White, Stephen H.; 1949 –

    Beyond the numbers : making data work for teachers & school
leaders / Stephen H. White

      p. cm.

Includes bibliographical references and index.

    ISBN 978-0-9644955-4-8 (pbk.)

    1. Educational statistics—United States. 2. Educational indicators—United
States. 3. Educational evaluation—United States. 4. Educational accountability—
United States. I. Title

LB2846.W439 2005

379.1'58—dc22   2004062677

Printed in the United States of America

12 11 10 09 08   04 05 06 07 08 09

Dedicated to

Jonathan—

Back from the brink

Acknowledgments

Beyond the Numbers is based on more than thirty years of experience in public education and the expertise, insights, and faith in students and teachers that are so evident at The Leadership and Learning Center. My association with this extraordinary organization has had a dramatic influence on my thinking about leadership, teaching, and learning. *Leadership,* because the example of The Center's chairman, Dr. Douglas Reeves, has been one of transparency, encouragement, and a relentless focus on building a better future. Dr. Reeves lives as if education were the most important ingredient for personal success, independence, and our future democracy. *Teaching,* because the examples of Nan Woodson, Larry Ainsworth, Donna Davis, Anne Fenske, Jill Unziker-Lewis, Michelle LePatner, Tony Flach, David Nagel, and others have elevated the field of performance assessment to reflect the complexity, challenge, and dedication of the profession of teaching. *Learning,* because each and every Center seminar is designed to respect adult learners, encourage participants to apply their best thinking to the lessons of research, and challenge educators everywhere to adopt practical and user-friendly strategies to improve their practice individually and collectively.

My experience has blessed me with the opportunity to work with thousands of dedicated professionals at all levels who have been asked to respond to light-speed societal and political changes, dramatically improve student achievement, and generally save the world. The vast majority have responded with love for children, a healthy capacity to laugh at themselves, and an undying optimism in their students. Some of their stories are included in *Beyond the Numbers,* and I acknowledge their contributions and ask their forgiveness for blending stories across school systems and even across decades in the composite scenarios.

My wife, Linda, loved me through every page and tolerated the preoccupation with data and minute details that dominated my thinking at all hours of the day and night during the creation of this book. Her ability to laugh at my foibles and encourage my best work at the same time is a gift I continue to experience and treasure.

Analysis of data is inextricably linked to accountability, assessment, and standards in the pursuit of effective means to make the promise to leave no child behind a reality. It is not an idle promise, nor an easy challenge, but data analysis that reaches "beyond the numbers" offers principles, frameworks, tools, and a conceptual basis to assist educators in making data work for teaching and learning, rather than working for the data.

About the Author

Stephen H. White, Ed.D.

Stephen White, Ed.D., is no stranger to data analysis. His career spans more than thirty years in three countries and four states, serving preschool to graduate students in public and private education since 1972. Raised in Montana, he received his Doctorate in Educational Leadership from Montana State University in 1989.

Dr. White's career has been characterized by creation of innovative programs in response to emerging needs, high-quality fiscal stewardship of limited public resources, and a consistent focus on professional development and best practice. As a teacher, counselor, coordinator, director, high school principal, chief executive officer of a higher education BOCES, executive director, assistant superintendent, and superintendent, Dr. White has had the privilege of being involved in significant reform initiatives and hands-on experience with the day-to-day challenges of leadership in public education, all of which required insightful data management and analysis.

Previous publications include ten journal articles and a contribution to a university textbook, addressing subjects as diverse as the transition from school to work, performance excellence, and finding common ground in a diverse and divided society. Dr. White is the author of The Leadership and Learning Center's seminar on "Advanced Data-Driven Decision Making," and he is proud to be associated with the world's preeminent source of professional development in the areas of standards, assessment, and accountability.

Beyond the Numbers represents his practical experience, depth of knowledge, and innovation in this timely and challenging topic.

He resides in Highlands Ranch, Colorado, with his wife, Linda, and youngest son, Jonathan, enjoying skiing, cycling, grandchildren, and a good spy novel whenever time allows.

Dr. White can be reached at swhite@LeadandLearn.com.

Contents

Introduction

Data-driven decision making has become an axiom in public education over the last decade. Spurred by the movement toward standards and accountability, educational systems today are under much greater pressure to produce measurable results than ever before, particularly since passage of The No Child Left Behind Act of 2001 (Pub. L. No. 107-110). Educators are realizing that failure to make changes that improve student achievement, as measured by specific, external measures of performance, will not be tolerated. Thus, the ability to make quality decisions based on local data is a commodity in great demand.

At The Leadership and Learning Center seminars, participants have indicated a real hunger for skills and understandings that go beyond the numbers. Astute educators remark, "I know how to collect the data and develop improvement plans. What I need is the ability to make sense out of data that doesn't tell me enough. I need tools that allow me to know why I'm getting the results I'm getting and what I need to do to get better results." Using *Beyond the Numbers* and its handbook companion, *Show Me the Proof!*, teachers, principals, and even board members won't need a Ph.D. in Educational Tests and Measurement to become experts in data analysis.

Beyond the Numbers describes the foundational principles for data analysis and provides the strategies necessary to turn that analysis into action. For too long, data has been associated with statistical tests, p values, and sampling error rather than professional judgment, discoveries, decisions, and innovation. It provides those new to data analysis with tools they can use tomorrow in their schools and classrooms, but it has been created for savvy educators who are looking for more.

The first two chapters set the stage for a comprehensive program of data analysis, introducing readers to the rearview-mirror effect, bureaucratic creep, the importance of routine continuous improvement cycles, and the need to establish assessment calendars. Chapters 3 through 5 describe key principles of effective data-driven decision making, and Chapters 6 through 9 offer powerful methods to translate data into decisions. The final chapter, "The Teacher as Expert," summarizes the lessons of *Beyond the Numbers,* underscoring the capacity and talents teachers have at their fingertips right now in terms of data analysis.

Beyond the Numbers provides several appendices of tools and insights about data analysis and a glossary of terms to capture the many acronyms that have been used in the text. The text uses scenarios extensively and hypothetical data based on the author's real experiences during more than thirty years in the field. Its message can be summed up in the five Rs of data analysis:

1. **Recognize** the influence of the rearview-mirror effect on our current practices, policies, and values about teaching and learning.

2. **Realize** that data provide opportunities that require thoughtful analysis, infusion of our own experience and insights, and decisions that change how we practice the craft of teaching.

3. **Reflect** on available data with other professionals, engaging the power of collaboration to examine student work, implement and monitor insightful changes, and improve student achievement.

4. **Respond** to urgent challenges.

5. **Replicate** practices that work to share the wealth of knowledge and expertise that exists in every school.

The instructional strategies that really lift performance in this new century will emerge locally, will represent replication of highly effective practices, and will come from the collaborative wisdom of teachers and school leaders in our schools today. The ideas in this book represent different ways to look at ourselves and our craft; they call us to get beyond the numbers to strategic and powerful analyses that result in actions that change our paradigms and make sustained differences that improve student achievement. I am convinced that the collective strengths of my colleagues in schools and classrooms everywhere are sufficient to understand where we have been, to chart a path leading to where we need to go, and to know why and how we will get there, until the promise of leaving no child behind becomes a reality.

Beyond the Numbers:
The Rearview-Mirror
Effect

Most people are more comfortable with old problems than with new solutions.

—ANONYMOUS

Data-driven decision making has become an axiom in public education over the last decade. Spurred by the movement toward accountability and establishment of standards in every state, educational systems today are under much greater pressure than ever before to produce measurable results. Twelve states have charter-school takeover provisions in their accountability systems, and twenty-five have sanctions ranging from closure to reconstitution to charter takeovers (Quality Counts, 2004). States are becoming much more active about intervening in low-performing schools—a distinct shift from their former tendency to defer to districts' handling of their own affairs (Olson, 2004). Consequently, all across the nation, results in student achievement are driving responses by teachers and principals. Educators are realizing that failure to make changes that improve student achievement, as measured by specific, external measures of performance, will not be tolerated. The No Child Left Behind Act of 2001 (Pub. L. No. 107-110) has had a dramatic impact on the use of data in our schools, and has served as a catalyst for many of the changes states have initiated in terms of curriculum, standards, accountability, and assessment. Thus, the ability to make quality decisions based on local data is a commodity in great demand.

At seminars presented by The Leadership and Learning Center, participants have indicated a real hunger for skills and understandings that go beyond the numbers. Savvy educators remark, "I know how to collect the data and develop improvement plans. What I need is the ability to make sense out of data that doesn't tell me enough.

I need tools that allow me to know why I'm getting the results I'm getting and what I need to do to get better results." Hence, this book about data analysis. This chapter examines the old problems that hamper the efforts of dedicated public servants to get better, and suggests methods to achieve new solutions, some of which are less than comfortable but nonetheless necessary. Consider the experience of one such dedicated and capable public servant, someone not so different from you or me.

C A S E   S T U D Y

Superintendent Ellison was not looking forward to that night's board meeting, and for good reason. The local paper had published the results of the statewide assessment test that morning and the district average had fallen below the state average for the second consecutive year. Last year, Dr. Ellison had persuaded a reluctant school board to double its investment in professional development; adopt a model computer program that provided multiple assessments for students at every grade in math, reading, and language arts; and institute a pay-for-performance system for administrators based solely on improved student test achievement. It had been a bold move, and as Dr. Ellison reviewed the agenda, she knew there would be a number of pointed and angry questions—and not a few board members looking for a scapegoat.

"Carol, please excuse yourself early tonight. I have a feeling the board meeting will go a little longer than usual. Go on home and put your feet up. We're as ready as we're going to be."

"Are you sure? I've got plenty to keep me busy. Should I call the people who are presenting and remind them?"

"No thanks, Carol. We're all set. Tell John hello for me."

"Thanks, I'll be back at 6:30 to start the coffee."

Dr. Ellison smiled, then gently shut her office door behind her, clutched her coffee cup, and put her own feet up. "Where did I go wrong?" she asked herself, looking back over the past eighteen months. "What gets measured gets done; focus on student achievement; maximize learning opportunities; accountability is about improvement."

She recalled the recent *Education Week* article that reported a link between closing the gap and attention to data (Viadero, 2004). She could picture her staff, the software program salesman, the consultants, and remember the pride of the staff members who had presented with her at the national conference she attended with three board members last year. Yet here she was, without answers, wondering how much of all she had learned had been little more than hype. Dr. Ellison had made it a point to review school improvement plans at each cabinet meeting, showcase schools that showed gains last year, and require each school to submit data by student and classroom from the software program twice a month. Every principal and school improvement team had designed goals, activities, and training in response to last year's scores, and Dr. Ellison had given them great latitude to adjust times and schedules to address the skill deficits indicated by the state tests. Her curriculum director could provide data for every subgroup in math, reading, and language arts by grade level and by school without opening a file or book. She was that good, that organized, and that well-informed about student achievement results. Never in the seventy-six-year history of the district had so much data been collected by so many with as much purpose and intensity.

"For what?" she thought, closing her eyes and savoring the heat of her pre-meeting Starbucks. "I should have left things the way they were," she thought briefly, realizing that she was on the verge of self-pity.

She recalled the frequent attacks by the Teacher's Association, the complaints about being overwhelmed and about how unfair the tests were, and especially the complaints about being out of the classroom for training. She remembered the comment in November that had almost moved her to laughter: "We have enough trouble implementing the homework grading policy and sending out progress reports on time!"

Dr. Ellison wasn't laughing this night. She had been most certain about the positive impact of professional development . . . perhaps she had moved too quickly? Just then, the phone rang, and Dr. Ellison knew it was her board president.

"Dr. Ellison, my phone's been ringing off the hook . . ."

Dr. Susan Ellison got through her board meeting and conducted herself with the courage and dignity necessary to maintain her support from the board and even support for her initiatives. She drew from a reservoir of inner strength and love of children to weather this storm, articulately revealing the reality of learning as a complex and multifaceted process; the reality that state test data by grade measures location, not cohorts; and the reality that it takes time to make improvements. The meeting ended on a sober (if not somber) note, and although the local reporter cooperated with softball questions, Dr. Ellison's private assessment of the situation during her drive home was not nearly as uplifting and positive as the carefully worded presentations of her staff had suggested. She glanced frequently out the rearview mirror, trying to imagine what could have been, what should have been.

The most disconcerting thought for Dr. Ellison was none of the above, however. It was the fact that for the first time in her professional life, she really did not know where to turn. Deep down, she was even more incensed than her lay board or the public about the results, and she feared that another year of swimming against the tide would only produce all-too-similar results.

REARVIEW-MIRROR EFFECT

Dr. Ellison was experiencing the full brunt of the rearview-mirror effect, although she did not realize that she had succumbed to it. The *rearview-mirror effect* is defined simply as planning the future on the basis of events past, and it has four debilitating characteristics.

The first harmful characteristic of the rearview-mirror effect is responding to a rapidly changing reality based on past events. The rearview-mirror effect fails to anticipate urgent challenges and fails to elicit fresh feedback from students, parents, and teachers about the reality they are experiencing now. A common example of the rearview-mirror effect in action is educators waiting for instructional practices to be verified in the educational literature before they allow changes to be introduced. How many schools or school systems insist on 80 percent faculty approval before instituting a new approach? How often are school improvement goals developed from popular conceptions rather than informed examinations of trend data about student performance?

Like the view through the rearview mirror, we see what allowed us to get where we are today—but little more. Schools commonly write improvement goals such as "80% of students will demonstrate one or more years' growth on the state assessment or standardized achievement test." Measurable? Yes. Realistic? Probably. Helpful? No way. This goal effectively defines *success* as one student in five falling further and further behind. Rather than closing the learning gap, this plan accepts its opening even wider.

A very popular superintendent in the 1990s had a long and distinguished career characterized by a refusal to jump on the bandwagon of popular practices. By avoiding what he perceived as the fads of his day, the district stayed the course with instructional practices validated in the 1970s and early 1980s. Schools performed at an achievement level expected for the district's demographics, and parents, teachers, and patrons were satisfied with the results. In today's environment, this wait-and-see attitude will not produce the breakthrough results that educators everywhere are being challenged to create. Rearview-mirror thinking will not move educators one iota closer to meeting standards for all students, nor will it close the learning gap. The analogy of driving illustrates the challenge all too clearly: One does not consider what is ahead when driving by looking out the rearview mirror, and anyone who does so for more than a split second is inviting disaster, even on the quietest country road.

The second debilitating characteristic of this effect is waiting for the road to reveal itself, by depending on and waiting for annual assessments. Reliance on state assessment results as the single most important dimension of learning invites the very dilemma Dr. Ellison's district experienced, simply because data is examined after the fact. In many states, this rearview-mirror effect is exacerbated by a wait of several months for results that span two different school years. In addition, a common and legitimate complaint from those held accountable for such results is that scores are compared from year to year with completely different students. This is one reason the No Child Left Behind Act (NCLB), and several states before the passage of the

NCLB, instituted annual testing to facilitate examination of test results by student cohorts. Unfortunately, even with this capacity, states continue to report scores in the most cost-efficient manner, which is annual test results. Annual assessments can be valuable for analysis, but reliance on annual assessments contributes to the rearview-mirror effect because it creates a situation in which any response to the data is too little and too late. All too often, educators chart a path of action, close their eyes, hold their noses, and jump—and then wait patiently for positive results until the annual test results roll in. The most detailed school improvement plans sometimes periodically err in this way, glancing through a rearview mirror of data.

The third unhelpful characteristic of the rearview-mirror effect is its focus on a single dimension of the highway; that is, a focus only on what students do. This is not the same as focusing on student achievement, through a system where decisions are calibrated and measured against their impact on student achievement. The most successful school systems understand that teacher behaviors, professional development, learning conditions, resources, teacher qualifications, curriculum alignment and development processes, assessment variety, common planning, and a host of other antecedent conditions and structures influence student achievement. Teachers and administrators in these schools gather, analyze, and monitor data to determine the degree to which these practices and structures are implemented. Superintendent Ellison looked only at student achievement data, and at that data only annually. Is it any wonder that the important changes she initiated felt like a bold gamble? The same reality exists in schools across the country, as well-intentioned efforts to respond to the lessons of the data are hampered by an inability to look beyond a narrow definition of the data. Data is not just numbers, and examining only student achievement data is a recipe for frustration. Proactive, safe drivers in the twenty-first century anticipate what is ahead; they attend to speed, driving conditions, the condition of the vehicle, and the surrounding traffic. They pay attention to the drivers in front, behind, to the right, and to the left of the vehicle. In this century, schools that rely solely on student achievement data to make decisions shortchange themselves and fail to access the expertise, wisdom, and intelligence of their faculties.

The fourth debilitating characteristic of the rearview-mirror effect is a wistful looking-back to a time when things were simpler. Few teachers and administrators would admit it, but Superintendent Ellison's reaction to less-than-favorable results was not so unusual, especially with the heightened accountability that exists today. Criticisms abound about the unfairness of state assessments: "If only I could be left alone, I could go back to teaching!" Experience working with schools and teachers all over the country suggests that such responses are fairly common.

Let me be perfectly clear: The teacher who feels this way cares about students and wants them to perform at a high level. I am *in no way* passing judgment on these teachers' professionalism or dedication. I *am* pointing out that looking back, whether done by the superintendent, classroom teacher, parent, or board member, is counter-productive. It is very much akin to driving via the rearview mirror, with all the attendant consequences. Sustained, breakthrough improvements in student achievement that outperform expectations will never occur when those responsible for making the improvements look backward for answers.

We all know the adage, "If we continue to do what we've been doing, we will continue to get what we've been getting." An adaptation might read, "If we do something different, we'll get something better." There is no guarantee of the latter. Is it any wonder that the district Dr. Ellison served produced the same results from one year to the next? In fact, if her district had achieved its goals in such a rearview-mirror context, that would be a real cause for wonder. What can be done to diminish the rearview-mirror effect? The answer can be summed up in five Rs (to be examined in greater detail later):

- **Recognize** the influence of the rearview-mirror effect on our current practices, policies, and values about teaching and learning.

- **Realize** that data provide opportunities that require thoughtful analysis, infusion of our own experience and insights, and decisions that change how we practice the craft of teaching.

- **Reflect** on available data with other professionals, engaging the power of collaboration to examine student work, implement and monitor insightful changes, and improve student achievement.

- **Respond** to urgent challenges.

- **Replicate** practices that work, to share the wealth of knowledge and expertise that exists in every school.

A major focus will be to eliminate, as much as possible, the rearview-mirror effect, and to equip educators to understand the reasons for the results their students achieve. Only when educators look beyond the numbers to examine the dynamics of teaching and learning will schools, systems, and states make the dramatic improvements that must be commonplace in the future. When professionals examine student work, when they take a close look at correlations and ask why, and when antecedents of excellence that precede improved performance are revealed and institutionalized, students will surprise us and colleagues will surprise each other. The 90/90/90 schools, identified several years ago by The Leadership and Learning Center (Reeves, 2004b), continue to confound the skeptics because their results challenge the conventional wisdom about race, ethnicity, and poverty. (The 90/90/90 schools have enrollments in which 90 percent or more are students of color, 90 percent come from families that qualify for free or reduced-price lunch, and 90 percent meet district and state academic standards.)

DATA EVERYWHERE, BUT NOT A DROP TO USE

Today's technology offers educators opportunities to monitor student achievement, give quality corrective feedback, and adjust instruction to meet individual needs in ways only imagined by the previous generation of teachers. Data, like paperwork, increased exponentially prior to the accountability mandates that exist now in virtually every state. Our lives are inundated with data in print and electronic media, across every industry, and in every home. Surveys are taken at fast-food restaurants and hospitals, and charts and graphs are much more prevalent in the daily work life of employees than ever before.

Dr. Douglas Reeves astutely observed that although students may be "over tested" in today's climate, they are much more apt to be "under assessed" (2004a, p. 71). In other words, performance is rarely examined in terms of proficiency or to offer insights that can help us improve. Test data and even more benign assessments are used to compare rather than improve performance. Is this judgment too harsh? Before you decide, consider whether your school:

- Deliberately sets time aside for reflection on actual student work.
- Has a process to ensure that teacher reflections and insights are used to modify current practices.
- Takes action as a result of patterns and trends that emerge from the data.

Far too often, these sources of quality analysis are overlooked or omitted. Experience at The Leadership and Learning Center indicates not so much a lack of data as an absence of analysis, and an even greater absence of action driven by the data. It is not unusual for school districts to require reports for safety, attendance, behavior, demographics, budgets, school improvement, professional development, Title I compliance, facility usage, parent visits, volunteers, committee meetings, staff observations, summative evaluations, activities, accidents, field trips, immunizations, special education referrals, intervention efforts, technology purchases, email use, and the amount of toner used or copies made. This list, however lengthy, is not exhaustive, and readers who serve in schools today can easily identify other reports that were not listed here. Shouldn't we at least consider what is the point of all these reports?

NOW WHAT DO I DO?
THE DILEMMA OF DATA COLLECTION

Few of us intentionally add or require superfluous data and recordkeeping, but it is an easy trap to fall into, particularly if employees in your school or district are typical of educators everywhere: dedicated, thorough, hard-working people committed to doing the best job they can, particularly in terms of complying with expectations for production. The dilemma of data collection can best be illustrated by a look at the various data requirements of the NCLB (Exhibit 1.1).

The list in Exhibit 1.1 does not include additional data requirements imposed by individual states or districts. Nor does it reflect the "bureaucratic creep" so common in federal initiatives. In our form of government, separation of powers prevails in more than just the legislative, executive, and judicial branches; additional requirements or expectations can be imposed at each level of implementation. Exhibit 1.2 graphically describes the process.

The mere fact that departments of education (local, state, and federal) add requirements does not make those requirements onerous, in and of themselves. Whether local board policy or acts of Congress, an appropriate balance is needed between administering the spirit of a law and defining the process that will govern implementation of that law. The problem emerges only when each level, in its effort to add value, also adds complexity. What does bureaucratic creep have to do with data? Using the No Child Left Behind Act as our frame of reference, consider the following not-so-far-fetched scenario.

Exhibit 1.1

No Child Left Behind Requirements

Standards and Assessments

Reading standards
Mathematics standards
Science standards
Annual assessments in reading
Annual assessments in mathematics
Assessments in science
Assessment of English language proficiency
Inclusion of limited English proficiency
   (LEP) students
Inclusion of students with disabilities
Inclusion of migrant students
Disaggregation of results

NCLB School Improvement

Timely identification
Technical assistance
Public school choice
Rewards and sanctions
School recognition
School restructuring
Corrective action for local educational
   agencies (LEAs)

NCLB Safe Schools

Criteria for unsafe schools
Transfer policy for students in unsafe
   schools
Transfer policy for victims of violent crime

NCLB Accountability

Single accountability system
All schools included
Continuous growth to 100% proficiency
Annual determination of adequate yearly
   progress (AYP)
Accountability for all subgroups
Primarily based on academics
Graduation rates and additional indicator
Separate math and reading objectives
95% of students in all subgroups assessed

NCLB Report Card

State report card

NCLB Teacher Quality

Highly qualified teacher definition
Subject matter competence
Test for new elementary teachers
Highly qualified teacher in every classroom
High-quality professional development

NCLB Supplemental Services

Criteria for supplemental services
Approved supplemental services providers
Monitoring of supplemental services
   providers
Implementation of supplemental services

Note: Go to http://www.nclb.ecs.org for details of how all states compare on these topics
   (and the actual NCLB question/standard formulations).

Exhibit 1.2

Bureaucratic Creep

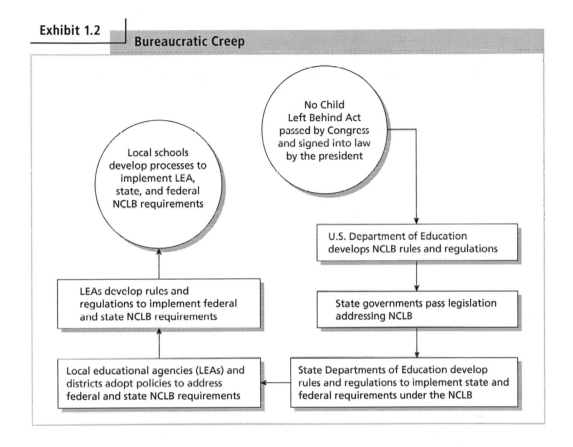

Mr. Hutchinson teaches seventh-grade social studies in a small, rural midwestern community. Until three years ago, his students did not have to take a standardized test or measurement of any kind. The district was satisfied with screening at kindergarten; use of a norm-referenced test at grades 3, 6, and 8; and reliance on ACT and SAT scores and completion rates at the high school to monitor the quality of the district's curriculum and its ability to challenge students to strive for their potential. All that has changed: There now is an annual district writing assessment that all content-area teachers administer and score; the state has required a reading and math assessment at every grade; the district curriculum director has insisted that every secondary course (grades 7 through 12) have an end-of-course assessment; and the social studies department has elected to use a multiple-choice, criterion-referenced exam as a pre- and posttest. Mr. Hutchinson feels that all he does now is test students. Gone is his opportunity to delve deep into world geography, develop student-generated units on various cultures, and take several (two per nine-week grading period) field trips to the state capital to visit museums and meet with people from a wide variety of

(continues)

CASE STUDY *(Continued)*

ethnic, religious, and cultural groups from around the globe. In addition, because his major was psychology, the state is now requiring him to take courses in geography and pass a state test if he wants to continue to teach social studies next fall. Mr. Hutchinson is angry, especially about the NCLB requirements.

Is bureaucratic creep evident in Mr. Hutchinson's life? Very few of these new demands were required by the NCLB. True, the use of end-of-course assessments helps align and focus the curriculum, and there is ample evidence that a writing assessment that engages all classroom teachers is good for students and good for teaching (Leadership and Learning Center, 2004c), but neither of these innovations are required by the NCLB. What about the licensure problem? Even that requirement has some latitude, and if his state were to license teachers by a broad discipline designation (e.g., social studies), Mr. Hutchinson's psychology major could suffice. The use of standardized, norm-referenced assessments is not required, as long as the state math and reading assessment requirement is met, and Mr. Hutchinson's rich world geography units with hands-on interviews, multiple applications, and quality team learning could be incorporated into a meaningful performance assessment that aligns with standards.

The example illustrates how bureaucratic creep is a natural outgrowth of our federal system of separation of powers, and how easy it is for schools and school systems to respond with additional requirements that tax teachers in counterproductive ways. Bureaucratic creep begs the question, "What can I get rid of? What should I stop doing and how?" The following true story drives home the point.

CASE STUDY

A supervisor included in each payroll record for her department a form listing current department employees, their social security numbers, and start and end times for each day. This handwritten report was attached to time cards, which had been modified in 1999 to identify only days absent or out of the district for school business (e.g., a training seminar). After three years, an inquiry was made to the supervisor and to the accounting department. To accounting: "Was the additional form required by accounting?"

"No, we thought the supervisor needed to submit the report for someone else."

To the supervisor: "Who required you to append the department list to the time cards?"

"We've done this since I arrived here eleven years ago, and I assumed accounting needed the data."

No one used the information, and no one made a decision resulting from the additional data, but the supervisor spent at least thirty minutes every two weeks,

C A S E　　S T U D Y　*(Continued)*

and nine employees within her department spent fifteen minutes each, on a form whose origin no one remembered. The math would be funny if it weren't so representative of busy school systems that don't slow down long enough to subtract unnecessary reports, paperwork, and just plain busy work. Over that eleven-year period, almost twenty weeks of time had been wasted on that activity.

Was this an isolated case? Are there procedures or forms that either duplicate current effort or hang on because "we've always done it that way" in your setting? All too often, the candid response is yes. As professional educators, we cannot see the forest for the trees if we don't find ways to subtract some of the data we gather at least every time we add something new.

THE NEED FOR SUBTRACTION

The need to subtract redundant practices or duplication of effort resonates with almost everyone. It's a little like asking, "Do you want clean water?" Most would agree that a subtraction mechanism is absolutely essential for any accountability- or data-driven decisionmaking system. Unfortunately, organizations bound by policies, rules, and regulations require explicit permission for subtraction. The surprise for the individuals in the preceding example occurred because assumptions were made, and permission to stop doing something was not spelled out, or more appropriately, shouted from the rooftops. Leaders must be intentional and explicit in their communication of the subtraction principle if schools are to cease obsolete practices that take time away from the important work of improving student achievement and staff performance. Responsibility for results is meaningless without the authority to make changes. The following scenario brings it back to the classroom.

C A S E　　S T U D Y

Mrs. Andrew's twenty-four third-graders were expected to score as high or higher on the state reading assessment as her previous class. Unfortunately, Mrs. Andrew also knew that this year's students were starting at entirely different places in terms of reading ability than the previous year's, when all but two students were reading at or above grade level by the end of the first nine-week period. Nonplussed, Mrs. Andrew initiated several differentiation strategies and increased the quantity and quality of writing by insisting that every culminating activity in every subject have a

(continues)

writing component and by using very explicit analytical writing rubrics (preferably stated in terms generated by the students themselves). This worked very well, and despite the facts that four students were being served on Section 504 plans (non-eligible students with disabilities) and three others were English-language acquisition students with only minimal literacy in their first language, Mrs. Andrew was seeing progress. By the end of the second nine-week grading period, however, it was clear that five of her students needed more direct intervention for the integrated curriculum strategies and differentiated instructional strategies. Without additional time for small-group or even one-to-one instruction in the skills of reading for these five students, she was certain they would not come close to proficiency on the state assessment in the spring.

Mrs. Andrew approached her principal with her dilemma, but the district had a board-approved schedule for the elementary curriculum that prescribed minutes for art, music, health, physical education, peer mediation, and social studies to complement the areas tested by the state: language arts (including reading and a writing assessment), mathematics, and science. Citing board policy, the principal would not allow her to deviate for these five students. Mrs. Andrew was responsible for improved student achievement, and she was committed to helping every child achieve at the highest possible level, but she did not have commensurate authority to adjust time or content, except in terms of homework. Was this master teacher as effective as she could have been? She improvised and was resourceful, but was restricted as to options.

The authority to act requires permission to subtract. Teachers and administrators, in both formal and informal settings, almost universally identify the need for more time as one of the most pressing challenges today. It is very likely that the angst felt by Mr. Hutchinson in the earlier example was as much about the need to reinvent how he teaches as it was about the apparent marginalizing of his craft. Both examples require teachers to change what they are doing, based on evidence of how students are achieving—and therein lies the rub. No longer is our business about our "teaching" per se. Standards have forever changed the equation; teaching is more and more about what students are learning and why. Quality data analysis can yield insights about individual students and teaching skills that are not evident or visible unless data is reflected on, examined, probed, and questioned from various perspectives. Schmoker (1999) speaks of how data, when analyzed in a collaborative way, "makes visible the invisible," leading us to make changes that improve performance. Data provides information we otherwise would not have. It behooves us to stop and reflect on what student achievement data, antecedent data, teaching data, and all kinds of data tell us.

I have found the following rule of thumb particularly helpful in counseling schools and school districts around the country:

Data that is collected should be analyzed and used to make improvements.

The bureaucratic creep depicted in Exhibit 1.2 illustrates how easily data can be multiplied but not necessarily improved. A second, unavoidable reality of data systems in public schools is that data is collected for compliance purposes. Many times, statutes and regulations require reporting of data that is never analyzed and never used to improve processes, let alone student achievement. Consider the following description of a 1992 state school finance requirement:

CASE STUDY

To protect the taxpayer and ensure transparent financial management of schools, legislation was passed to provide the legislature with annual fiscal reports that included each and every transaction for each and every school district. Because public K–12 education was the state's largest expenditure (all fifty states share that distinction), it was believed that a complete electronic transmission of expenditures would provide insights and highlight potential savings for future legislatures. Since that time, data has been collected but never analyzed for that purpose. The state education department implements the law, and local districts commit inordinate amounts of labor to submit and resubmit the detail. The information is used just to verify compliance.

This example shows striking costliness to all parties. It is also striking because it represents one of the worst instances of data being collected just because it has to be collected. It makes the case by omission: If data is collected, it should be analyzed and used to make improvements (or analyzed to affirm current practices and stay the course). *It should invite action.* Data for compliance purposes is a reality that professionals often must contend with, but all other data should be scrutinized using another rule of thumb:

If the data is not being used, stop collecting it.

SUMMARY

Superintendent Ellison had ample data at her fingertips, yet she knew the data was driving her and her staff, rather than improving her ability to make decisions. Achievement of results is not enough if one has no idea how to replicate those results. Teaching and learning are complex endeavors that require the best thinking of practitioners, accountability that empowers, and strategic implementation of instructional strategies. We collect lots of data, sometimes using hundreds of person-hours (as in the district budget example, where data was collected but never analyzed or used). In an era of standards, schools are swimming and sometimes drowning in data, but systematic analysis is often lacking or altogether absent.

Effective decision making, driven by data, requires active involvement of educators in the field. By understanding analysis as well as lesson plans, educators can make data come alive with insights and understandings that empower teachers and improve student achievement. The discussions of the rearview-mirror effect, the challenge of having too much data, and the need for subtraction provide a preview for the remainder of this book. Classroom teachers and hands-on building principals all over the nation possess—right now—the expertise to make decisions on the basis of sound data. The following chapters are designed to unlock that expertise for every reader and for the students each reader serves.

DISCUSSION

BIG IDEAS

To get beyond the numbers, educators must be as intentional about analysis as they are about lesson plans.

Data that is collected should be analyzed and used to make improvements.

If the data is not being used, stop collecting it.

QUESTIONS

1. *What is the rearview-mirror effect?*

2. *What are some of the limitations of annual testing? Of school improvement planning?*

3. *Do you have a process in your school, classroom, department, or system for subtracting obsolete practices?*

Analysis: Key to Data Management and Decision Making

Men occasionally stumble over the truth,
but most of them pick themselves up and hurry off
as if nothing had happened.

—Sir Winston Churchill (1874–1965)

If effort to collect and manage data resulted in improved student achievement, there would be little reason to worry about leaving anyone behind. Schools invest considerable resources, time, talent, and technology to collect data, manage it effectively, and complete required reports. It is fair to ask whether the same schools invest a fraction of the time, talent, or technology to analyze the data they collect. This chapter is devoted to making a conscious and deliberate effort to ensure that such an investment in data pays dividends in achievement. Consider the example of Timberline Middle School.

CASE STUDY

Timberline Middle School serves a diverse student population and community, with sufficient numbers of students to compare all NCLB subgroups. Its 1,150 students (grades 6 through 8) come from middle-income working families. The school serves an older, inner-suburb community that has seen a dramatic change in demographics over the past decade, as families that raised children in the 1960s have been replaced by families new to the community, many of which are also new to the nation.

Principal Smith is in her third year as a principal, having served in the adjacent school system as an assistant principal for the previous eighteen months. She has

(continues)

C A S E   S T U D Y   *(Continued)*

finished a masters program, and is acutely aware of the high stakes involved in the state accountability system and the No Child Left Behind Act (NCLB). As in eleven other states, failure to make adequate yearly progress (AYP) for three consecutive years would mean essentially that her school would be reconstituted under an autonomous charter with entirely new staff and a new focus that might or might not be related to the local community. For Principal Smith, this possibility is totally unacceptable, and her leadership is recognized for high expectations, extensive data systems, and accountability for students, teachers, and parents. Adapting lessons from a successful inner-city academy model, Principal Smith offers after-school and Saturday opportunities for students to demonstrate proficiency. Students, teachers, and parents realize that advancement from grade to grade and into Timberline High School requires a clear demonstration of proficiency for each standard.

Data is important at Timberline Middle School, and a wide range of student assessments is administered. For example, Timberline sends home progress reports every three weeks, and parents can access data regarding attendance, behavior, classroom assignments, and grades online. This has proved to be an excellent means of communication for parents whose work makes it difficult to attend the trimester parent conference meetings, which are held in the evenings. Timberline's range of student assessments are presented in Exhibit 2.1.

Principal Smith is very proud of the range of data collected, and classrooms that show the greatest improvement on writing assessments are recognized on her "Data Wall" outside the office. Student attendance, tardies, and school improvement targets for the statewide tests and the norm-referenced test (NRT) results are displayed in the same area. Students are expected to maintain self-assessment notebooks to chart their own progress, especially for timings, end-of-course (EOC) assessments, performance assessments, and unit tests.

Principal Smith is committed to collecting data and having her staff and even students manage their performance with charts and graphs. She is convinced that "what gets measured, gets done," and each department is expected to be prepared to offer evidence of progress for each student, in each subject, at any time. Results data are disaggregated by subgroup at faculty meetings (data varies), and each department identifies students who need additional help at least monthly, submitting a report on students when data shows flat or negative trends in two or more core subject areas or just one state indicator.

At Timberline, students consistently outperform the district and state averages, and Ms. Smith has had no problem identifying classrooms that are showing growth or scoring well above their peer groups for recognition purposes every month and at each assembly. To her supervisor, Principal Smith is very much a data-driven principal. Teachers and some parents have begun to ask for data to verify positions or viewpoints throughout the school.

C A S E   S T U D Y   *(Continued)*

Exhibit 2.1   **Hypothetical Student Assessments**

Assessment	Frequency
Skills timings (reading speed, math computation)	At least weekly in language arts and mathematics; teachers differentiate timing requirements to build skills with massed practice
Progress reports	3 per trimester
Grades	Trimester report cards
End-of-course multiple-choice assessments	1 per core subject per trimester
Performance assessments	1 per course per trimester, all courses
Unit tests	6 per year for core: language arts, math, science, social studies
District writing assessment	Pre- and post, K–10, fall and spring testing
Statewide writing assessment	Fall, grades 3–10
Statewide academic content standards assessment	Spring, Grades 3–10, math, reading, writing
Standardized norm-referenced test (NRT)	Grades 2, 5, 8, 11; spring
Postsecondary assessments (SAT, ACT, and ASVAB for the armed services)	Grade 11, fall and spring; Grade 12 for SAT and ACT; Grade 10 for ASVAB
Computerized basic skills testing in math and reading	Ongoing. Students access reports in weekly computer labs after each test administration, and teachers have desktop access to monitor progress

Of late, Timberline has been vulnerable to failure to meet AYP goals, simply because the learning gaps for some subgroups have actually widened with reference to the overall student population. A large English Skills Acquisition (ESA) group (175 students) has shown only slight improvement for three consecutive years, something Ms. Smith attributes to an influx of students from Kazakhstan and Honduras who arrived with very limited literacy in their first languages. Asian students scored at considerably higher levels on state and EOC assessments than their peers, and the persistent learning gap between boys and girls remains a concern, with boys falling far behind their female peers in all core subjects.

Principal Smith is not sure what to do. She commissioned a school improvement team to work on goals and prepare the application every spring, and every department complied with the requirements for EOC and performance assessments. She also provided training in key instructional strategies. At the same time, teachers are unabashed about the fact that they don't have time to get everything done. Veteran

(continues)

CASE STUDY *(Continued)*

teachers complain about the time required to test students and maintain data records. Principal Smith has viewed this concern as typical resistance to change, but now she is beginning to wonder.

This example illustrates the need for deliberate and collaborative analysis. The efforts of Timberline Middle School are commendable and they represent attempts to avoid or mitigate the rearview-mirror effect discussed in Chapter 1. Supported at the district level, Timberline has involved parents, and technology is leveraged to improve achievement. A concerted effort is being made to develop powerful performance assessments in every classroom; quality scoring guides align instruction with standards; assessments are embedded into instruction. Few schools have data like Timberline—but the value of the data does not lie in the fact of its collection or even graphs that display trends and patterns. The value of the data emerges only when analysis provides insights that direct decisions for students. Take a few moments to assess your knowledge and skills on the scoring guide for data management (Exhibit 2.2), before proceeding to learn about the fundamentals of data-driven decision making.

DATA-DRIVEN DECISION MAKING: PRINCIPLES THAT MAKE IT A REALITY

Numerous systems promote data-driven decision making in schools. Brazosport, Texas, was an early proponent of systematic decision making, whose success in the 1990s had a direct influence on the No Child Left Behind Act of 2001 (Pub. L. No. 107-110). Brazosport was able to affect results in such a way that over a seven-year period, students in every ethnic group and students from every income level showed dramatic improvement on the state assessments (Schmoker, 2001). Brazosport officials attributed their success to a continuous assessment and reteaching system known simply as the "Eight-Step Process." Joan Richardson (2000) of the National Staff Development Council (NSDC) described a similar ten-step process for an effective data plan. The Leadership and Learning Center implemented a very successful seminar on data-driven decision making (DDDM) that is also characterized by a continuous improvement cycle. Literally hundreds of schools and thousands of teachers have adopted this seven-step process. These three cycles are compared in Exhibit 2.3.

Schmoker noted that "[a]lmost any successful system, including a school system, is characterized by" improvement cycles (Schmoker, 2001, p. 108). In describing effective accountability systems, Dr. Reeves recommended a feedback cycle for continuous improvement that involves (1) formative and summative evaluations, (2) decisions

Exhibit 2.2

Beyond the Numbers: Scoring Guide for Data Management 2.0

Analysis Dimension	Meeting the Standard	Progressing Toward the Standard	Not Meeting the Standard
2.0 Data Management			
2.1 Data Collection	The educator makes informed decisions at all levels based on formative assessments of prior learning, embedded assessments during instruction, and summative assessments of results following instruction. Data collection demonstrates understanding of antecedent data, including administrative structures and conditions and cause data (teacher behaviors that engage students in thinking and learning). Results (effects) data includes student performance; pre- and post data; use of longitudinal cohort data for patterns and trends; embedded performance assessment data; and common assessments by department, grade, or discipline. Data provides evidence of antecedents and instructional strategies. Data collection minimizes interruption of instruction, with data collected limited to critical variables that lend themselves to triangulation.	The educator ensures that teachers and support staff collect and monitor data associated with goals, and that data is maintained for both summative and formative purposes. Emphasis is primarily on collect on of results (effects) data, with limited evidence of cause data measures or programmatic and administrative antecedents (conditions and structures that correlate with excellence ir student achievement). Educator attempts to schedule data collection so it does not interrupt instruction.	The educator's data collection system is limited to external requirements for compliance in annual student assessment results. No evidence of attempts to link cause and effect; institute continuous assessment measures before, during, and after learning; or address timing issues of data collection.
2.2 Improvement Cycles	The educator employs improvement cycles for all major programs and unit teams Cycles ensure that plans are formed by data, implemented to address gaps and opportunities, analyzed, and routinely and systematically revised for improvement (e.g., 7-step DDDM, PDSA, etc.).	The educator is beginning to apply an improvement cycle to assess student achievement across state or local requirements (e.g., seat time, Carnegie Units, state assessment). Application to adult practices or administrative and programmatic structures has yet to be attempted.	The educator reacts to state or local requirements for data and does not employ improvement cycles that link data to planning and implementation.

(continues)

19

Exhibit 2.2 | Beyond the Numbers: Scoring Guide for Data Management 2.0 *(Continued)*

Analysis Dimension	Meeting the Standard	Progressing Toward the Standard	Not Meeting the Standard
2.0 Data Management			
	The educator examines test scores for trends within subjects, relationship to grades and state assessments, internal consistency across subjects, unanticipated gains, and outlier performers that score well above and well below standard. Data is routinely triangulated with antecedent, collaboration, and accountability data to reveal insights not available from examining single data points. The educator has formed teams and meeting times to examine data for improved student achievement.	The educator has formed teams and meeting times to examine data for improved student achievement. The educator examines test scores for trends within subjects; relationship to grades and state assessments; and internal consistency across subjects; and to identify students with unanticipated gains.	Data is collected and recorded, but seldom analyzed to improve student achievement.
2.3 Analysis/ Reflection/ Action	The educator sets aside specific times and formats to ensure that collaborative analysis takes place; that quality data tools are applied to facilitate that analysis; that insights from reflection are recorded; and that action is planned, implemented and monitored on the basis of the analysis.		

Exhibit 2.3

Continuous Improvement Cycles

	Brazosport Eight-Step Process	Ten-Step Data Plan	The Center's Seven-Step DDDM Process
Steps of Continuous Improvement Cycles	▪ Test score disaggregation ▪ Timeline development ▪ Instructional focus ▪ Assessment ▪ Tutorials ▪ Enrichment ▪ Maintenance ▪ Monitoring	▪ Collect basic information ▪ Identify additional data ▪ Disaggregate the data ▪ Analyze the data ▪ Summarize the data ▪ Brainstorm causes ▪ Collect more data ▪ Analyze and summarize data ▪ Identify a goal ▪ Repeat the process	▪ Treasure hunt ▪ Analyze data ▪ Prioritize ▪ Set, review, revise goals ▪ Select instructional strategies ▪ Determine results indicators ▪ Implement action plan (implied seventh step)

informed by that feedback, and (3) actions taken on the basis of that feedback to make improvements and establish new initiatives (2004b, p. 122). Rick DuFour, a leader in professional learning communities, stressed the need for leaders to create a systematic process in which teachers work together to analyze and direct professional practice to improve their individual and collective results (2003, p. 64). Each of the models presented in Exhibit 2.3 offers systematic processes with explicit steps, and there are several other examples in the literature (Wade, 2001; Killion & Bellamy, 2000; Shipley, 2000). To better understand these cycles, The Leadership and Learning Center process for data-driven decision making is described here.

Step 1: The Treasure Hunt

The term *treasure* was chosen to communicate a sense of discovery, great value, and the unknown. In treasure hunts, we don't know for certain where it is or what we will find, but we know we must be attentive to external factors if we are to discover it, and we know it is valuable enough to pursue with our best efforts and best thinking. This is the key to data analysis: not just that we disaggregate it, but that we examine it for insights. "Data-Driven Decision Making" seminar participants are directed to examine trends by looking at data over time, preferably a series of scores or data points over a year or more. Schools like Timberline, with a wide variety of data, have a much greater opportunity to discover treasures of real value than schools that are limited to annual, rearview-mirror data. Effective treasure hunts examine more than student achievement data, looking also at teaching strategies, behaviors, conditions, and structures that affect results. Exhibit 2.4 shows a treasure hunt that begins with state assessment data.

Exhibit 2.4

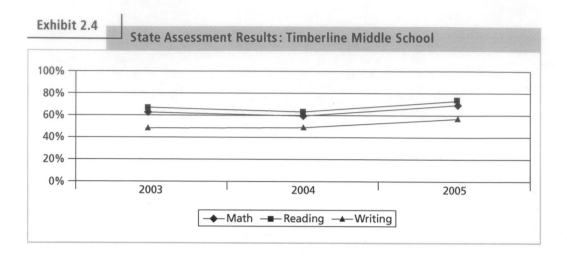

State Assessment Results: Timberline Middle School

Math scores improved from 62 percent to 70 percent proficient during the period, reading proficiency ranged from 67 percent to 73 percent, and writing proficiency increased from 48 percent to 57 percent. Timberline appears to be making steady growth, but the data doesn't tell us why. Exhibit 2.5 depicts the percentage of teachers trained in a number of instructional strategies, to add to the student achievement data and continue our hunt for treasure.

Almost 80 percent of teachers were trained in "Five Easy Steps to a Balanced Math Program," 86 percent in "Effective Teaching Strategies" (ETS), and 45 percent in the "Writing Process." The school gained only 8 percent more proficient students in math, with 30 percent nonproficient. The training in ETS was at the time almost universal at the school, yet only 6 percent of the students not proficient in 2003 were added to the proficient column by 2005. In writing, the school increased the number of proficients by 9 percent, but trained an additional 30 percent of teachers to get there. Perhaps Timberline erred in implementing such training? Examine Exhibit 2.6,

Exhibit 2.5

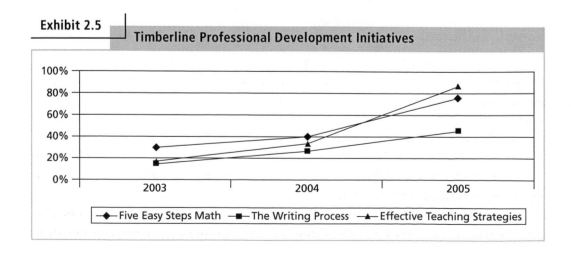

Timberline Professional Development Initiatives

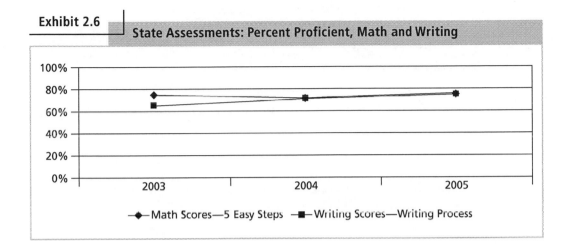

Exhibit 2.6

State Assessments: Percent Proficient, Math and Writing

as our treasure hunt continues. The percent of students scoring at the proficient level in both math and writing with teachers trained in these strategies was higher every year than the school average. We can infer at least that the professional development was having some positive influence on improved student achievement scores.

In this brief and simplified treasure hunt, we were able to identify trends and draw some inferences by looking only at professional development with instructional strategies. If Timberline would examine its rich treasure chest of student achievement data, and monitor key teaching strategies, routine behaviors, conditions, and structures that influence results, the school would be well positioned to make all kinds of adjustments that would lead to improved student achievement. "Wait a minute," the skeptic demands. "The percent proficient is still under 80 percent, meaning that almost one student in four is still not achieving where we want them to. How can we make the case that this strategy makes a difference?" Good question. Move to step two, analysis.

Step 2: Analysis

Analysis answers the questions:

- What did you discover during your treasure hunt?
- What can you learn from what's working?

Analysis is designed to identify strengths and successes to celebrate, challenges to be met, and trends across subjects and grades. This aspect of analysis is extended later in this chapter when we introduce a four-part process to "'unwrap'" assessments, to identify their strengths and weaknesses.

Analysis is simply examining data to improve the decisions we make based on that data. Currently, we know that Timberline invested a lot of time, effort, and money in

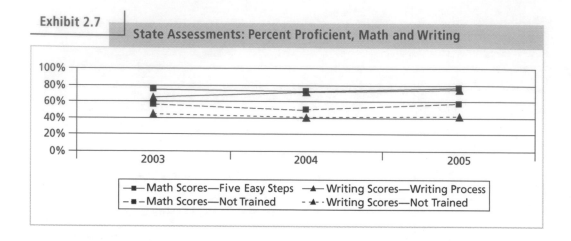

Exhibit 2.7

State Assessments: Percent Proficient, Math and Writing

Legend:
- ■— Math Scores—Five Easy Steps
- ▲— Writing Scores—Writing Process
- ■- Math Scores—Not Trained
- ▲·· Writing Scores—Not Trained

particular staff development programs. We know that just under 80 percent of students in classrooms where teachers have been trained are now proficient, and we know that the school saw an 8 percent increase in proficients in math, and gains in both reading (6 percent) and writing (9 percent) from 2003 to 2005. Is this program really working? How can we find out?

Exhibit 2.7 adds student scores where teachers did not receive training in "Five Easy Steps" or the "Writing Process." Students were much less likely to score at the proficient level than their counterparts in both subjects, with variation greater than 20 percent of students enrolled. The more teachers were trained, the greater the number of students scoring proficient or better. Absent the training, student performance stalled or declined. With the professional development, student scores were consistently high, much higher than the school averages shown in Exhibit 2.4. Our treasure hunt and brief analysis clearly indicate that participation in professional development (specifically, in "Five Easy Steps" and the "Writing Process") was a powerful contributing influence. It served, in this case, as an antecedent or predictor of improved performance. Let us now turn to see how Timberline might set its priorities when armed with this information.

Step 3: Setting Priorities

Setting priorities requires careful scrutiny of what has to be done, including consideration of external factors, urgencies on the horizon (e.g., AYP status), and selection of the most pressing needs on the basis of existing strengths or capacity and the areas of greatest weakness. Given the little we know about Timberline Middle School, we can nonetheless identify some training that has been beneficial to student achievement, and we can identify which area offers the greatest opportunity for growth (in terms of state assessments).

Setting priorities merely means responding to the reality in schools that faculty cannot address every need all at once. The data provided so far only indicates student achievement on state assessments and the degree to which certain professional development activities have influenced that achievement. Given this data, Timberline might continue its focus on improving writing scores. Fewer teachers have received training in the writing process, and writing scores without training for teachers have been static at best. Nevertheless, each year a greater proportion of students scored proficient on the writing assessment. However, quality prioritization would require a thorough understanding of the student population, the curriculum, the antecedents that are affecting student achievement, and the quality of program implementation.

Step 4: Setting, Reviewing, or Revising Goals

The key in this fourth step is to make sure that any and all goal statements are specific, measurable, achievable, relevant, and timely. Once again, The Leadership and Learning Center process for continuous improvement is more explicit and more focused than simply implementing instruction. It ensures that for every goal, there is a baseline to work from, and that every goal is important (relevant) to the challenges at hand. The discussions on accountability (Chapter 5) and replication (Chapter 9) offer insights into pursuing goals methodically and deliberately until they are realized. They also provide a number of strategies for timely review and revision of goals to minimize the rearview-mirror effect.

Step 5: Instructional Strategies

This fifth step corresponds to Brazosport's steps 3 through 6, in that it stipulates adult actions to deliver instruction related to needs and goals. The Leadership and Learning Center's "Data-Driven Decision Making" seminar adroitly distinguishes strategies from activities or programs or textbook adoptions. For instance, purchase of an instructional program—even a high-quality, research-supported program—would not constitute an instructional strategy. School improvement plans all too often identify such purchases or plans to purchase as instructional strategies in themselves, when in fact they are resources that may not affect instruction at all.

Powerful instructional strategies require training and practice by the adults who use and implement them, and we should be able to expect that such strategies will enhance student achievement when implemented well. Our Timberline examples include focused professional development designed to equip professionals to implement and refine effective instructional strategies with three broad applications: mathematics instruction, writing instruction, and systematic selection of proven and effective teaching strategies.

Step 6: Results Indicators

This sixth step is a key aspect of data-driven decision making because it insists on interim measures to determine (1) if the strategy is being implemented correctly, and

(2) if the strategy is having the intended effect on student learning and improved performance. Hence, *results indicators* may be measures of teacher actions or probes that indicate student performance to date. Quality performance assessments, for example, include performance tasks with scoring guides that reveal to what degree students are progressing toward demonstrating proficiency for content-area standards.

Results indicators are critical to extract educators from the rearview-mirror effect. They offer ongoing and interim measures that allow the education professional to make midcourse corrections and to do so systematically. Exhibit 2.8 offers two practical examples of results indicators within excellent performance assessments. Both examples have detailed scoring guides to accompany each results indicator or task, and both series of results indicators have been carefully designed to capture an increasingly rigorous application of Bloom's taxonomy.

Exhibit 2.8

Results Indicators as Components of Performance Assessments

Overview of Performance Assessment: Students will use a variety of reading comprehension skills and materials to better understand and relay information about Mexico and its culture.

Grade Three

Task 1	Recognize important facts and create a biography	Bloom's Taxonomy: Knowledge & Comprehension
Task 2	Analyze information to create a schedule	Bloom's Taxonomy: Analysis & Application
Task 3	Use atlas to plan concert city and city map in Mexico	Bloom's Taxonomy: Analysis & Synthesis
Task 4	Judge and evaluate restaurant reviews and formulate opinion in a written essay and in class presentation	Bloom's Taxonomy: Synthesis & Evaluation

Source: Mia Dellanini, Chris Droge, and Liz Hunt, The Leadership and Learning Center, Colorado Springs, Colorado (October 2003).

Overview of Performance Assessment: Through photographs, interviews, artifacts, and documents, students will create a family history illustrated with a timeline and beautifully crafted paragraphs in a student book, explaining work for family to enjoy.

Grade Two

Task 1	Students will create a timeline of their lives using tools of an artist; use information from timeline as prewriting to craft a thoughtful paragraph about their lives, written for future relatives in 2103	Bloom's Taxonomy: Knowledge & Comprehension
Task 2	Students interview parent or grandparent; organize information in graphic organizer of choice; create focused paragraph; create frame around	Bloom's Taxonomy: Analysis & Application

Grade Two *(Continued)*

paragraph with things the loved one enjoyed doing

Task 3 Students review paragraphs to evaluate progress; apply information in input chart to create a compare-and-contrast paragraph of student's life to that of parent or grandparent; using artist tools, students will create self-portrait

Bloom's Taxonomy: Analysis & Synthesis

Task 4 Students will compile family member interviews; use information to display materials in form of a book; write introduction, explaining the project, keeping in mind importance of presentation

Bloom's Taxonomy: Application, Synthesis, & Evaluation

Source: L. M. Van de Merghel, Adams Elementary, Santa Ana Unified School District, California (May 2003).

Step 7: Quality Action Plans

Continuous improvement cycles must be explicit and have sufficient backing from administration to ensure that they are implemented and sustained. Exhibit 2.9 provides another look at continuous improvement cycles.

Exhibit 2.9

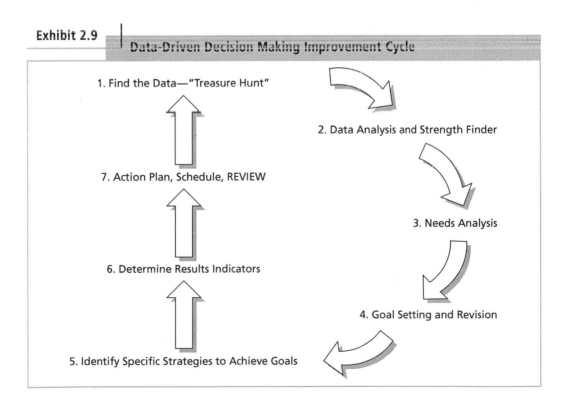

Data-Driven Decision Making Improvement Cycle

1. Find the Data—"Treasure Hunt"

2. Data Analysis and Strength Finder

3. Needs Analysis

4. Goal Setting and Revision

5. Identify Specific Strategies to Achieve Goals

6. Determine Results Indicators

7. Action Plan, Schedule, REVIEW

Implementing decisions driven by data analysis is often seen as the last step rather than a midcourse step in a continuous improvement cycle. Examine the seven-step DDDM process in Exhibit 2.9. Although the action plan (implementation) is the final step, review, revision, and modification are also included. All seven steps are a single application of one continuous cycle. Improvement cycles require leadership follow-up and relentless efforts to maintain the focus on data if decisions are truly going to be driven by informed data.

PRINCIPLES OF DATA-DRIVEN DECISION MAKING

We have learned that a systematic process is required to ensure that informed decisions flow from a thorough analysis of data. Variations of all kinds can be made to accommodate local differences and preferences, but it is essential that a continuous improvement cycle of some sort be implemented and adhered to. This section introduces three key principles of data-driven decision making, which are investigated in greater detail in Chapters 3 through 5.

Antecedents

The first principle is a focus on *antecedents,* structures and conditions that precede, anticipate, or predict excellence in performance. Antecedents to excellence are the strategies employed by a specific school that lead to academic achievement and the attainment of other system-wide goals. Antecedents include causes, instructional strategies, administrative structures, and conditions for learning. The best way to understand this principle is to be mindful of what antecedents are *not.* They are not measures of student performance, and they are not actions of students. They can never be test scores, but they can be measures of adult behaviors or numbers of teachers with training and certification in specific methods, such as "6 +1 Trait Writing," "Differentiated Instruction," or "Making Standards Work." Antecedents are the researcher's independent variables that are modified in the quest for improved student achievement. To successfully use them in data analysis, one must measure and monitor antecedents with as much regularity as student achievement results. Numerous Leadership and Learning Center seminars (2001 to 2004) emphasize the management of antecedents to improve student achievement (the seminars include "Effective Teaching Strategies (ETS)," "Making Differentiated Instruction Work (MDIW)," "Data Teams," "Data-Driven Decision Making (DDDM)," "Making Standards Work (MSW)," "Writing Excellence (WE)," and "Advanced Data-Driven Decision Making (ADDDM)."

A very simple rule of thumb will help illustrate why antecedents are a fundamental principle of data-driven decision making and so many other high-quality instructional programs:

Understanding of the effect (results) requires
understanding of the cause (antecedents).

To successfully understand antecedents, we must be able to measure what is modified. How many times do we point to strategies, programs, resources, and specific teacher behaviors that were implemented to effect a change in student achievement without measuring the degree to which those antecedents were implemented correctly or whether they were actually used during instruction? This author has observed countless instances of frustration by educators who attempted to implement a program or strategy that was reportedly capable of effecting dramatic changes, but abandoned the program or strategy when the positive results were not evident, and dramatic, right away. The strategy or program may not have been the problem. The teacher was not the problem either, as the strategy required more intensive coaching, feedback, and modeling than anticipated in the professional development plan. Without adequate monitoring, we just won't know. All we will know is that student achievement is not improving rapidly enough. Antecedents must be identified, directed, and measured every bit as often and thoroughly as the results we seek.

Accountability

The second principle of data-driven decision making is *accountability.* Much has been written about quality accountability systems. For example, in *Accountability in Action,* Douglas Reeves outlined seven critical elements of such a system: congruence, respect for diversity, fairness, specificity, accuracy, universality, and feedback for continuous improvement (2004b). Accountability systems are part and parcel of school improvement plans in virtually every school in the United States, and they invariably identify both expected performance for students and those responsible for producing those results, or at least implementing key activities.

Here is a very simple definition:

Accountability *is the authority to act and permission to subtract.*

Accountability systems must ensure that action follows analysis; that roles and responsibilities are assigned to individuals and to teams; that user-friendly timelines for data management are established; and that accountability is integrated into every data-driven decision. Accountability is a construct that applies as much to the work of individuals as to schools and school systems. It applies as much to the context of one's work as to a school's or school system's duty to the public.

Collaboration

Collaboration, the third and final principle of data-driven decision making, becomes operational in three ways. First, collaboration has to be built into every step of data management: collecting, disaggregating, analyzing, setting priorities, setting goals, establishing strategies, identifying indicators, and planning action. Every step requires at least two sets of eyes, ears, brain matter, and heart.

Second, collaboration necessitates deliberate efforts to facilitate team thinking and candor in our interactions regarding data, learning, and teaching. This author has observed many leaders who genuinely promote and proclaim candor, but there is a natural reluctance among staff to be candid, and it takes only a few instances in which candor is discouraged or punished to shut it down completely within any organization. For candor to be present in discussion about results and the causes that precede them, a culture of no blame and no excuses must be modeled, communicated, celebrated, and explicitly promoted. This element of collaboration is particularly difficult to effect, but it is necessary if data is to drive our decisions.

Third, collaboration must be integrated into every data-driven decision. Rick DuFour summed it up in this way, "[T]rue collaboration does not happen by chance or by invitation. It happens only when leaders commit to creating the systems that embed collaboration in the routine practices of the school and when they provide teachers and teams with the information and support essential to improve practice" (2003). Timberline did not lack data or even a number of effective antecedents. What was lacking was a means to ensure sufficient analysis of antecedents, collaboration, and accountability to learn lessons that would help students learn. Each data point listed in Exhibit 2.1 can be used to inform instruction, design curriculum, and respond to student needs. The problem is not the availability or even collection of data; the problem is the absence of analysis.

ANALYSIS: THE "UNWRAPPING" OF DATA

Analysis is defined by *Webster's* (1983) as "a separating or breaking up of any whole into its parts so as to find out their nature, proportion, function, relationship, etc." The process of analysis, then, is to examine any whole by dividing it, breaking it into component parts, and looking for relationships and functions. Readers familiar with the "unwrapping" process (Ainsworth, 2003) will quickly recognize that unwrapping of standards is really a very simple and effective method of analysis. The following excerpt succinctly defines the unwrapping process:

> "Unwrapping" the academic content standards is a proven technique to help educators identify from the full text of the standards exactly what they need to teach their students. "Unwrapped" standards provide clarity as to what students must know and be able to do. When teachers take time to *analyze* each standard and identify its *essential* concepts and skills, the result is more effective instructional planning, assessment, and student learning . . . (2003, p. 1; emphasis added).

This powerful technique has created literally thousands of "ah-hah" moments for teachers and administrators across the country. Its basic premise is that analysis is needed to identify the essential concepts and skills in each and every standard. Just as unwrapping of standards offers teachers a tool to integrate the key academic content with the most powerful instructional strategy, unwrapping of data offers teachers a means to make visible the invisible and trigger insights on the dynamics of teaching and learning. Analysis, rather than collection or even disaggregation of data, is the catalyst for improvement.

Analysis is best when it is collaborative. This is especially true in education, a business Linda Darling-Hammond refers to as "work characterized by simultaneity, multidimensionality, and unpredictability"(1997, p. 69). Statisticians consider education the most difficult of the social sciences on which to conduct research, because of all the uncontrolled variables that affect virtually any research design (Kerlinger, 1986). Hence, statisticians have developed elaborate and sophisticated statistical multivariate analyses to control for variances attributed to unknown or uncontrolled variables.

Is it possible to collect too much data? As we learned in Chapter 1, any data that is collected but never analyzed or acted upon is an added burden and little more. Nevertheless, it is to our advantage as educators to be able to reduce everything of any importance that happens to our schools and classrooms into meaningful information. Reliable observations of events and behaviors that affect learning can help us make improved decisions when the information from those observations is translated and analyzed for patterns or trends or relationships. End-of-course assessments help align the curriculum and draw teachers together to collaborate on what is important in each course. Proactive performance assessments ensure that standards are addressed. Assessments that provide incremental evidence of proficiency assist teachers in minimizing the rearview-mirror effect and in making appropriate modifications for each student. Timberline had all of these elements, but erred by emphasizing the collection of data, and did so at the expense of helpful analysis. In schools, where the nanosecond is a reality and interruptions legendary, one can easily find ways to lose the forest for the trees. Let's reexamine Timberline's data and see if we can help the school find time for quality analysis through a relatively simple, three-part unwrapping of required student assessments.

Function

When we look at function, we examine both the nature and the purpose of assessments in terms of what they measure and what we hope to accomplish with them (*validity*). What do the progress reports measure? Are assessments designed to test knowledge, or skills, or both? By examining the purpose of assessments, areas of redundancy are identified. What is the purpose of EOC assessments? Is it content knowledge, or achievement of standards, or the application of skills? What about performance assessments? Consider the hypothetical Timberline data in Exhibit 2.10 for the entire K–12 district; this is included to reveal differences across grades and to show how quickly an assessment program can become unwieldy.

Emphasis

The greatest emphasis will always be on those assessments that take more time and effort, so we unwrap them to know with certainty the reasons for doing them. In our

Exhibit 2.10

Timberline School District K–12 Assessment Emphasis by Grade

Assessments per year	K1	2	3	4	5	6	7	8	9	10	11	12
Trimester Assessments												
Basic skills/Weekly	30	30	30	30	30	30	30	30	30	30		
Skills timings	24	8	8	8	8	8	4	4	—	—	—	—
Progress reports	3	3	3	3	1	1	1	1	1	1	1	1
Content performance	4	4	4	4	4	4	6	6	7	7	7	7
End of Course/Semester												
Grades	2	2	2	2	2	2	2	2	2	2	2	2
EOC—Core academics	4	4	4	4	4	4	4	4	4	4	4	4
All subject unit tests	6	6	6	6	6	6	6	6	6	6	6	6
Annual Assessments												
Statewide writing—Fall		1	1	1	1	1	1	1	1			
Statewide standards—Spring		3	3	3	3	3	3	3	3			
NRT—Spring testing		1			1			1			1	
Annual Pre- and Posttests												
District writing	2	2	2	2	2	2	2	2	2	2		
Postsecondary											2	1

example, there is pressure for testing all year long, with twelve assessments per trimester and six additional unit tests per year, or fourteen per trimester. The result in our Timberline hypothetical is a school that emphasizes so many assessments that it emphasizes none. Imagine the reactions of students! Unwrapping examines assessments by month, season, trimester, and by grade to provide a baseline for making changes and developing a comprehensive assessment calendar.

Relationship

This final step in unwrapping provides a much clearer picture of the entire assessment program in terms of alignment and degree to which assessments complement one another, create unnecessary redundancy, or corroborate other assessments. What is the relationship between progress reports and unit tests? Unit tests and EOCs? Do we really need all three? Relationships help us prioritize and simplify assessments.

Exhibit 2.10 clearly showed that Timberline had a huge number of assessments, that it was very top-heavy with skills timings and computerized basic skill assessments, and that very little had been done to delineate the nature of the assessments. As is so often the case, Timberline added NCLB requirements to the assessment battery but apparently did not subtract any testing. Further unwrapping by time periods for test administration would reveal very test-heavy months around trimester time in the fall and in the spring, especially for NCLB grades 3 through 10. One might also surmise that so many content-level assessments could actually inhibit the presence of writing or constructed-response assessments in this school system. Does the system lend itself to quality assessments that stretch students to apply higher levels of thinking consistent with Bloom's taxonomy?

Unwrapping to determine assessment emphasis should create an awareness about the impact and value of current assessment practices and raise questions about adjustments that may be needed. An analysis of the degree to which assessments are related assists by clarifying similarities and differences between assessments, revealing areas of conflict and duplication, identifying areas and items that should be subtracted, and highlighting assessment needs that have not been addressed. One can see clearly from this hypothetical example how important it is to determine where and how to scale back.

It is just as important to unwrap data and assessment systems as it is to unwrap standards. Without the analysis that emerges from unwrapping, decision makers are just as limited as teachers and specialists who attempt to design quality instruction without a clear understanding of the requirements and expectations of various standards. Without unwrapping, decision makers are left to assume that assessments measure what educators expect them to; that assessments are administered proportionately;

that the purposes of assessment are clearly defined and complementary; and that assessments are aligned to focus instruction and generate reliable data for curriculum design, differentiation of instruction, and professional development. These assumptions are much more apt to be true after an unwrapping process or assessment audit has been completed.

TIME FOR REFLECTION

Timberline Middle School's assessment battery was over the top in terms of time demands, and allowed very little time for reflection. Unfortunately, few school systems deliberately or explicitly set aside times to analyze data and then reflect on it.

When the time and resources required to administer assessments, surveys, or studies of any kinds are calculated, the need to take time for reflection becomes an ethical issue about public stewardship. The unwrapping exercise to identify areas of concern, raise questions about the scope of Timberline's data system, and focus efforts on aligning the assessments should have taken each reader no more than ten minutes. Even brief time frames of thirty minutes can accommodate analyses that will make a difference (Schmoker, 2001, p. 119). Schools may consider setting aside times in department, grade, or faculty meetings as soon as possible after assessment results become available. Formal, explicit, and protected time periods to do nothing but apply the best thinking of school teams and faculties to the analysis of data is time well spent. Assessment calendars provide such a structure by establishing time for both analysis and reflection for every assessment in the district's battery.

ASSESSMENT OR DATA CALENDARS

An assessment calendar (see Exhibit 2.11) establishes time frames, accountability, and collaboration to conduct the following nine steps to quality analysis and decision making:

1. A time frame for administration (implementation of any new practice)
2. A precise and published window for collecting the data
3. A precise and published window for disaggregating the data
4. A precise and published time for analysis
5. A separate time to reflect on the data after it has been analyzed, graphed, and charted for trends and patterns
6. A precise window for recommendation of changes of any kind or maintenance of the status quo
7. A specific date when decisions will be made regarding the recommendations

Exhibit 2.11 | Assessment Calendar Template (Part 1)

Describe each assessment by specifying times when steps are to be accomplished. Use precise dates when available or windows of time (range of days, month)

Assessment	Administration	Collection Date/Window	Disaggregation Date/Window	Analysis	Reflection	Recommendation of Changes	Decision Point	Written Rationale	Dissemination to Stakeholders
NRT									
State assessment									
CRTs									
Writing assessment									
EOC assessments									
Common assessments									
Performance assessments									
Unit tests									
Other									

- Scheduled times to collect, aggregate, and disaggregate data
- Required time for analysis, reflection, and recommendations for changes
- Decision points to proceed with status quo or implement change recommendations
- Written rationale for each decision
- Disseminate rationale driven by data to all affected parties

(continues)

35

Exhibit 2.11 | Assessment Calendar Template (Part 2)

Recommended times when steps are to be accomplished are provided. This example includes a recommended assessment to subtract from the district battery (see strike-through). Assessment calendars should be tailored to the realities of external mandates and still provide time for quality data collection analysis, reflection, recommendations, decisions, and action.

Assessment	Administration	Collection Date/Window	Disaggregation Date/Window	Analysis	Reflection	Recommendation of Changes	Decision Point	Written Rationale	Dissemination to Stakeholders
NRT	Sept. 10–14	Sept. 17–21	Sept. 17–21	Sept. 24	Sept. 25	Sept. 27	Sept. 28	Oct. 3	Oct. 5
State assessment	Mar. 4–18	Mar. 21–28	Mar. 29–Apr. 8	Apr. 11	Apr. 12	Apr. 13	Apr. 14	Apr. 18	Apr. 20
~~CRTs~~	~~Oct. 1–8~~ ~~May 2–4~~	~~Pretest~~ ~~May 5~~	~~Pretest~~ ~~May 6~~	~~Pretest~~ ~~May 9~~	~~Pretest~~ ~~May 10~~	~~Pretest~~ ~~May 11~~	~~Pretest~~ ~~May 12~~	~~Pretest~~ ~~May 13~~	~~Pretest~~ ~~June 10~~
Writing assessment	Oct. 15–19 Apr. 25–29	Pretest May 2	Pretest May 3	Pretest May 4	Pretest May 5	Pretest May 6	Pretest May 9	Pretest May 10	Pretest June 10
EOC assessments	Jan. 21–23 May 9–11	Jan. 24 May 12	Jan. 24 May 12	Jan. 25 May 13	Jan. 25 May 16	Jan. 28 May 17	Jan. 29 May 18	Jan. 30 May 18	Feb. 5 June 10
Common assessments	Last Fri. of Sept./Nov./Feb.	1st Mon. Oct./Dec./Mar.	1st Mon. Oct./Dec./Mar.	1st Tues. Oct./Dec./Mar.	1st Wed. Oct./Dec./Mar.	1st Thurs. Oct./Dec./Mar.	1st Fri. Oct./Dec./Mar.	1st Fri. Oct./Dec./Mar.	Optional
Performance assessments	Ongoing, at least 1/term/core subject	Ongoing, seamless	Ongoing, seamless	Ongoing, seamless	Ongoing, seamless	Ongoing, seamless	Ongoing, seamless	Ongoing, seamless	Ongoing, seamless
Unit tests	No more than 2 Weds./month	Same day	Same day	Same day	Same day	Same day	Second day	Second day	Optional
Other	Teacher-determined	N/A	N/A	N/A	N/A	N/A	N/A	N/A	N/A

■ Scheduled times to collect, aggregate, and disaggregate data ■ Required time for analysis, reflection, and recommendations for changes ■ Decision points to proceed with status quo or implement change recommendations ■ Written rationale for each decision ■ Disseminate rationale driven by data to all affected parties

The criterion-referenced test is recommended for elimination for the following reasons: (1) competition for testing windows with other assessments more aligned with standards, such as end-of-course and writing assessments; and (2) the opportunity to fold CRTs into EOC, textbook, and unit common assessments.

8. A specific time for providing a written rationale for the selected decision

9. A time when data is disseminated to stakeholders, including parents and even students, depending on the data

Assessment calendars are very useful in keeping all parties focused on the real purpose of data: to provide meaningful information that "makes visible the invisible" (Schmoker, 2001) and leads to improved performance. Assessment calendars anticipate discovery of antecedents that can lead to improved performance, and they include two other key principles of data-driven decision making, accountability and collaboration. Notice how the nine-step cycle is designed to create a culture that expects assessments to be completed at one time, analyzed at another, examined for usefulness (reflection) at another, and have results and decisions published at another. The value of having explicit time frames and communication structures is that such a structure invites external scrutiny and awareness while ensuring that action is taken as a result of the data. Recommended dates are provided, but many dates are mandated externally, and a quality calendar spreads time frames to ensure that action follows analysis.

Our example provides specific dates to spread the testing battery throughout the school year. Note that the date for reflection is distinct from the analysis date, and that the dates for making a decision differ from most of the recommended change dates. The reason for this is simply pragmatic: specific dates for specific purposes help ensure that sufficient time is given to each critical step in data analysis. Each date is calendared well in advance so stakeholders and those involved will be able to devote the time and effort needed for the particular step; this minimizes the likelihood that team members will have something else competing for their time.

Establishing a specific date for completion of each step in data analysis builds in an accountability factor and increases the likelihood that action will follow analysis. At the very least, an effective assessment calendar can reveal redundancy and the overtesting represented by the hypothetical Timberline Middle School. Few procedures, practices, or programs are ever subtracted in education, but an assessment calendar forces decision makers to examine the entire testing battery and weigh the value of NRTs, criterion-referenced tests (CRTs), and other assessments in this era of accountability. It behooves those involved to consider the costs and benefits of administering all of the historical assessments in terms of adding value to the organization's ability to make decisions, and ability to devote sufficient time to remaining assessments. As you examine the recommended calendar, note the relationship between the time allocated and the types of assessments.

Did you recognize a pattern in Exhibit 2.11? The assessments closest to the classroom have the shortest time frame from administration to change implementation. This distinction does not mean that any of the nine steps should be eliminated, simply that the cycle can be compressed and accomplished much quicker when fewer people are involved.

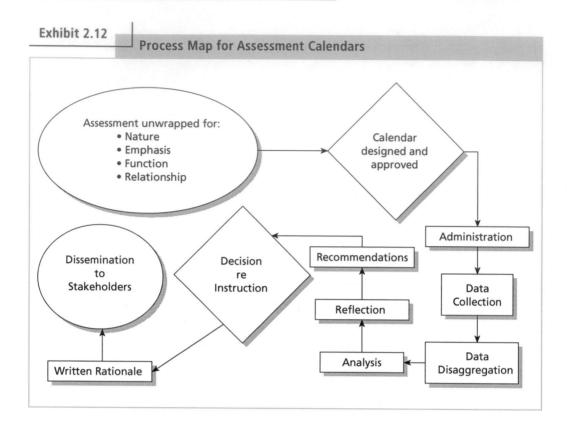

Exhibit 2.12

Process Map for Assessment Calendars

Exhibit 2.12 describes how to apply the assessment calendar through a step-by-step process map or flowchart to examine individual assessments. The process is equally applicable to data other than assessments, such as the degree to which classrooms are standards-based in their implementation (Reeves, 2002a). Steps to analyze, reflect, recommend, and decide with a written rationale have numerous applications that can assist faculty throughout a school or school system in responding to emerging challenges or refining established processes. Ovals indicate start and finish, diamonds show decision points, and rectangles are steps in the process.

SUMMARY

Timberline Middle School had exceptionally detailed and comprehensive data systems capable of disaggregating on the basis of all NCLB factors, and capable of providing such information quickly to the desk of every teacher, principal, and district administrator. Absent intentional reflection periods and an effective and practical means to analyze data, however, Timberline Middle School was unable to fully benefit from the wealth of data at its fingertips. Rather than lessons learned and applied, data was shelved, staff and stakeholders became frustrated, and reliance on past traditions for decisions prevailed.

This chapter defined analysis in the context of the unwrapping process, stressed the need to explicitly set aside time for reflection, and introduced the concept of assessment or data calendars. Unwrapping helped reveal the nature, emphasis, function, and relationship of assessments to a school's entire assessment program. The assessment calendar illustrated the importance of collaborative structures to encourage teacher judgments, team insights, and decisions driven by the data rather than implemented in spite of the data. Both set the stage to examine what works and what doesn't work as we pursue ways to achieve success and discover how to replicate that success again and again. Exhibit 2.2 provided a scoring guide for self-assessment of proficiency in terms of data management. The next chapter describes the role of antecedents in data analysis, and the need to measure the behavior of adults every bit as much as student achievement results.

DISCUSSION

BIG IDEA

Analysis requires time, improvement cycles, and explicit structures to leverage data into action. In other words, take time to smell (analyze) the roses (data).

QUESTIONS

1. *What inhibited Timberline Middle School from making more progress than observed?*

2. *What is "unwrapping"?*

3. *How does the unwrapping process assist in examining the various student assessments in your school?*

4. *What benefits can you expect from establishing an assessment or data calendar in your school or district?*

CHAPTER

Antecedents of Excellence

*We are free to choose our actions, . . . but
we are not free to choose the consequences of
these actions.*

—Stephen R. Covey (1996)

A photograph shows a young lady who lost twenty-five pounds. We know the result precisely, and the data is unequivocal. We even know that she lost the twenty-five pounds in three months. Should we celebrate because she reached her goal through exercise and nutrition, or should this be serious cause for alarm, because the weight loss was a product of anorexia or drug abuse? Without the capacity to determine what actions resulted in the weight loss, we cannot know.

This illustration makes the case for knowing the causes that produce results, for understanding the antecedents that lead to improved student achievement. *Causes* are routines that create specific effects or results. When a strong correlation exists between a cause and an effect—one that is strong enough to predict with some confidence—we refer to the cause as an *antecedent*. This chapter answers the question: How do I determine what to select and monitor to produce the desired effects that will ensure continuous improvement?

CASE STUDY

Dennis was a highly respected elementary school principal. A leader among his peers, he was first to pursue emerging best practices but the last to jump on fads and bandwagons. He viewed his teaching faculty as the most important people his students would encounter in terms of learning, and he realized that if his efforts at

(continues)

this Title I school failed to excite students about learning, a majority would drop out before completing high school. Seventy-five percent of his students received free and reduced-price lunches, 47 percent were minority students from limited English-speaking families, and even more families had parents with less than a high school education. Dennis was determined to turn the tide; long before the phrase "leave no child behind" came into popular parlance, Dennis was committed to the concept.

The number of teachers with masters' degrees increased from 23 percent to 57 percent in 5 years, and the district's first National Board Certified teachers were from his school. Dennis's heart was as large as his commitment, and he was very collaborative in making decisions, painstakingly waiting for consensus when hiring new teachers, and making sure every school improvement goal had 80 percent faculty support.

Dennis was principal of Woodside Elementary, a school that outperformed its demographics so dramatically that test scores improved at all grades (2, 4, and 6) in both math and reading. Woodside's third- and fifth-graders had the second highest percent proficient on the district writing assessment, even though its poverty, transient, and English as a Second Language (ESL) populations were also the second highest in town. This year a challenge was made to every school to improve test scores, and Woodside earned $5,000 to be used on anything but salaries (prohibited by the negotiated agreement). A larger-than-life facsimile check was to be presented at a school assembly. Parents were coming, and the media was on hand for photo opportunities and a human-interest story for the six o'clock news.

In the privacy of his office, he told his supervisor, "All this is very nice, and we have lots of needs for the money, but quite honestly, I don't know why our kids did so well this year. I guess we were lucky." Dennis was communicating, in a not-too-subtle way, that Woodside's results may be great this spring, but don't expect the same results next year. He had been around long enough to witness lots of peaks and valleys in terms of test scores, and explanations that rarely satisfied.

"Wait," his boss countered, "you introduced common planning periods, extensive professional development in balanced literacy, and your investment in technology and literacy coaches with discretionary Title I funds was quickly replicated by your peers. Your efforts made a difference. Take some credit for the results."

Dennis smiled, "I know, but we've been working on the same thing for years and this is the first bump we've seen. We need to clone our sixth-graders!" Then the assembly bell rang . . . .

This author has met leaders like Dennis in more than twenty-five states: principled principals, modest about their accomplishments, devoted to their staff and students. Instructional leaders, when they are as candid as Dennis, admit that they just don't know what produced changes in student achievement. Kids are so complex, the argument goes, and there are so many variables! Nonetheless, we can identify factors that are highly correlated with improved performance. Schools all across the United States demonstrate how common antecedents make it possible to predict improved student achievement with some certainty. Exhibit 3.1 is provided so you can assess your current knowledge and skill regarding antecedents of excellence.

Dr. Douglas Reeves, founder of The Leadership and Learning Center, developed the brilliant L^2 Matrix for leadership and learning that links understanding of antecedents of excellence with sustained results. Those who wish to replicate success year after year must understand the conditions, structures, and strategies (*antecedents*) that correlate with improved student achievement and learning. See Exhibit 3.2.

In the L^2 Matrix, understanding of antecedents is viewed as the distinguishing variable between leaders who experience success and those leaders who do not. The L^2 Matrix suggests that those who understand the conditions and structures (antecedents) that lead to success and know how to avoid those antecedents that perpetuate mediocrity or static student performance will be able to sustain improvement year after year, despite cohort changes. It behooves us, then, to understand what antecedents are and how to distinguish them.

Antecedents are those structures and conditions that precede, anticipate, or predict excellence in performance. They lead to excellence in student achievement, excellence in implementing a new program or strategy, or excellence in performing routine tasks. Dennis applied antecedents when he created common planning times, focused professional development, and devoted resources to create literacy coach positions. Antecedents are teaching strategies such as questioning, reinforcing effort, rewarding achievement, and instruction in nonlinguistic representation. Antecedents are also causes that correlate with effects in student behavior and achievement (*results*), such as classroom routines, grading procedures, and teacher-student relationships and connections. The degree of consistency with which standards are implemented in the classroom has a direct effect on student behaviors. Hence, we refer to these routine practices and teacher behaviors as *causes*. Antecedents also include conditions such as class size, technology literacy, availability of textbooks, and structures such as continued education unit (CEU) requirements, block scheduling, data teams, and prescribed data reflection times. All of these influence achievement.

Antecedents precede something. In mathematics, antecedents are the first term of any ratio. In science, the first and conditional part of a hypothesis is the antecedent (e.g., If the sun is fixed, the earth must move). Regarding data, antecedents both precede and predict results. Antecedents are those causes that have a strong correlation (negative or positive) with results. If we desire sustained improvements in student achievement, it would be wise to identify antecedents, structure their deployment, and test their veracity for replication.

Exhibit 3.1 | Scoring Guide for Antecedents of Excellence 3.0

Analysis Dimension	Meeting the Standard	Progressing Toward the Standard	Not Meeting the Standard
3.0 Antecedents for Excellence			
3.1 Cause Data and Instructional Strategies	The educator provides evidence of specific antecedents used in classrooms or school to increase student achievement effects (*results*) through teacher behaviors in the classroom (*causes*), and systematic teaching strategies. The educator modifies and adjusts antecedent cause data (teaching behaviors and practices), and shares with colleagues current research findings describing causes that produce the greatest gains in student achievement for all subgroups; effective cause strategies are implemented in classrooms or the school, and the Hishakawa Fishbone is frequently used to examine current data, determine root causes, and take action through effective intervention plans.	The educator recognizes effective teaching strategies that impact student thinking and reasoning as causes that lead to achievement effects (*results*), and is conversant with current research about the causes most apt to produce the greatest gains in student achievement for all subgroups. The educator recognizes that cause/effect data represents strong correlations, not actual causes; The educator is beginning to identify antecedents to improve student achievement based on available data.	The educator is not able to identify antecedents or leverage them to increase student achievement.
3.2 Administrative Structures and Conditions	The educator leverages a wide range of antecedent conditions and structures to increase student achievement, and monitors their impact with user-friendly data. The leader is adept at creating antecedents that increase student achievement, leveraging time, settings, and resources to align and focus efforts (i.e., technological capacity, time and opportunity issues, staff training, levels of implementation in specific teaching strategies, attendance).	The educator recognizes antecedents in terms of time, technology, training, logistics, and level of implementation, and applies them periodically to improve student achievement based on external research findings and antecedents employed in neighboring or comparable schools.	The educator does not view administrative structures of time, technology, textbooks, or training as possible antecedents for excellence that can be modified for improved student achievement.

Exhibit 3.2

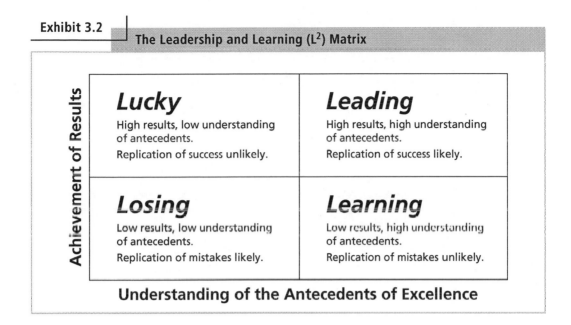

The Leadership and Learning (L²) Matrix

Achievement of Results

Lucky
High results, low understanding of antecedents.
Replication of success unlikely.

Leading
High results, high understanding of antecedents.
Replication of success likely.

Losing
Low results, low understanding of antecedents.
Replication of mistakes likely.

Learning
Low results, high understanding of antecedents.
Replication of mistakes unlikely.

Understanding of the Antecedents of Excellence

DIFFERENTIATING ANTECEDENTS, EFFECTIVE INSTRUCTIONAL STRATEGIES, AND CAUSES

Antecedents are predictors of results. Some that lead to excellence are precursors of improved student achievement, whereas other antecedents may effect less desirable outcomes. Exhibit 3.3 describes types of antecedents. Each term meets the definition of *antecedent* as a predictor of results, but they are differentiated to provide greater precision in planning and implementing changes driven by analyzed data.

Causes are routines that create specific effects or results. Every result has been caused by certain conditions, and a practical tool that helps identify causes of desired results (effects), and results to be reduced or eliminated is the Hishakawa Fishbone. Causes have a specific effect on classroom performance and student achievement. Cause data can always be linked to effects (results) at the classroom level or at the individual student level. Cause data helps determine what to replicate and what to subtract, and reminds us that the interaction between teacher and students in the classroom holds the greatest promise for improved student achievement. Exhibit 3.4 provides examples of causes (routines). These examples have been deliberately chosen to illustrate the distinction between teacher behavior cause data and instructional strategies. They do not necessarily influence student thinking or require extensive training for teachers to implement well, and may or may not lead to improved student achievement.

Instructional strategies are distinguished by the capacity to engage students in thinking, and the need for training, practice, and professional development. We will want

Exhibit 3.3

Antecedents, Differentiated

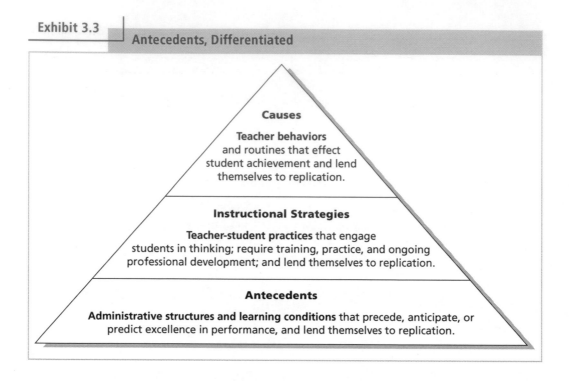

Causes

Teacher behaviors and routines that effect student achievement and lend themselves to replication.

Instructional Strategies

Teacher-student practices that engage students in thinking; require training, practice, and ongoing professional development; and lend themselves to replication.

Antecedents

Administrative structures and learning conditions that precede, anticipate, or predict excellence in performance, and lend themselves to replication.

Exhibit 3.4

Common Examples of Cause Data

- Transitions between activities
- Closing activities
- Routines for asking questions
- Collecting assignments
- Routine for opening every class
- How classroom rules are established
- Teaching classroom procedures
- How teams and groups are formed

to replicate, refine, and multiply this type of antecedent to better predict improved student achievement and excellent performance. Examples include summarizing and note taking designed to connect prior learning to new applications, or the use of corrective feedback that is meaningful, accurate, and timely. Another powerful category of instructional strategies is the generation and testing of hypotheses. At The Leadership and Learning Center, the "Making Standards Work" seminar draws on the research regarding student engagement to include the "engaging scenario" in every performance assessment (Ainsworth, 2003). Engagement has been associated with improved student achievement at all levels (Fredricks, Blumenfeld, & Paris, 2004). When faculty understand the strategies that are most effective for specific students under specific conditions, they begin to be able to predict and create excellence in student performance. Exhibit 3.5 identifies instructional strategies that engage students cognitively and require training, practice, and professional development to implement well:

Exhibit 3.5

Examples of Instructional Strategies

- Written "ticket out the door" every day for every student
- Identifying similarities and differences
- Teaching "up"
- Self-assessment
- Pervasive use of scoring guides
- Systematic use of graphic organizers for creating, planning, collaborating
- Engaging scenarios
- Homework for thinking with practice
- Flexible grouping
- *Five Easy Steps to a Balanced Math Program*

In fact, all of these examples require training of some sort to implement well. They are usually more than one single cause or routine, and in all cases produce a cognitive level of engagement from students. For example, *Five Easy Steps to a Balanced Math Program* (Ainsworth & Christinson, 2000) is a complete training program with five discrete and effective strategies.

Even the most effective instructional strategy, however, will not produce breakthrough results if it is not employed as intended. Too many dedicated educators experience confusion and frustration when they adopt a proven practice without sufficient training and skill development. When student growth fails to equal that achieved by the originators, the proven strategy is often blamed or criticized rather than the degree and quality of implementation (Evans, 1996, pp. 137–140).

Instructional strategies are distinguished from causes and structural antecedents by a connection to professional development and quality implementation. Data about strategies helps determine whether a strategy was implemented and whether the strategy had its desired effect. As antecedents, strategies offer practitioners the ability to identify on the front end data that will provide the most information and value, rather than discovering the need for different data after the fact.

ANTECEDENTS AS CONDITIONS AND STRUCTURES

One can hope that all learning conditions and administrative structures are designed and implemented as antecedents of excellence that result in improved student achievement. Unfortunately, antecedents can also institutionalize ineffectiveness. Transferring teachers or administrators who perform at marginal levels, rather than assisting them to improve, counseling them to change careers, or showing them the door through dismissal, is just one example. Increasing the length of the instructional day without providing time for collaboration is another; our middle school example in Chapter 2 failed to identify the time required to comply with reporting requirements, even though the additional time required resulted in reduced instructional time with students. The result showed that this was hardly an antecedent for excellence.

Many other conditions for learning and administrative structures are adopted or adapted randomly or based on tradition, rather than being thoughtfully selected as potential antecedents of excellence. Teachers and principals often select and apply antecedents independently; if they are successful, they may see such practices replicated voluntarily by peers and colleagues. A better approach that advances best practices on a faster track is to examine the research for what works. Exhibit 3.6 identifies fourteen practices that are clear examples of antecedents that align closely with standards and improved student achievement.

These antecedents, such as reinforcement of writing conventions, flexibility for teacher management of the curriculum, assessments, collaborative scoring, and meaningful feedback, have powerful support throughout the research (Reeves, 2004a, pp. 79–82; Langer, Colton, & Goff, 2003, p. 13; Reeves, 2004d, pp. 111–113; Marzano, Pickering, & Pollock, 2001a; Calkins, 1994). Some items reflect best practices, alignment of effort, and just plain professionalism (e.g., item 13 in Exhibit 3.5). Let's apply what we've learned about the different types of antecedents by categorizing a sample of the antecedents described in Exhibit 3.6 (see Exhibit 3.7).

Presence of highly visible standards in the classroom is definitely an antecedent condition for learning, probably an antecedent that engages student thinking, and most definitely one that could and should be replicated. It does not, however, qualify as a teacher behavior (cause), because we have insufficient information to attach it to a specific classroom effect. Flexibility to vary content is a structural and administrative antecedent that will require professional development, but until the teacher develops a strategy that engages students, it is not an instructional strategy. Neither is it a cause, because flexibility alone does not mean that the teacher actually applies it in the classroom, nor does its presence mean that the teacher has changed her behavior to produce a specific result or effect. Flexibility in curriculum is something that can be replicated and applied with all three forms of antecedents, but it must first be refined into a strategy and then applied in the classroom to produce a desired outcome.

Exhibit 3.6

Classroom Checklist for Standards Implementation

1. Standards are highly visible in the classroom.

2. Standards are expressed in student-accessible language.

3. Examples of proficient and exemplary student work are displayed throughout the classroom.

4. The teacher publishes in advance the explicit expectations for proficient student work.

5. Student evaluation is always done according to standards and a scoring guide.

6. The teacher can explain to every parent or stakeholder the specific expectations of students for the year.

7. The teacher has flexibility to vary the length and quantity of curriculum content daily.

8. Students can spontaneously explain what *proficient* means for any assignment.

9. Commonly used standards are reinforced in every subject (e.g., conventions, organization of writing).

10. The teacher has created at least one performance assessment in the past month.

11. The teacher exchanges student work with a colleague for review and collaborative evaluation at least once every two weeks.

12. The teacher provides feedback to students and parents about the quality of student work compared to the standards, not in relation to a curve.

13. The teacher helps to build community consensus in the classroom with other stakeholders for standards and high expectations for *all* students.

14. The teacher uses a variety of assessment techniques.

Source: Douglas B. Reeves, *Making Standards Work,* 4th ed. (Denver, CO: Advanced Learning Press, 2004), 269–273.

Exhibit 3.7

Antecedent Matrix

Antecedent	Replicable	Causes—Teacher Behaviors		Instructional Strategies		Administrative Structures and Strategies
	Replicable	Classroom	Specific	Professional Development	Thinking	Can Be Mandated
1. Standards are visibly displayed	✔				✔	✔
7. Flexibility in curriculum	✔			✔		✔
11. Collaboration	✔			✔	✔	✔
12. Feedback	✔	✔	✔	✔	✔	✔

Collaborative scoring is both an instructional strategy and an administrative structure, but until teacher behaviors in the classroom change, it cannot be identified as a cause that produces a particular effect with students. Only the feedback item meets the criteria for all three antecedent forms; it is provided to students and linked to a specific effect (work production); it requires professional development to do well; and it engages student thinking. Provision of feedback is something that can be mandated and instituted in a systematic way.

The strongest antecedents reflect the components of all three antecedent forms. The cause demonstrates that teachers are employing the antecedent, not just that they are aware of its utility. The instructional strategy demonstrates that the antecedent is something that must be mastered if teachers are to fully engage students with their best thinking, and the administrative structure ensures that the strategy and classroom application will be established to advance student learning and achievement. Antecedents offer a wealth of possibilities in data analysis unavailable to those who limit their understanding of data to results only.

ANTECEDENTS YOU CAN BANK ON

Are some antecedents more valuable than others? If I were to suggest that every classroom needed a large-screen color television more than Internet access for students, or that the televisions were more important this year than professional development in "Making Standards Work" or "Writing Excellence," I would hope my colleagues would challenge my assumptions and ask me for evidence that supports my recommendations. I am always surprised at how many classrooms in countless schools have expended precious resources on large-screen TVs while staff get by with inadequate content materials or limited access and literacy in technology. Is the presence of the TVs an antecedent? The question should be: "How confident are we that large-screen TVs in each classroom will precede, predict, or produce improved student achievement results?"

Consider incorporating the key components of antecedents into your review process for purchase and adoption of significant antecedent programs and services. Rather than asking for research findings from every product representative (they will surely have them), consider the following questions:

- How will we leverage _____ for student achievement?

- How will we ensure that _____ will promote proficiency?

- What effect can we expect in classrooms that adopt _____ ?

- What instructional strategies have been most effective with _____ ?

- What professional development requirements are needed to ensure staff proficiency with _____? What measures have been developed for implementation quality?

- Describe how adoption of _____ will engage student thinking.

- Does _____ lend itself to systematic introduction through administrative structures and conditions for learning? If so, what structures would you recommend and why?

These questions are useful when examining a novel idea, new program, or resource. They are designed to help educators at all levels select the antecedents most likely to produce desired improvements and avoid those that do little to focus effort, improve instruction, or predict excellence in performance.

CAUSES AND HUNCHES

Causes rarely are spoken of in data analysis, in part because of the complexity of teaching and learning, and in part because few educators systematically and consistently take the time to identify causes, especially root causes. Moreover, true cause-and-effect relationships are virtually impossible to find, because of a myriad of variables that are outside our control. Cause antecedents have the advantage of revealing very strong correlations, both positive and negative, helping to achieve goals and solve problems. Anderson and Fagerhaug (2000) suggest two characteristics of a problem: (1) having a problem is by nature a state of affairs plagued with some difficulty or undesired status; and (2) a problem represents a challenge that encourages solving to establish more desirable circumstances. The identification of causes, even root causes, then, is very important to our profession. Exhibit 3.8 shows a modified Hishakawa Fishbone, a popular tool for examining cause and effect to achieve goals and solve problems. The Fishbone is a quick and useful tool for data analysis; this cause–effect diagram organizes the antecedent skeletons around the four key dimensions of people, structures, resources, and processes so as to guide brainstorming around the selected effect, and address administrative structure, conditions of learning, instructional strategies, and teacher behaviors. Exhibit 3.8 provides a template and Exhibit 3.9 offers an example based solely on data described in the narrative about Dennis, the principal of Woodside Elementary School. Applying his story will make the benefit of this graphic organizer apparent.

Tools like the Hishakawa Fishbone help "make visible the invisible" and stimulate insights that achieve goals and overcome persistent challenges. Although we don't know everything that contributed to success at Woodside, we can see the connections between

Exhibit 3.8

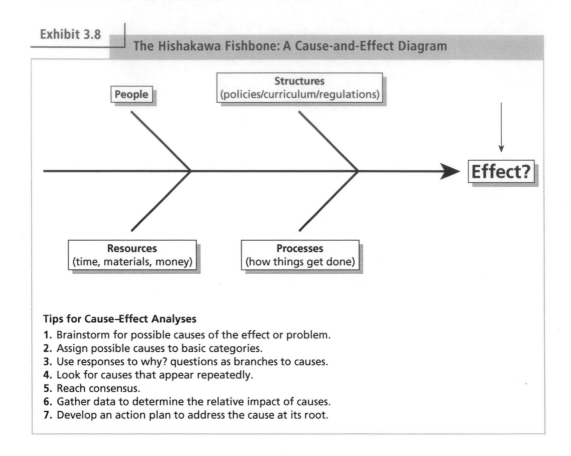

The Hishakawa Fishbone: A Cause-and-Effect Diagram

People

Structures
(policies/curriculum/regulations)

Effect?

Resources
(time, materials, money)

Processes
(how things get done)

Tips for Cause–Effect Analyses

1. Brainstorm for possible causes of the effect or problem.
2. Assign possible causes to basic categories.
3. Use responses to why? questions as branches to causes.
4. Look for causes that appear repeatedly.
5. Reach consensus.
6. Gather data to determine the relative impact of causes.
7. Develop an action plan to address the cause at its root.

resources, staff, policies, and processes, and we can see how leadership marshaled those resources, created those processes, and engaged staff to make a difference.

SUMMARY

The rearview-mirror effect is difficult to escape without a clear understanding and application of antecedents. The L^2 Matrix is based on a hypothesis that those who understand and apply antecedents of excellence are better able to replicate successful practices and sustain success as cohorts of students advance to their next environment. Without that understanding, educators with only student achievement data are every bit as much at a loss as someone trying to interpret a twenty-five-pound weight loss without information as to what transpired.

Antecedents are strategies, causes, structures, and conditions that precede, anticipate, or predict excellence in performance. There are three forms of antecedents: (1) cause antecedents that lead to results, (2) instructional strategies that require mastery and engage students in thinking, and (3) administrative structures and conditions for learning. In this chapter, the aspects that define a standards-based classroom were

Exhibit 3.9

The Hishakawa Fishbone and Woodside Elementary School: A Cause-and-Effect Simulation

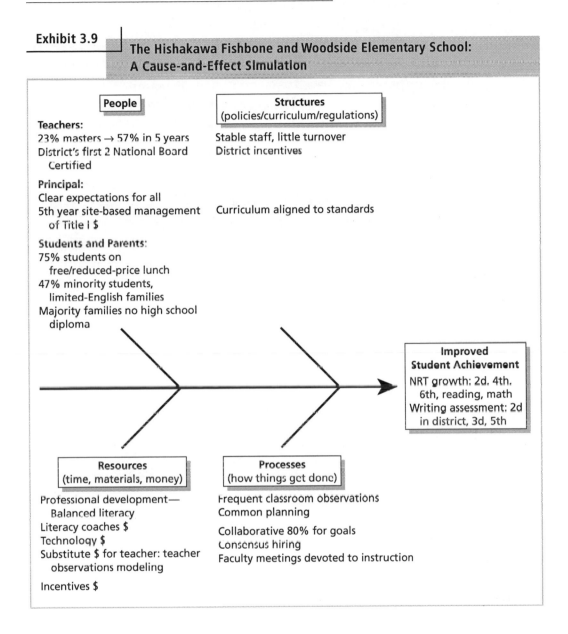

People

Teachers:
23% masters → 57% in 5 years
District's first 2 National Board
  Certified

Principal:
Clear expectations for all
5th year site-based management
  of Title I $

Students and Parents:
75% students on
  free/reduced-price lunch
47% minority students,
  limited-English families
Majority families no high school
  diploma

Structures
(policies/curriculum/regulations)

Stable staff, little turnover
District incentives

Curriculum aligned to standards

**Improved
Student Achievement**
NRT growth: 2d, 4th,
  6th, reading, math
Writing assessment: 2d
  in district, 3d, 5th

Resources
(time, materials, money)

Professional development—
  Balanced literacy
Literacy coaches $
Technology $
Substitute $ for teacher: teacher
  observations modeling
Incentives $

Processes
(how things get done)

Frequent classroom observations
Common planning

Collaborative 80% for goals
Consensus hiring
Faculty meetings devoted to instruction

analyzed as antecedents and a process was provided to help practitioners select antecedents capable of predicting success and preceding improvement in student achievement. The same process was employed to scrutinize large-scale antecedents that teachers and school leaders make decisions about every day. A cause-and-effect diagram was presented as a means to identify and select antecedents when faced with challenging goals that must be achieved or when persistent barriers and problems require solutions.

Woodside Elementary, a fictional school, represents the experience of capable, dedicated professionals thrust into a paradigm where results and numbers seem to be all that matters. Dennis needed to understand that he was capably creating antecedents that did precede excellence, and that could predict improved student achievement. Unfortunately, those who analyze data are far too often preoccupied with getting results, without the benefit of data describing and monitoring the causes that produce them. Therein lies our hope that educators who read and apply the lessons of *Beyond the Numbers* will take the time to analyze what adults do, identify the connections with student achievement, and carefully select antecedents with the greatest capacity to engage students to think, improve their classroom performance every day, and set in motion structures and learning conditions that can be widely replicated by teachers who embrace their obligation to learn and to lead.

DISCUSSION

BIG IDEA

If continuous improvement is to occur, cause, effect, and antecedent data must be identified, collected, analyzed, and acted upon.

QUESTIONS

1. *Describe the steps you would take to select the essential data you need to ensure continuous improvement in your school.*

2. *What role should antecedents play in data analysis? Why isn't it sufficient to concentrate on student achievement results alone?*

3. *What distinguishes cause–effect antecedents from instructional strategies? An instructional strategy from an administrative condition of learning?*

4. *Describe the benefits of using a cause–effect diagram.*

5. *How can early identification and monitoring of antecedents prevent unnecessary data collection?*

The Power of Collaboration

Plans fail for lack of counsel, but with many advisors comes success.

—PROVERBS 15:22

Educators have long been proponents of collaboration. Labor negotiations are collaborative and interest-based. Education has promoted shared decision making for years, and policies across the nation have detailed descriptions of the means and format for making decisions, as well as definitions of consensus, parity, collaborative, and executive decisions (for those rare emergencies when one voice is needed). Collaboration ensures that multiple viewpoints are available and that all voices are heard. In public education, collaboration has become as much a function of fairness and application of democratic principles as it is a practical approach to gathering information and making decisions.

Collaboration is essential in data analysis if we are to get beyond the numbers. Data rarely provides a blueprint for improving instruction or modifying antecedents; you cannot find the ways just by examining a table or a chart or a worksheet. Data we collect are invariably limited, as we discussed in Chapter 3 on antecedents. The most accurate data is even more limited if educators succumb to the rearview-mirror effect. The incomplete nature of the data we have available is the very reason we need to add the human perspective, and it is the reason collaboration is so critical in data analysis.

In *Accountability in Action* (Reeves, 2004b), data is described in three levels. Tier 1 is the district and state assessments and related mandated data; Tier 2 represents the wealth of data (antecedent and results data) available at the school level to leverage in pursuit of goals and improvements; Tier 3 data offers the narrative story that numbers are unable to describe. Tier 3 data provides the context for learning—the data that requires professional perspective, hunches, and opinions about Tier 1 and Tier 2 data. Surowiecki describes this data as "private information," the results of interpretation, analysis, and even intuition (2004, p. 41). Tier 3 data is every bit as critical and reliable as the numbers we crunch, and quality analysis is incomplete without the insights that emerge when teachers work together. Data of any kind is meaningful only when professionals collaboratively examine, analyze, reflect, and ultimately decide to act on the data available to them.

Frequently used models of collaboration have been developed by well-respected scholars in the field. Surowiecki (2004) identified three conditions necessary for a "crowd" or group to be wise: diversity, independence, and decentralization. *Diversity* promotes wisdom through the meeting of differing ideas and perspectives and by "making it easier for individuals to say what they really think" (p. 39). *Independence* means relative freedom from the influence of others. It is a capacity to rely on one's own thinking, including the independence to withhold judgment and resist innovation until it resonates with one's own experience and observation. *Decentralization* means that authority for decision making has devolved from a central authority to other units and that specialization and division of labor are prevalent. School systems possess each of these ingredients for wisdom when decisions are made at various levels, when specialization occurs, and when opportunities exist to benefit from diverse ideas and perspectives.

Schmoker (2001) reported how collaboration became a central tenet of reform at Adlai Stevenson High School in Illinois, under the direction and vision of Rick DuFour:

- Teamwork is scheduled and structured. There are team norms, scheduled times, and formats.

- Teamwork is focused on improving teaching strategies that promote better results on the common end-of-course assessments.

- Teamwork is focused on the development and refinement of the end-of-course assessments (pp. 11–13).

The approach employed at Adlai Stevenson High School was "Teamwork: If you require it, they will come." A focus on collaboration redirected staff to pay attention to student learning, and the structured format helped produce a truly "collaborative culture" in which student achievement results were dramatic and sustained over time.

Reeves (2004e, pp. 99–100) recognized collaboration as key to effective professional development, describing a collaborative model of professional development with the following four characteristics:

1. The model depends more on teachers teaching teachers and less on outside assistance. It is primarily an internal, established process that recognizes teachers as experts.

2. The collaborative model depends upon context. Integrated curriculum, standards, and leadership must all be addressed simultaneously.

3. Attention is paid to individual needs. Collaborative professional development is not one size fits all.

4. Collaborative staff development is sustained internally.

Professional development works precisely because of collaboration in this model, which is sustained internally and relies on teacher-to-teacher instruction and practice. The model attends to the context of teaching and learning through collaborative conversations and dialogue, and enriches understanding by capturing individual differences in experience, training, and perspectives of individual teachers.

Collaboration requires practice if it is to yield the synergy and gestalt of "the whole is greater than the sum of its parts." Langer, Colton, and Goff (2003, p. 163) put it succinctly: "[T]oo often we expect collaborative tasks to be natural and convenient for teachers. The task may get done, but sometimes at the expense of precious time, lack of collegiality, and bad feelings." Educators will not routinely, predictably, or deliberately be able to get beyond the numbers without approaching collaboration in a systematic way.

These examples underscore the need to make sure collaboration is explicit, structured, and embedded. The same call for precision is echoed by Rick DuFour: "[T]rue collaboration does not happen by chance or by invitation. It happens only when leaders commit to creating the systems that embed collaboration in the routine practices of the school and when they provide teachers and teams with the information and support essential to improve practice" (2003, p. 63). Peter Senge adds, "At its core, team learning is a discipline of practices designed, over time, to get the people of a team thinking and acting together. The team members do not need to think alike" (2000, p. 73). Collaboration, then, is really all about data and using the insights of experience and diversity to help us make the best decisions possible.

Collaboration is so important that it is central to application of analysis methods, choice of data tools, and triangulation. Collaboration powerful enough to effect excellence in student achievement has three characteristics that form the basis for our discussion here:

1. Collaboration must be present from planning to execution in data-driven decision making.

2. Collaboration is the means to develop team thinking and candor in data-driven decision making.

3. Collaboration must be integrated into every data-driven decision.

These characteristics are described in terms of leadership competencies in Exhibit 4.5 at the end of this chapter. We will address each of these characteristics of effective collaboration in data-driven decision making, but first let us visit two teachers of high school science.

CASE STUDY

Mary Ann has taught chemistry at Maple High School for the past seven years, after accepting a change in assignment from the biology and earth science classes she taught for the previous five years to help the department. Mary Ann was an excellent teacher, loved by her students and their parents, and respected by her peers. Before coming to Maple, she had taught elementary school, primary level, rotating from kindergarten to second to first grades for twelve years, again helping whenever requested. Each of her five principals loved to observe her classroom, where every event and transition was purposeful and connected. She understood reading and she understood children, and for most of her career remarked, "I can't believe I get paid to do what I love." The fact that she taught high school students with the same passion, humor, and skill as demonstrated at the elementary level made Mary Ann a teacher to reckon with, especially when changes were proposed. If her principal convinced Mary Ann of the need for change, it was easy sailing from then on.

Mary Ann is not pleased with the changes being implemented now, though, and they are causing her to consider a change herself. She had never had issues with accountability, and approached every fall confident that her students would learn the material and be more than ready for the next grade or next course. She is insulted by the state assessments and NCLB requirements, and believes that the enrollment in her classes and feedback from students and parents is the real measure of accountability. Since she began at Maple twelve years ago, students have twice voted for her to make the faculty commencement speech, and in her twenty-four years, she has twice been elected the association's teacher of the year.

Now the district is getting in on the accountability act and Mary Ann has had it. She tolerated the seven days of state assessments (class periods), but now the district is insisting that each department create its own end-of-course assessments based on the standards. "We can't call them tests anymore," she was heard saying. The district already required teachers to collaboratively score monthly writing assessments and to adhere to an instructional calendar beginning next year. The instructional calendar required departments to determine what standards would be addressed each week and to agree to develop instructional units and performance assessments together for each course. Mary Ann really bristled at this requirement, as she long ago had developed quality units for her courses. Kids knew they were challenging, and she updated them frequently; she had no problem with new textbooks, as she always served on the committees that recommended selections to the school board.

"Whatever happened to academic freedom? I am not about to take my valuable time to have to explain or justify my work to novice teachers or to spend unnecessary time always having to 'reach consensus' with teachers who are just figuring out how to manage behavior in their classrooms. It's not that I'm not willing to help," she would tell her best friend at the gym, "but I've got students that come in before and after school to see me. See how messed up their priorities are!"

Even worse, the "head shed," as she calls the administration building, now expects faculty to evaluate the end-of-course assessments and review them annually for improvements. Mary Ann told a colleague, "Now the district expects us to do the jobs of the curriculum department. How in the world do they expect us to do anything of significance for kids when we are responsible for everything, but have no authority?"

Mary Ann knew herself well enough to notice the impact of the added stress. Several times, when she previously would have used humor with students, she had been abrupt instead, sending three of them to the office this year alone—a number equal to the eleven previous years combined. She didn't like the cynicism and sarcasm that she felt and expressed. Mary Ann decides that if her principal follows through on requiring departments to develop the same tests, and require collaborative scoring of writing assessments each month, this year will be her last. Early retirement she does not want, but she knows that the changes planned are untenable, so it may mean leaving the profession.

C A S E   S T U D Y

Georgia proudly received her "Maple High School Family" plaque at the end-of-year banquet, having successfully completed her third year in the district. It hadn't been easy, as she had had to take the state examination for teacher proficiency in earth and biological sciences twice. She finally passed just under the wire before the district's policy would have required her dismissal. Georgia hadn't been the best student. In fact, her first degree was in speech therapy, but she had been unable to pass the state exam even after three tries. So, because she wanted to work with kids, she went back to school long enough to take a few content requirements, complete student teaching, and earn her teaching certificate. Georgia recognized the same characteristics in many of her students: they just weren't test takers, so she went out of her way to make sure they were exposed to various assessments. Georgia made it clear to all her students that they would have multiple opportunities to succeed, and she was determined that every student would be proficient, even on district and state assessments.

Every evaluation spoke of her willingness to learn, her dedication to students, and her powerful work ethic. Georgia was the department's earliest arrival, and she was like a sponge in learning from her colleagues—people she struggled to call peers because she had such respect for their knowledge, experience, and skills. Mr.

(continues)

CASE STUDY (Continued)

Ino, the assistant principal who had observed and evaluated Georgia since day one, had assigned a great mentor coach to help her, although Lisa was from the cross-town high school. This was a little awkward, and Georgia never really understood why her coach was from another school. The great thing was that Lisa helped her understand how to ask for and receive help from her colleagues. Over the three years she had been at Maple, Georgia had also received help and assistance from her department, especially by observing Mary Ann. The department chair also provided lots of instructional materials and great Internet resources.

Georgia shook Mr. Ino's hand to the applause of the faculty, whispering as she crossed the banquet dais, "Mr. Ino, thanks for assigning Lisa to me. She was so helpful getting me enrolled in just the right in-services and courses. And thanks for being so encouraging while letting me know where I needed to grow!" Georgia returned to her seat as other Maple High School family members took their turns.

"This is the best job in the best school in the best district anywhere," she thought gratefully. She remembered Allen's encouragement to have her develop the first draft of the biology EOC assessment, and the way every team member had contributed great changes without putting her down. She really liked the collaborative writing requirement, because she had learned that she expected too little from her students, and that her own understanding of the writing process and 6+ Traits was below standard and warranted additional training and support. As she looked back, she was amazed at how much she had learned. She sometimes wished her university had been so helpful, but she was confident that she was becoming more proficient every day. As the last teacher accepted his plaque, and everyone rose in applause for the twenty-three new "family" members, Georgia was moved to tears and determined right then and there to be the best biology teacher ever, maybe even better than Mary Ann.

Both of these teachers taught in the same department and same school. Both were dedicated to their craft and loved their students. Mary Ann was a talented and gifted teacher, while Georgia was learning how to become one. Mary Ann preferred her autonomy, resenting the intrusion of colleagues, her department, school, and district, and viewing the issue as one of academic freedom. Georgia needed assistance, knew it, and welcomed it. Their experience will form the backdrop of our discussion throughout this chapter.

EVEN THE LONE RANGER HAD TONTO

Mary Ann viewed her profession as one where she had the obligation to independently develop her skills and content knowledge to the best of her ability; it is also a profession where she had the latitude to develop her own style, set her own pace, and enrich the district's curriculum by providing in-depth units of her choice. The result: Mary Ann adhered to the "Lone Ranger" isolation that has characterized teaching and learning in the United States for more than a century. Teaching is an inherently lonely profession and teachers usually feel isolated enough as it is, but some very effective teachers have grown accustomed to this model and actually prefer it. Although some may find ways to be effective within the four walls of their classroom and the limits of their respective curriculum, students are shortchanged in the process. Teachers who collaborate learn from each other, and support each other by bringing their special individual talents and skills to the process. Collaboration is fundamental to data analysis because it produces better decisions, provides the context needed for insight, and allows those engaging in it to discover solutions and identify challenges that otherwise would go unnoticed. Georgia, in contrast to Mary Ann, wanted to collaborate and was like a sponge when others offered assistance and feedback.

Peter Senge refers to the "deprivatization of practice and critical review" (2000, p. 327) as a characteristic of schools that learn—schools that have discovered ways to reduce the teachers' ability and need to function as Lone Rangers. Senge suggests that teachers need to share, discuss, and observe the practice of teaching with colleagues daily, and that they share responsibility to provide feedback. This is the essence of every model discussed earlier. Specialization or decentralization allows individuals to increase their expertise in certain areas because colleagues share responsibility to develop expertise in other areas. The result is that faculty provide helpful, corrective feedback in the process. Even Tonto advised the Lone Ranger as to his most effective decision or strategy by anticipating dangers and communicating strategies.

Collaboration provides a forum to sanction or legitimize proposed changes. It is powerful because it promotes insights that numbers alone are unable to produce. Collaboration also provides an opportunity for educators to benefit from the collective wisdom of professionals and, in so doing, discover how the whole really is greater than the sum of its parts. Exhibit 4.1 depicts how collaboration in data analysis can produce high-quality insights just by collaborative examination of critical incidents. The data is made up of *private information,* contextual narrative data that is seldom quantified but helps identify needs and develop strategies for improvement. Not one shred of student achievement data is introduced initially, although the process will help identify just what student achievement and antecedent data will be needed to address those incidents that are critical for school success.

The process for determining a *critical incident* is simple and effective. A large-group exercise can be used, or teams as small as two persons. Teams examine each dichotomy separately, then prioritize from the four choices what is most urgent, most compelling, and most important to address first. Further analysis is likely within any size of organization, to quantify the team's perceptions and test their biases. The process communicates the importance of collaboration in any deliberation on data, as

Exhibit 4.1

Critical Incident as a Collaborative Tool

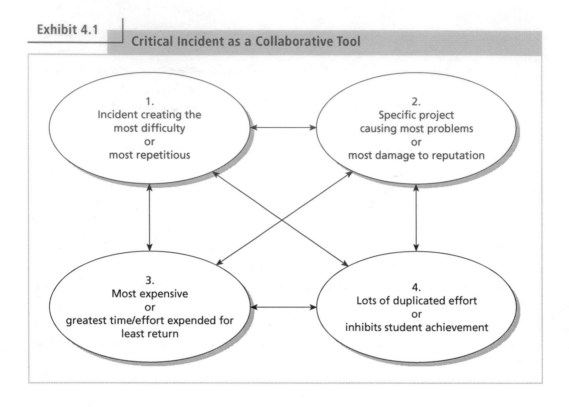

completion of the activity outside of a collaborative group yields merely one's individual opinion. Critical-incident identification jump-starts data analysis by immediately identifying priorities from the collective wisdom of the group. Let's assume the following results:

1. Most difficult: Reliable scoring on 6 + 1 Trait Writing
2. Cause of most damage to reputation: Volleyball team suspended for drinking
3. Greatest time/effort expended for least return: Homecoming parade
4. Inhibits student achievement: Policy requires homework as 25 percent of all grades

Which incident should be addressed? Are all these incidents sufficiently critical to require a systematic effort to prevent their reoccurrence? Leaders at this juncture frequently ask for student achievement data or antecedent monitoring to verify that these anecdotal incidents are indeed critical. Even without such data, the collective wisdom of the group is its own validation for some of these issues. As a school, the group members experienced the damage to their reputations; they recalled the work requirements of the homecoming parade; and they labored under the prescribed homework policy, even though it was implemented with such variability as to render it meaningless in terms of proficiency. The collective and collaborative judgment (*assessment*) that these incidents are critical is a measure of the context within which the school operates and the private information each professional brings to the table.

The critical-incident data tool offers a dramatic example of collaboration because of its ability to help professionals get to the heart of issues that affect their work lives. It also reveals how powerful collaboration is: the Lone Ranger could not have achieved these insights independently, regardless of how skilled and talented the Masked Man may have been. He, or Mary Ann in our example, needs the perspective of others to identify what is really critical, simply because our information is limited by our experience. The business manager might know with some certainty the program that was most expensive in a per-pupil cost formula, but she would be less likely to know what was most costly in terms of expenditure of staff effort. The same is true for the department head, superintendent, board member, or classroom teacher. Surowiecki notes that when it comes to solving problems or identifying solutions, groups of even less informed individuals, if they are acting on their own best independent judgment and if the group represents a sufficiently diverse group of thinkers, will invariably offer better solutions than the expert (2004, pp. 35–39). But let's return to our critical-incident discussion.

The high school team decides to address all four incidents simultaneously. Number 1 indicates a need for follow-up in terms of professional development to improve the quality and reliability of collaborative scoring. Number 2 indicates a need to reexamine eligibility rules, establish very clear protocols for each activity sponsor and coach, and monitor implementation of those rules to prevent a similar incident in the future. Number 3 indicates that a great deal of time and effort continue to be expended with limited perceived benefit. Perhaps a solution is to further engage the community in operating the parade, or to increase the academic incentives and sanctions associated with it. Although a multifaceted problem, introduction and identification of this as a problem sets in motion actions to improve its effectiveness, clarify its relationship to student achievement, and redirect internal resources to other areas. Finally, Number 4 is viewed as a hindrance to student achievement because homework effort and cooperative behavior mask a lack of proficiency on state standards. This recognition, too, puts into motion actions to correct and improve the homework process, and perhaps to clarify expectations and introduce strategies and solutions that better align student and teacher efforts on the standards.

In some instances, only one of the identified issues would be addressed, but the example is provided here to illustrate how critical-incident data initiates very important actions to improve the climate and performance of any school or school district—*without* examining achievement data or even numbers about antecedents. How much better informed and more reliable could our decisions be if we added meaningful quantitative student achievement data and insights from antecedents to collaborative analysis of data and events? We will now turn to the need for collaboration from start to finish, planning to execution.

COLLABORATION: FROM PLANNING TO EXECUTION

Collaboration has to be built into every step of data management: from data collection to action planning to implementation to monitoring to evaluation. Every step requires at least two sets of eyes, ears, brain matter, and heart. One of the most useful ways to ensure that collaboration occurs at every step is through the use of an assessment calendar like that depicted in Exhibit 2.4, or through instructional calendars where curriculum content is aligned with standards and addressed during a specific window of time for all teachers. Both of these approaches require teachers to work together at critical junctures in time, and both require explicit actions to take place. The assessment calendar in Exhibit 2.4 insists on a window for administration, data collection, and disaggregation of data, and ensures that faculty are focused on the tasks of data management at prescribed times. Presumably, they will also adhere to similar protocols for administration and for data collection, and be offered the same training and resources to disaggregate their data. That alone gets teachers together. By setting aside specific times for analysis, one creates an expectation that the interaction of professional experience, insights, and perspectives will produce more than what the data alone reveals. This is the essence of collaboration.

Four remaining categories in the assessment calendar establish points in time to recommend changes, make a decision, create a written rationale, and publicly disseminate decisions (with rationales therefor) to affected stakeholders, including parents and students as appropriate. Each step in the assessment calendar is a collaborative process, from planning to execution, in driving decisions based on data. Recommended changes following reflection require educators to do more than see data as a report card, and to do something with the results. The point of decision should also be collaborative when those with authority to make a decision weigh its potential benefits, barriers, costs, and training requirements to implement the recommendation. The written rationale serves as a record of the collaborative processes and also as a report back to those involved at every step of the process. Should the recommendation and decision be to make no changes, a written rationale compels those involved to justify that decision on the basis of their analysis. It objectifies the process, especially if decision makers are at another organizational level, by requiring communication of the process used to select the course of action. It also communicates to those involved in the tedium of collecting and disaggregating data that their work is important, and that the fruits of their efforts are at least examined seriously. In this way, collaboration is made part and parcel of all aspects of data-driven decision making, from planning to execution.

Meaningful collaboration that captures the best thinking of staff to improve student achievement can be achieved by building a number of antecedent structures into the daily routines in schools. Seven antecedent structures are recommended:

1. **Action planning and continuous improvement cycles.** The scenario at Maple High School will be used to illustrate how much more successful collaborative processes will be when a continuous improvement cycle for data-driven decision making is employed.

2. **Collaborative improvements.** A very simple means to promote collaboration in data-driven decision making is to insist that any planned improvement, including those at the classroom level, be supported by data and one other colleague before it can be implemented. Undoubtedly, some of these data requirements will raise the ire of teachers like Mary Ann, and it may require time and effort to bring her along. Mike Schmoker (1999) speaks of the "high maintenance" aspect of building teams and professional learning communities—but if Mary Ann were convinced, her credibility would make that support a real asset for change.

3. **Lesson logs.** When shared and distributed by departments or grade-level teams, lesson logs create opportunities for teachers to collaborate. Given the opportunity, the vast majority of teachers are energized to model lessons or observe others, and the distribution of lesson logs provides a means for teachers to voluntarily be enriched by each other's work.

4. **Common assessments.** Common assessments are those created, evaluated, and revised by teacher teams; they function as a catalyst antecedent for excellence. Common assessments require discussion, debate, and dialogue among peers about the heart of their business. They also serve as a means to institute standards-based assessments to replace less-demanding multiple-choice assessments of content knowledge without the applied learning.

5. **Instructional calendars.** Calendars represent the intent of grade-level and department teams to map out when and how standards will be demonstrated throughout the school year. Many educators are surprised to find out how poorly their curriculum and instruction are aligned with state standards; such calendars assist teachers to drive instruction and apply curriculum strategically, rather than be driven by textbook sequences.

6. **Data teams.** Data teams offer schools a format for submitting challenges and problems, as well as insights and questions, to a group of teachers who agree to monitor outlier student performance and efforts to close learning gaps in the school. This experience really should be common to every classroom teacher, but creation of school-wide data teams can act as a launching point for future

expansion. Data teams are by definition collaborative, and schools may want to create systems that refer difficult data challenges to the data team for analysis, reflection, and recommendations. It is recommended that every teacher serve on a data team that examines actual work of students with real names, real needs, and real faces, and that schools offer as much latitude as possible in responding to those needs. This aspect of data-driven decision making is addressed further in Chapter 5 on accountability.

7. **Program evaluation.** A clearly defined evaluation process offers a means to benefit from the collective wisdom of faculty. When a team of teachers is established who routinely examine the effect of programs and strategies implemented in the school, a culture that is open to modifications based on results emerges.

Any one of these structures will improve the school's capacity for collaborative data analysis. It is collaboration that translates the numbers of data into actions of adults. Data cannot improve instruction; only teachers have that capacity. This is true for every collaborative process, as the insights that emerge from discussions—from hunches to opinions to awareness of best practices to experience—are the insights that drive planned changes in curriculum, antecedent management, and instruction.

WHY THREE HEADS ARE BETTER THAN ONE

Remember Mary Ann, who preferred to be a Lone Ranger, and Georgia, the novice who desired greater collaboration and more explicit mentoring and coaching? Let's examine Georgia's program in detail to illustrate how collaborative processes can add value, even when they are applied informally. We will examine Georgia's grading system to determine its relationship to the biology EOC assessment and ascertain whether writing scores correlated with the state writing assessment. Her data is displayed in Exhibits 4.2 and 4.3.

Exhibit 4.2

**Biology Outcomes by Teacher G: Percent Proficient
Maple High School 1998–2000**

	Caucasian	Hispanic	African-American	Asian
Biology EOC 1998	67	31	28	67
Biology EOC 1999	71	44	41	33
Biology EOC 2000	69	67	63	83
Department Average 1998–2000	75	55	43	81
Biology performance assessment 1998	N/A	N/A	N/A	N/A
Biology performance assessment 1999	73	61	66.7	10

Exhibit 4.2

Biology Outcomes by Teacher G: Percent Proficient
Maple High School 1998–2000 *(Continued)*

	Caucasian	Hispanic	African-American	Asian
Biology performance assessment 2000	78	78	58.3	100
G's district writing assessment 1998	N/A	N/A	N/A	N/A
G's district writing assessment 1999	73	14	23	60
G's district writing assessment 2000	53	35	39	58
District Writing Assessment 2000	52	25	19	71
G's state writing assessment 2000	33	31	36	47
State Writing Assessment—District	45	19	17	53

Exhibit 4.3

Antecedent Measures: Teacher A,
Maple High School Tenth-Grade Biology

	Teacher Attendance %/days	Standards-Based Classroom Components: % Implemented/14	Correlation of Grades with EOC r value	Professional Development Days, Including Summer	Graduate Credits Earned
1997/1998	99%	N/A	.06	7	3
1998/1999	97%	50%	.46	11	6
1999/2000	100%	79%	.39	5	3
District Average	88%	n/a	.14	5.5	1.3

CASE STUDY

Georgia worried about the writing assessment because her state used a holistic scoring guide for each genre and annual tests rotated from one of six genres at random. Mr. Ino assured Georgia that if she could get her students proficient in biology content, and they understood the writing process and 6+1 Traits, even in part, they would do well. Both Mr. Ino and Lisa encouraged Georgia to analyze the data and bring her conclusions to them. They also examined the results for Georgia's students and developed recommendations on their own.

Georgia was overwhelmed with just about everything in year one, so she could not capture many antecedent measures. Exhibit 4.3 describes the measures that Lisa (the mentor/coach) helped identify and monitor during Georgia's three years of

(continues)

noncontinuing contracts. Georgia was shocked to hear Mr. Ino say that no other teacher had monitored these outcomes. She had assumed that everyone would do so, especially great teachers like Mary Ann. Lisa helped Georgia secure other data from human resources and the curriculum department.

Georgia was encouraged that her students outperformed the district on six of eight measures; this year (2000), her students outperformed the department on the biology EOC exam. She wondered if her input in drafting that assessment would not be viewed favorably because of such results, and because her first-year students had struggled so. She had no idea what that might mean in terms of her contract renewal. Overall, Georgia believed the data showed she was learning and getting better at helping her students, but she worried especially about the fall-off in 1999 for her Asian students and the cliff that Caucasian students fell off this year. They were the vast majority of her students, and she knew it was problematic when almost one-third were not proficient. Georgia was also concerned that her professional development days were fewer than the district average this year, something the "head shed" might frown on when they were considering her contract. When the Friday review arrived, she was more than a little anxious. Though she knew Lisa would be supportive, she also knew that Mr. Ino was accountable to others and feared he would have to deliver unpleasant news.

Mr. Ino's task was to review Georgia's data and offer up any insights he had regarding it. He knew Georgia was committed and a dedicated learner, but because she had struggled during the first year and a half, the positive outcomes, especially for minority students, were surprising. The gap for Hispanic and African-American children closed dramatically, and Asian and Caucasian students still met state standards. She monitored results on her performance assessments, and her commitment to professional development was extraordinary. His only concern was that her classroom management was characterized by a lax tardy policy that resulted in a disproportionate number of her students in the principal's office. He pulled the data to verify: seventeen children last year alone were in the halls when they should have been in Georgia's class, but were not counted as tardy or absent. Still, he was proud that he could encourage her, as she was becoming a fine science teacher in the tradition of the best at Maple High.

Lisa was also pleased with Georgia, especially with the progress her minority students had made each year. She knew the performance assessments had helped Georgia's students on the EOC and even the writing assessments. Her one concern was the fact that both Caucasian and Asian students seemed to have reached a plateau in terms of writing, and she wondered whether Georgia's emphasis on a five-step writing process might have become a little wooden, limiting student performance in terms of holistic writing by genre. Lisa felt responsible for the fact that Georgia had adopted her suggestion to require nonfiction writing every day, something that was at least achievable in biology. Students were now expected to react to current events

CASE STUDY   *(Continued)*

that had to do with biology and present succinct paragraphs recounting the news event. Lisa wondered whether that approach had resulted in domination of the written work by lower levels of Bloom's taxonomy, and whether sufficient time had been spent eliciting analysis, synthesis, and evaluation. That was also one of the criticisms and eventual revisions made of Georgia's draft EOC assessment. Still, Georgia's students had done well and her professional development had come a long way.

Georgia's nervousness and lack of confidence were noticeable, so she was surprised at how pleased her mentor and principal were with the student achievement scores in every area. Lisa was taken aback when Mr. Ino made no mention of the static growth in writing for Caucasian and Asian students. She knew that whenever significant differences exist among subgroups, it is prudent to examine for patterns in terms of antecedents that are operating. Both veterans brought different perspectives and experiences to the task, and each perspective was helpful to the other in understanding the data. They added the "data in their heads" to the discussion, and after forty-five minutes, decided to make a serious effort to replicate Georgia's performance assessments in other departments and to survey students to determine what assessments were most useful to them. They also decided to interview students who had made the most growth and students who had yet to achieve proficiency, applying the following rule of thumb:

Examine outlier data whenever subgroup differences are significant.

Finally, Lisa agreed to interview at random a dozen students over the summer for suggestions on how Georgia's class could be improved. The conference ended with Georgia ecstatic at the praise and encouragement provided and excited to receive the data from Lisa when she returned in the fall.

This story illustrates the power of collaboration when professionals gather around student work. Lisa, Mr. Ino, and Georgia viewed the same data and were able to reach consensus on key elements. However, until they participated together in the analysis of those results, their perspectives were very different, and no action was initiated. Neither did any of them consider the actions they later planned. Collaboration around data should result in action that clarifies understanding, replicates successes, and responds to remaining needs—critical elements that Georgia, Mr. Ino, and Lisa accomplished without any real structure. However, the next time this team or an expanded group looks at data, they may neglect to apply the rules of thumb that were helpful the first time. They may be tired, have conflicting priorities, or someone may say something that is taken as an insult or put-down rather than the constructive criticism it was meant to be. Because the collaboration was not explicit, required, and recognized for its power to produce quality change through shared accountability, they missed real opportunities to improve instruction, not only for Georgia's students but for the rest of the school, despite the thoroughness of their analysis and the personal benefit of the collaboration that was present.

COLLABORATION TO DEVELOP TEAM THINKING AND CANDOR

Deliberate efforts to facilitate team thinking and candor in interactions around data, learning, and teaching are necessary to realize the true benefit of collaboration in schools. Collegiality and learning how to respect one another and work cooperatively should be the baseline for collaboration in our schools, not the end product. This author has observed many leaders who genuinely promote and proclaim candor, but there is a natural reluctance among staff to be candid, and it takes only a few instances in which candor is discouraged to shut it down completely with any organization. For candor to be present in a discussion about results and the causes that precede them, a culture of no blame and no excuses must be modeled, communicated, celebrated, and explicitly promoted. Collins (2001) found that this characteristic was more important than vision in distinguishing good organizations from great ones, and he devoted considerable time and effort to what he called "confronting the brutal facts." In a very tangible way, *candor* is personal humility extended to the work of groups, teams, and even organizations. Confrontation of the facts does not happen in isolation; it happens in a collaborative context. Collaboration is the naked-truth level that leaders hope functional teams will strive for. How do we get where we all know we should be, but where we all recognize we are not? Here are some suggestions.

ESTABLISH NORMS. Langer, Colton, and Goff (2003, pp. 47–49) suggest that a culture for collaboration requires norms to help participants function collaboratively and use communication skills that promote inquiry and reflection. This can go a long way toward establishing trust, but setting norms only puts in place a potential for candor. It is the testing of the norms that will establish candor, so leaders and facilitators may even need to create situations to test the norms. Norms for data may include an expectation that members will merely ask for evidence to support any opinions or declarations made at meetings, or that a defined purpose, recommended process, and desired results for a meeting will always be published in advance. Another norm might be that participants are expected to request clarification whenever things are not evident, and to do so by paraphrasing back to the affected colleague their current understanding.

DIVERSITY OF IDEAS: DON'T MEET WITHOUT THEM. Structure meetings to elicit differences, not similarities, in thinking. In *The Wisdom of Crowds*, James Surowiecki discusses the power of "cognitive diversity," a conscious effort to bring together individuals with diverse experiences and perspectives who are encouraged to consider speculative ideas and function freely enough to choose good solutions over bad (2004, pp. 28–39). The business of education is a nurturing and positive profession in which educators seldom confront one another. The stakes are much too high to confront a colleague about data, especially when the data appears to be so lacking in any advice to teachers about their craft. For this reason alone, we need to structure meetings to elicit what differences we do have and to encourage more diversity in ideas and interpretations. Why not structure meetings to elicit differences before rushing to consensus? A data norm might be: "Expression of different viewpoints will be identified, examined, and discussed before any recommendation or decision is made." Such a process would at least invite alternative viewpoints and communicate to all team members the value of stretching for differences.

HOMEWORK: COME PREPARED TO TEACH. This is a particularly effective norm for data analysis, because it encourages participants to know their data so well that they can explain patterns and trends and address antecedents affecting the results. Meetings of busy professionals seldom extend beyond an hour; two at the most. It is not too much to expect each other to come prepared, especially when the decisions the team will make could affect a large number of students who are in real need of interventions that work.

ROLES TO ELICIT CANDOR: MAKE SURE NO STONE (GEM) IS LEFT UNTURNED. This may be the most effective strategy to elicit candor. By assigning roles and rotating them from meeting to meeting, participants learn to assist the group in very distinct ways. For example, the following roles could be very helpful: skeptic, proponent, analyst, change agent, and end-game champion.

- The skeptic is responsible for challenging the team to make a persuasive argument (based on the data) that proposed changes will actually be better than the current state of affairs. The skeptic protects the status quo.

- The proponent makes the case for changes, describing anticipated benefits and reasons for that hypothesis.

- The analyst constantly reminds participants to ask themselves, "Where is the evidence to support that viewpoint?"

- The change agent facilitates the group's decision making and helps them take action on the basis of the data.

■ Finally, the end-game champion promotes the desired results by insisting on a measurement that accurately reflects the end desired.

When these roles are formally rotated, data team meetings have a greater likelihood of being productive and developing real candor that leaves no stone unturned.

NUMBERS YIELD HUNCHES: DON'T LEAVE MEETINGS WITHOUT ONE. This operational norm invites participants to take a chance, to link their own experience with the data presented, and to venture out on a limb to suggest what the data may mean. This is every bit as important as the other norms, as our profession is far too reluctant to interpret data and offer hypotheses with peers. If the meeting is important enough to take professional time to examine data, analysis and reflection should offer up insights and hunches, if not recommendations.

TOOLS ARE TO USE. This norm refers to a set of data tools, several of which are introduced throughout this book. The companion handbook, *Show Me the Proof!* (White, in press) provides a detailed set of graphic organizers, analysis methods, and data analysis tools designed specifically for educators. Data teams should be at least conversant with, and preferably fluent in, the use of such collaborative tools; willing to develop new tools that promote analysis; and come to every meeting prepared to apply them. Effective data teams collaborate often to develop new graphic organizers and data tools.

PUBLISH AND DISSEMINATE MEETING RESULTS. Sharing results of meetings with those affected by them ensures quality attention to discussions and adherence to operating norms of all kinds. Although confidentiality is an issue for students, there is no room for adult confidentiality in data-team or data-driven meetings. Other process norms can facilitate candor, such as guidelines for conflict management, and ways to celebrate success or provide feedback.

These guidelines both value and celebrate diversity of ideas. When team thinking and candor produce solutions that are valued by others, especially those generated from within one's immediate professional support group, effective collaboration is evident. When team members proactively analyze data for discussion in advance of meetings, and when team processes routinely identify changes that result in improvements in the classroom and in student achievement, effective collaboration will again be evident. Collaboration will become part of the culture when training is pursued, provided, and encouraged in mental models, team learning, and cognitive coaching, and when teams are provided periodic training updates on the use of data analysis tools (see Exhibit 4.5 on pages 76–77).

Cognitive Coaching (Costa & Garnston, 1994) reminds us of the need for meta-cognition and the ability to suspend judgment while weighing the merits of ideas and proposals. Cognitive coaching has made good use of graphic organizers to guide student and adult thinking, and the nonlinguistic representations promoted by Costa and Garnston are supported in the literature as powerful instructional strategies and tools for students and adult learners, as well (Marzano, Pickering, & Pollock, 2001a, 2001b). Graphic organizers and data tools are identified as key elements of proficiency in Exhibit 4.5.

COLLABORATION IS INTEGRATED INTO EVERY DATA DECISION

Like the other principles of data-driven decision making, collaboration must be integrated into every data-driven decision. We have reviewed how assessment or data calendars ensure collaborative analysis, and our discussion of Georgia's experience at Maple High School illustrates how important it is to collaborate on every step of the improvement cycle employed. There was considerable excitement about very positive achievement results in Georgia's classes, but because the participants did not have a systematic process in place, they missed a number of opportunities to make the data Georgia collected work for her and for her school, or to suggest ways to ensure that the process remains collaborative. How can data be managed within your school or system to integrate collaboration into every data-driven decision you make? Consider the possibilities in Exhibit 4.4.

TEAM RECOMMENDATIONS FOR CHANGE. The plan to review recommendations only when accompanied by support from a peer facilitates dialogue and discussion among faculty, providing a crack in the structure that has created such teacher isolation and the tendency toward private practice. Support from a peer for a recommendation presumes thoughtful dialogue between at least two persons, if not other faculty and staff. It communicates volumes about the importance of sharing practices, debating strategies, and employing only the most powerful interventions available to the entire faculty. As noted earlier, education is extremely complex and multifaceted. As teachers, we all need the collective wisdom of our peers, and the skills and talents outstanding teachers possess should become skills and talents that all teachers can acquire and master. A recommendation from two staff members is a very simple intervention that moves us in that direction.

COLLABORATIVE SCHEDULES. Schedules that provide common planning and teaming times have become very widespread in recent years, as school leaders recognize the value of collaboration. These valuable investments of time can be made even more valuable by expectations for sharing strategies, analyzing data, and designing and refining classroom assessments. Many teachers will choose to collaborate during these times if doing so is optional; many more will do so if the expectations are communicated with a compelling rationale.

Exhibit 4.4	Methods of Integrating Collaboration into Data Systems
Integrating Collaboration into Data Systems	**Additional Ways to Integrate Collaboration?**
1. Recommendations are reviewed only when submitted with peers.	1.
2. Collaborative schedules are used to provide common planning, teaming.	2.
3. Teacher teams examine student work; leader requests analysis/recommendations for specific students.	3.
4. Assessment calendars establish times for collaboration in analysis, reflection, action planning, and implementation.	4.
5. Early release times are allotted for collaboration around student work.	5.
6. Time and effort are reallocated to respond to urgent challenges, through collaboration that develops powerful instructional strategies.	6.
7. A data analysis road map is put in place.	7.
8. Interim school improvement reports provide interim, midcourse data.	8.
9. Professional development is driven by data on student performance and teaching quality.	9.

DATA TEAMS. Data teams examine student work, develop interventions, adjust teaching strategies, and monitor results. Some teams are informal, some are formal, and some are optional. The most effective are formal enough to be scheduled and monitored, but collaborative enough for the teams to identify needs, develop interventions, commit resources, monitor results, and begin the cycle again. Meetings are typically held monthly or bimonthly; it is recommended that the meetings be as frequent as the data can be coordinated, analyzed, and reviewed. When a leader requests analysis and recommendations for specific students (preferably low-performing students at the margin of success or failure), it raises the importance of data teams by increasing expectations and focusing teacher efforts in powerful ways. Data teams represent a proven and collaborative antecedent for growth.

ASSESSMENT CALENDARS. We have discussed in detail the value of assessment or data calendars: They ensure that time is set aside for collaboration and that accountability structures are created to make sure when we take the time to gather and analyze data. We also schedule the time to respond with actions driven by that data.

EARLY RELEASE. Early release has become commonplace in recent years. Without explicit expectations and guidelines, however, this valuable resource can be diminished by the rampant private practice noted earlier and continued wide variation in student achievement.

TIME AND EFFORT REALLOCATION. When time and resources are reallocated, it is a strong indicator that collaboration around the difficult issues of data analysis and decision making has been established. The ability to commit resources is integral to the notion of accountability, and is studied in Chapter 5.

DATA ANALYSIS ROAD MAP. Schools are certainly not short of improvement plans, and a data road map is not suggested as a replacement for any plans. It *is* recommended to focus intervention efforts as needed, respond to urgencies, triangulate troublesome data, and move ahead with steps that anticipate and respond to emerging needs. A model road map is provided in Appendix H.

INTERIM SCHOOL IMPROVEMENT REPORTS. This recommended report is not unlike progress reports that offer parents and students interim data. Interim school improvement updates offer teachers the same opportunities to make midcourse corrections. Nothing precludes schools from so doing today, but as of this writing, they are as rare as early release programs were fifteen years ago.

PROFESSIONAL DEVELOPMENT. By 2004, more and more school systems have recognized the importance of investing in professional development, but many continue to make those investments on the basis of teacher choice alone, rather than a combination of district and school goals, teacher choice, and lessons from student achievement data. The most effective professional development programs examine antecedent data to determine why, what, when, where, and how professional development will be delivered, as recommended by the National Staff Development Council. Collaboration increases the adoption of best practices by increasing the likelihood that teaching practices will in fact be shared.

SUMMARY

Collaboration is more than a means to improve professional practice and student achievement where it occurs. Dr. Reeves described the craft of teaching in these terms:

Exhibit 4.5

Scoring Guide for Collaboration around Student Work 4.0

Analysis Dimension	Meeting the Standard	Progressing Toward the Standard	Not Meeting the Standard
4.0 Collaboration around Student Work			
4.1 Planning to Execution	The educator ensures ongoing, reflective, and meaningful collaboration that captures the best thinking of staff to improve student achievement through a variety of methods, such as: (1) *action planning*, including all steps of a continuous improvement cycle; (2) *lesson logs* shared and distributed by departments or grade-level teams; (3) *common assessments* created, evaluated, and revised by teacher teams; (4) *instructional calendars* that align curriculum and instruction with regent examinations; (5) development of *data teams* to monitor outlier student performance and close learning gaps, or (6) establishment of a clearly defined *program evaluation* process. Teacher-developed measures of collaboration complement those initiated by individual educator.	The educator promotes collaboration around student work by examining student work at faculty meetings and asking staff to identify solutions to patterns of lagging student achievement and strategies to replicate evidence of dramatically improving student achievement. The educator promotes collaborative data analysis by establishing one or more ongoing methods to examine student performance and implement strategies to improve that performance: (1) *lesson logs* shared and distributed by departments or grade-level teams; (2) *common assessments* created, evaluated, and revised by teacher teams; or (3) *instructional calendars* that align curriculum and instruction with regent examinations.	The educator looks for the path of least resistance in developing data monitoring systems; she or he frequently avoids collaboration beyond initial consensus to adopt a program or strategy; reflection is nonexistent.
4.2 Team Thinking	Solutions generated by others are valued, especially when generated from within the educator's support group. The leader ensures that team thinking permeates the data analysis process by requiring that: (1) all team members proactively analyze data for discussion in advance of meetings; (2) team processes routinely identify improvements; (3) training is provided and encouraged in mental models, team learning, and cognitive coaching; and (4) training updates on data analysis tools are provided to all teams.	The educator promotes team thinking in data analysis by providing and encouraging: (1) training in mental models, team learning, and cognitive coaching; and (2) training in data analysis tools for interested team members.	There is no evidence of a systematic plan to improve the quality of collaborative thinking in examining student work.

Exhibit 4.5 | Scoring Guide for Collaboration around Student Work 4.0 *(Continued)*

Analysis Dimension	Meeting the Standard	Progressing Toward the Standard	Not Meeting the Standard
4.0 Collaboration around Student Work			
	The educator integrates collaboration in data analysis into all key decisions through collaborative processes that benefit from the best thinking of classroom teachers. Evidence is demonstrated through a variety of means, such as: (1) recommendations are reviewed only when submitted with peers; (2) collaborative schedules provide common planning, teaming; (3) teacher teams examine student work; leader requests analysis and recommendations for specific students; (4) assessment calendars are required of all department/grade-level teams; (5) early release times are established for collaboration around student work; (6) time and effort are reallocated to respond to urgent challenges, through collaboration that develops powerful instructional strategies.	The educator attempts to integrate collaboration in data analysis into decision making by one or more of the following: (1) requesting that recommendations be submitted with support by two other peers; (2) establishing school schedules with common planning/teaming; or (3) providing data to teacher teams (flexible grouping) and requesting analysis and recommendations for specific students.	The educator views decisions regarding data analysis as the prerogative of administration or as isolated acts of leadership separate from lessons revealed by data.
4.3 Integration into Decision Making	*Assessment calendars* establish times for collaboration in analysis, reflection, action planning, and implementation.		

Ours is an inherently collaborative profession, and my respect for individual creativity does not reduce my demand for consensus on the essentials. Indeed, my commitment to fairness for students requires that educational opportunities, teacher expectations, and classroom assessment practices are never a matter of luck but a matter of right (2002a, p. 179).

We know that teaching practices are even more powerful than content preparation or professional development (Wenglinsky, 2002), and it has been well established that teacher quality has a direct relationship to a student's achievement for multiple years out (Sanders, 2001). We need to get to the point where we see the opportunity to benefit from great teaching as something for all our students, delivered by all our teachers, as a result of their collaborative efforts to improve. That will require collaboration in earnest.

Collaborative analysis is imperative as a matter of fairness and equity. It is the forum for examining student results and antecedents affecting those results. Collaboration puts in motion those changes in expectations, educational opportunities, and assessment practices that emerge as best in a collaborative context. It makes it easier for a group to make decisions based on facts and expands the set of possible solutions when a problem is present. Finally, collaboration introduces a new dynamic to data analysis, because the interaction among participants reveals solutions and strategies that could not have become evident without the diverse perspectives (and even preconceptions and biases) of those who examined the data together. Exhibit 4.5 provides a scoring guide for self-assessment by leaders, and Chapter 5 examines accountability as the third principle of data-driven decision making.

DISCUSSION

BIG IDEA

Collaboration is the platform that translates data into decisions.

QUESTIONS

1. *What is meant by the "power of collaboration"? Why should collaboration be considered a principle of data-driven decision making?*

2. *What did Georgia, her mentor Lisa, and her principal, Mr. Ino, fail to do in their analysis of Georgia's classroom and personal data?*

3. *How does collaboration enrich analysis of data?*

5

Accountability

Accountability for quality belongs to top management. It cannot be delegated.

—W. EDWARDS DEMING

Top management in the schools includes teachers, who by their presence, expectations, and clarity of communication let every student of every age know very quickly where the line is for acceptable quality. Accountability, then, is active and essential; it should come as no surprise that accountability is the third principle of data-driven decision making. Accountability and data are often used in the same breath, and the terms *data* and *accountability* are apparently inextricably linked in educational circles. Thus, a fair question to ask is, "Why?" Is it because accountability systems in all fifty states, the District of Columbia, and all territories use student achievement results data as measures of effectiveness? Is accountability a report card for adults and educational organizations? For the purposes of data analysis, accountability must become much more.

Accountability is taking responsibility to act on the basis of what data tells us. The medical analogy is a powerful one with profound implications for schools. When a child has a temperature of 103 degrees, few of us would wait until the next morning to take action, let alone the next week. To even consider waiting until next semester would be unconscionable—yet schools routinely make such decisions. When the restaurant we frequent is visited by the Health Department and found lacking as to hygienic food storage procedures, it would be foolish to continue to dine there. In schools, however, the rearview-mirror effect is all too pervasive: The data shouts, "Intervene, take action!," but we respond by noting that we tried that before or we are planning to adopt a new math textbook later this year. Accountability regarding data analysis is first and foremost taking action on the basis of what the data tells us and acting quickly on the diagnosis, rather than allowing problems to fester. Accountability is also student-centered (Reeves, 2004b), meaning that it relies on measures of both student achievement results and antecedents of excellence. Accountability for data analysis means that teachers provide leadership in the analysis process and that such leadership is fundamentally collaborative. We will define it this way:

> *Accountability* is authority to commit resources (**to take action**), responsibility to demonstrate improvement (**results**), and permission to adjust time and opportunity (**permission to subtract**) so that all students achieve beyond their expectations and the expectations of adults committed to their achievement (parents, teachers, other educators).

A thumbnail definition of accountability for data analysis is simply:

> *Authority to act, permission to subtract,*
> *and responsibility for results.*

This chapter discusses the authority to take action and the structures needed to ensure that accountability is proactive with regard to improved performance and quality. A scoring guide that describes proficiency in terms of data-analysis accountability is provided in Exhibit 5.1. Opportunities are available in every state and territory to create sound accountability systems that will allow practitioners to use data to drive decisions rather than be driven by data. To better illustrate this contention, we begin by describing a composite (and fictional) school system constructed from real observations made over the past fifteen years in public education across the nation.

NO BLAME, NO EXCUSES

C A S E   S T U D Y

Colson Independent School District (ISD) is a comprehensive preK–12 school system that served 23,415 students as of October 1 of last year. The district has been growing steadily for the past fifteen years, in large part because of suburban residential growth and high-tech, clean industries that multiplied with every innovation in technology. Even the economic downturn failed to slow the growth, and Colson developed a reputation as a high-quality school district. Even though its demographics

(continues)

Exhibit 5.1 Scoring Guide for Accountability and Data 5.0

Analysis Dimension	Meeting the Standard	Progressing Toward the Standard	Not Meeting the Standard
5.0 Accountability			
5.1 Authority to Act	The educator establishes written policies, within his or her direct control and influence, that provide teachers and other staff the authority to implement changes designed to improve student achievement based on a preponderance of the evidence revealed from data available at any given time. Preponderance of evidence is determined through triangulation of data and thoughtful collaboration around actual student performance.	The educator advocates for written policies, within his or her direct control and influence, that provide teachers and other staff the authority to implement changes designed to improve student achievement. Data provides some evidence to assist teachers and staff in making changes designed to improve student achievement; triangulation and thoughtful collaboration around student performance occur sporadically among teachers and staff.	The educator defers to popular opinion in making changes, with little evidence of efforts to extend authority for program or instructional changes to teachers or staff.
5.2 Accountability Structures	The educator integrates accountability into all major decisions by delineating explicit responsibilities for teams and individuals, establishing user-friendly timelines for data, and establishes multiple feedback systems, such as assessment calendars, formal listening systems for student, teacher, parent, and staff stakeholder groups, grade level/department teams, or data teams.	The educator has developed accountability methods that specify responsibilities for teams and individuals, establish timelines for data collection/ disaggregation, and provide at least one formal and responsive feedback system to improve student achievement.	Focus is on compliance with external requirements established by supervisor or institutional policy; little evidence exists to demonstrate a commitment or plan to add value with account-ability systems.

(continues)

Exhibit 5.1

Scoring Guide for Accountability and Data 5.0 *(Continued)*

Analysis Dimension	Meeting the Standard	Progressing Toward the Standard	Not Meeting the Standard
5.0 Accountability			
5.3 Accountability Reports	The educator publicly displays and communicates results of ongoing, monitored accountability measures for Tier 1 data (system-wide indicators), Tier 2 data (school-based indicators), and Tier 3 data (narrative description of school successes and challenges). The educator supplements measures at all levels with performance indicators that add value and focus efforts to improve student achievement.	The educator communicates the results of ongoing, monitored accountability measures that exceed Tier 1 (district-wide indicators) requirements, and supplements such measures with a number of performance indicators that add value and focus efforts to improve student achievement.	The educator communicates only those results mandated by external requirements (Tier 1 or compliance measures). There is no evidence of plans to develop, monitor, or communicate Tier 2 or Tier 3 data to staff, parents, students, or patrons.
5.4 Permission to Subtract	The leader establishes written policies, within his or her direct control and influence, that give teachers and other staff permission to eliminate, reduce, or omit historical practices or instructional strategies that inhibit improved student achievement, based on a preponderance of the evidence revealed from data **available** at any given time. Preponderance of evidence is determined through deliberate triangulation of data and thoughtful collaboration around actual student performance.	The leader has developed a policy giving teachers and staff permission to eliminate, reduce, or omit historical practices or instructional strategies that inhibit improved student achievement, but has yet to establish written policies, within his or her direct control and influence, to that effect, and has not yet developed a system to monitor implementation of the policy. Data provides some evidence of assistance to teachers and staff in eliminating obsolete, redundant, or neutral practices that do not contribute to improved student achievement. Triangulation and thoughtful collaboration around student performance occur sporadically among teachers and staff.	The leader is reluctant to share the authority to eliminate, reduce, or omit existing practices with staff, and is unable to identify current instructional strategies or antecedents (conditions and structures) that inhibit improved student achievement for groups or individuals.

Exhibit 5.1

Scoring Guide for Accountability and Data 5.0 (Continued)

5.0 Accountability

Analysis Dimension	Meeting the Standard	Progressing Toward the Standard	Not Meeting the Standard
5.5 Responsibility for Results	Performance goals are met for student achievement that meet AYP requirements and close the learning gap for all subgroups. Sustained record of improved student achievement on multiple indicators of student success can be verified. Explicit use of previous and interim data indicates a focus on improving performance. Efforts to assist students who demonstrate proficiency to move to the advanced or exemplary level are evident, and new challenges are met by identification of needs from existing data, creation of timely and effective interventions with monitoring data, and selection of meaningful and insightful results indicators.	Staff members report that they should be responsible for student achievement results, but have limited understanding of the factors (antecedents) that effect student achievement. There is evidence of improvement for one or more subgroups, but insufficient evidence of changes in antecedent measures of teaching, curriculum, and leadership to create the improvements necessary to achieve student performance goals for all subgroups.	Indifferent to the data; tendency to blame students, families, and external characteristics. Staff and leaders do not believe that student achievement can improve through their efforts. No evidence of decisive action to change time, teacher assignments, curriculum, leadership practices, or other variables of achievement.

83

were changing from white upper-middle-class to a mix more representative of the ethnic and racial makeup of the nation, achievement results continued to outperform the state average at all grades, and more than 85 percent of its students pursued a four-year college education upon graduation. In terms of free and reduced-price lunches, Colson had two elementary Title 1 schools in 1990, and only one other school has qualified since then (an older suburban school of 430 students).

The NCLB requirements and state accountability system are not popular at Colson ISD. Its relatively high performance—where 72 percent of the student body scored above the 50th percentile on the Iowa Test of Basic Skills (ITBS) and 67 percent passed the state assessment in reading and language arts last year—no longer warrants the praise and awards it once did. This year, the headlines identified seven schools that had failed to show improvement, and noted the learning gap for African-American students and the high dropout rate for Hispanic students. Five schools were in danger of being placed on AYP probation and board members, the superintendent, and every principal were getting calls from realtors and other business leaders demanding an explanation. The heat was definitely turned up this past summer, as constituents and even the district's most supportive parents began watching the school district as never before.

The board started the ball rolling by passing a resolution requiring schools to collect data and report student achievement data at least four times during the school year. This required schools to develop common assessments that could be reported, that were aligned with state standards, and that reflected the rigor and high expectations of the state assessments, which are reported annually by the state and included in each school's report card. The superintendent was also directed to create an accountability system that made administrator compensation contingent on improved test scores at each school. Furthermore, the system had to have the capacity to track student achievement at least quarterly for the board of education. Educators were on notice that they needed to be able to improve student achievement scores and to do so again and again over time.

Principals, particularly those in the seven schools facing AYP sanctions, collectively decided to publish student achievement results more frequently and to hold their teachers accountable by routinely monitoring grades and other classroom assessments. Principals shared strategies to monitor student performance in each teacher's class, conduct daily walk-throughs, perform desktop audits of grades and other assessments, and post student results by teacher, department, and grade on "data walls." They agreed that these strategies were the best ways to make the data work for them and share with teachers the accountability that the principals had been feeling for some time. One self-appointed leader proclaimed, "Teachers need to understand every bit as much as we do what is at stake, and we won't be here in three years unless we start seeing significant gains by subgroup."

Teachers were equally concerned with achievement results, but viewed the demands for more data and more publicly displayed data as insulting and intrusive. "The real issue is the need for support from parents and from administration to hold these kids accountable," said one teacher in frustration. "If students don't show up, wake up, or shape up, we get blamed." Teachers knew that the students who attended every day and were motivated just enough to do what was expected of them would perform well, regardless of subgroup. "It isn't as simple as test scores, and this new NCLB system that expects 100 percent of students to be proficient is humanly and statistically impossible."

The group of seven principals decided to develop common end of year and back-to-school agendas to set the tone with staff and to avoid the faculty fallout that might follow if one principal were more accommodating in his approach or appeared less urgent to get the scores up. The initial presentation was intended to drive home the "brutal facts" of the situation: Scores are way too low, they are even affecting homeowner choices, and the gaps among subgroups are widening. If things continue as they are now, we will find ourselves positioned to be reconstituted in three years, even if the neighborhood community objects. Each principal was to illustrate this reality with the same type of chart tailored to her or his individual school, although very little difference existed among the schools. Then the principals would present evidence of other schools in the state with equivalent free and reduced-price lunch numbers, and comparable second-language and minority populations, that had closed the gap and shown improvement for a number of years. At this point, principals would attempt to rally the troops by declaring "X Elementary School is better than that, and if Y Elementary upstate can do it, we can, too."

The attendees would then break into small groups by school and invite faculty to identify their school's strengths and strategies that could make a difference using the same resources available last year. This exercise was to take thirty minutes of the final day, including time to report out ideas. Care was taken to make sure that suggestions completed the following stems: "X Elementary will close the gap by _____," or "X Elementary will increase student achievement schoolwide by _____." Principals would then devote the rest of the meeting to securing volunteers for subcommittees that would come back in August with concrete changes that could make their suggestions a reality. The leaders felt pretty good about their initial salvo and knew in their hearts that their respective staffs would respond with enthusiasm and common purpose.

The actual reaction, however, was anything but enthusiastic. Comments from every school returned to the need for time, resources, and reduced class size. Suggestions almost universally called for greater autonomy, more time to work independently, and time to increase the rigor of course content. Principals facilitated the meeting as well as possible, closing with a reminder that next year must show improvement, that

(continues)

C A S E   S T U D Y   *(Continued)*

data would drive decisions, and that principals would be much more visible than ever before.

In August, five schools brought in motivational speakers from private industry unions or leadership consultants to stress the need to "work smarter, not harder" and to refine the school's vision with greater emphasis on continuous improvement. The remaining schools gathered input from teams for improving student achievement and closing the gap. They initiated after-school tutoring and made a commitment to use the five professional development days for common training in differentiated instruction, data-driven decision making, and effective teaching strategies. All seven schools ended the opening day with remarks about how data was going to drive everything and how everyone needed to pull together to make a difference this year.

Principals dutifully posted data and held conferences with faculty about what was going on and what the teachers were going to do to increase student achievement for specific subgroups or the entire student body. Most of the effort was devoted to increasing parent involvement and providing rapid notification of absences and tardiness. Teachers were also expected to develop charts and graphs that tracked student progress on standards.

By the end of the first term, teachers were exhausted and behind in their reporting. Principals' data walls were perceived as the school's version of "America's Most Wanted" rather than indications of growth and areas of celebration. Board members and central office staff, who previously had graced the doors of these schools about once every decade, now visited all the time, and staff were warned to be "on" at all times. Students wondered what all the charts were for, and mornings periodically saw graffiti on the charts, even though students created and updated these visuals. By semester's end, fewer students were earning Fs and attendance was up at the targeted schools from 91 percent to 94.7 percent. Teachers were much more cognizant of the standards addressed in various chapters and units, and the desktop audits did increase the alignment of lesson plans with the standards. Still, the tension was palpable, and even though teachers knew their students and their standards as never before, few believed that all this activity would produce the desired changes.

Although the principals did initiate some new procedures, the press of the new responsibilities, combined with ongoing demands on their time, made it very difficult for them to get into every classroom daily, and the visits were walk-throughs in a literal sense. By March, there was almost no dialogue or interaction with students or teachers in that process. Faculty resented the lack of integrity in these processes, which had been hailed as so critical and so important, and the data itself seemed to take away from instruction more every day. The central office upped the ante by requiring two administrator meetings monthly, and scheduled visits to all twenty-eight schools each year, with two visits minimum to the seven targeted schools and quarterly goal meetings for each of the seven principals during a scheduled cabinet meeting. This required the receiving schools to host eight formal visits annually, each of which typically required ninety minutes or more. The added meetings took principals out of their buildings for an additional ten and a half days for administrator meetings, and approximately two hours for each quarterly meeting—not to mention the preparation required or the follow-up needed to comply with requests from the superintendent and her cabinet.

AUTHORITY TO ACT

In the preceding scenario, faculties were given the authority to react, not to make instructional adjustments. Colson ISD's situation is a classic example of bureaucratic creep (Chapter 1), a scenario played out across the nation on far too many occasions. We have seen how easy it is to collect data and how unlikely it is that schools will act on the lessons of that data. The emphasis at Colson was on producing data that showed improvement rather than on data that instructed them *how* to show improvement. Even when schools measure the antecedents and the results well and accurately, if the insights gleaned and the programs implemented fail to change classroom practice, educators can be assured that student achievement will not improve measurably, and most definitely will not improve over time.

The authority to take action is central to accountability and an ethical consideration as well. Collecting, disaggregating, analyzing, and reflecting are important elements in the process of data analysis, but failure to take action and make necessary changes is patently unethical, in that it requires students and staff to behave as if something will be done with the test data, when in fact the data may be collected and shelved, or analyzed for the sake of analysis. The author, an administrator for eighteen years, found that it was not uncommon to hear parents counseled with the following: "We plan to change that [practice or procedure] next year" or "It will take us some time to make that change, but it will be in place for our incoming seventh-graders." Does it really take a year to ensure that instruction is purposeful and aligned to standards? Is it too much to ask that grades have a relationship to proficiency, or that work completed by students be returned with feedback that is corrective and instructive? One can only wonder how many administrators and teachers face parents who ask for changes that are entirely reasonable, yet find a way to avoid making changes because those changes do not fit into the current systems.

In the last chapter, we framed the notion that wide variance in teaching ability and skill is an example of unequal educational opportunity. As the craft of teaching and learning becomes more defined, and the connections and correlations between improved achievement and its antecedents become more established, acceptance of such inequality as chance or luck in terms of teacher assignment may even be actionable in a court of law. A recent and quite serious proposal was made to revamp how educators measure teacher effectiveness. By issuing each teacher a unique identification number and gathering the right data, states can assess the link between teacher performance and student outcomes over the course of many years (Raymond, 2003). The idea extends Sanders's seminal work in Tennessee on "value-added" instruction (1998), and it may very well be the future for educators everywhere. Exhibit 5.2 describes situations (opportunities) in which leaders of teachers and teachers of students need the authority to act and act now.

In practice, Exhibit 5.2 means that teachers and principals are given authority to change the time allotted for students to reach proficiency, adding time for those who need additional instruction or practice, and redirecting time for those who quickly demonstrate proficiency on a particular standard. For primary students learning how to read, this might mean giving those who have demonstrated the mechanics of reading the opportunity to read with a higher grade level or to apply their skill to acquiring content understanding in material that challenges them. For teachers in search of quality results indicators, it means having the authority to collaborate to create,

Exhibit 5.2

Ten Actions of Accountability

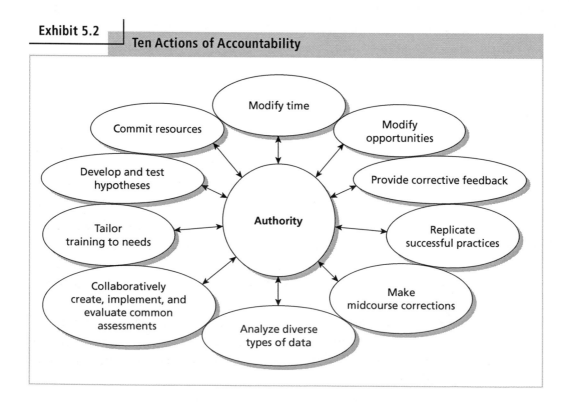

implement, and evaluate assessments. It means teachers and principals having sufficient resource capacity to make commitments for tutoring services or self-assessment software to respond to individual student needs. It means sufficient trust and safety to speak freely, providing peers and supervisors with quality corrective feedback, and creating a classroom climate in which students too are safe to speak freely, with candor. Accountability also means the capacity to develop and test one's hunches (hypotheses or intuitions) about teaching and learning. All of these capacities hinge not so much on greater resources, but on a sufficiently agile work environment that relies on the expertise of teachers to respond to the needs of students as revealed by data.

Why haven't educators been provided this authority to become accountable? The answer, in part, is that educators do not maintain sufficiently informative data to warrant the grant of that authority, or even to justify their recommendations. Data is as necessary for accountability to operate as accountability is necessary for a quality data system. Without data, one's desire to test a hypothesis will appear frivolous, even if the hypothesis has the capacity to dramatically improve public education across the school, district, or even nation. It is entirely reasonable to expect those with the authority to commit resources to be reluctant to delegate that authority, unless there is a strong, data-supported basis for the change recommendations. When data is available to support recommendations, most persons in authority are much more apt to delegate authority to act, and when a framework exists to test hypotheses and measures are available to provide baseline data, the opportunity for action research and innovations is also increased. Exhibit 5.3 identifies common barriers to accountability and suggests possible remedies that can help to ensure that educators have the authority needed for true accountability.

PERMISSION TO SUBTRACT

In Chapter 1, the concept of permission to subtract was introduced as key to effective data analysis. It is integral to accountability in our field because the authority to *stop* doing something—to stop doing *anything* in public education—is elusive for many. Lists of innovations introduced in public education that were never officially discontinued have become common in schools. Programs fall into benign neglect, with remnants of the program evident sometimes years after its demise. Why? The majority of innovations that make it to the radar screen in public education are based on sound pedagogy, validated in research settings, and offer powerful new strategies to improve student achievement. Hence, even when implementation is hasty, partial, or watered-down, those educational innovations add value. In fact, those who are most adept at implementing such reforms and innovations are more apt to realize their value and more reluctant to drop them altogether than those who resisted the innovations or were indifferent to them.

Exhibit 5.3

Barriers to the Ten Acts of Accountability

Act of Accountability	Barriers	Remedies
Commit resources	▪ One-size-fits-all work schedules for assistants ▪ Limited school or department budgets ▪ Negotiated agreement limits ▪ Transportation issues	▪ Allocate assistant time based on data trends for service needs ▪ Insist that discretionary dollars be allocated per needs verified by data ▪ Examine negotiated agreements for flexibility or waivers ▪ Reschedule student time consistent with transportation obligations
Modify time	▪ Uniform class periods ▪ Graduation requirements that limit opportunity to demonstrate proficiency in core standards ▪ Required time allotments in policy	▪ Construct dual classes for those in need ▪ Count dual courses in core competencies (math, English/reading, language arts/writing, science) ▪ Integrate content areas for instructional purposes
Modify opportunities	▪ Textbook-driven instruction ▪ Seat-time requirements for credits ▪ Limited course offerings or great variation in courses for same graduation requirement ▪ Prerequisites	▪ Collaboratively identify power standards ▪ Use standards-based grading ▪ Allow proficiency on standards to meet requirements for graduation ▪ Establish an opt-in provision for honors/IB/AP ▪ Change policies to open electives to all
Provide corrective feedback	▪ Fear or observation of retribution for speaking one's mind ▪ Culture of collegiality rather than collaboration ▪ Expectation of exemplary performance in all evaluations ▪ Candor viewed as threatening, inviting of grievances	▪ Establish operating norms for all teams that value candor, collaboration, diversity of ideas, corrective feedback ▪ Require data to support positions, recommendations ▪ Role-play format for team thinking ▪ Institute dialogue with association to set guidelines
Replicate successful practices	▪ Watered-down replication ▪ Path of least resistance ▪ Underestimation of training required ▪ Competing priorities that should be subtracted ▪ Push-back from unspoken and unwritten cultural expectations	▪ Replicate only when data warrants ▪ Provide in-depth training and modeling, and monitor quality indicators ▪ Consider context of replication in terms of work habits and processes, and identify what will be subtracted before adding anything new ▪ Establish clear norms for replication/innovation

Exhibit 5.3		

Barriers to the Ten Acts of Accountability *(Continued)*

Act of Accountability	Barriers	Remedies
Make midcourse corrections	■ Unrealistic curriculum coverage expectations ■ Single means to proficiency, such as written final exam ■ Grade expectations not based on standards ■ Traditions	■ Align curriculum and instruction to standards ■ Identify power standards that prioritize content ■ Develop scoring guides with multiple paths to proficiency ■ Align grades to standards ■ Gather data to verify traditional practices
Analyze diverse types of data	■ Existing data limited to student achievement ■ Teacher isolation and limited discussion of teaching strategies ■ Ignorance of power of classroom practices ■ Data examined annually; rearview-mirror effect prevails	■ Award staff development in data analysis with privileged choices to those who justify requests with diverse data ■ Have data teams examine and respond to actual student work ■ Discuss local strategies and expect that staff will become fluent with effective teaching strategies ■ Create structures to examine data routinely, at least twice per month
Collaboratively create, implement, and evaluate common assessments	■ Assessments limited to district requirements ■ Lack of common planning time ■ Professional development days committed to outside seminars, unrelated to local needs driven by data ■ Reluctance to accept collective wisdom of peers for individual classroom application	■ Create collaboration, common planning, early release times ■ Introduce collaboration at every faculty meeting ■ Align professional development to NCSD standards, student achievement gaps, and faculty needs to improve achievement ■ Build data system for teaching, curriculum, leadership, and a variety of student result measures ■ Train in group processes
Tailor training to needs	■ Optional training unrelated to vision, goals, student needs ■ Training unrelated to evaluation process ■ Data rarely disaggregated by antecedent strategies, structures, or teacher behaviors	■ Establish collaborative professional development ■ Have teachers teach teachers ■ Review context/integration: curriculum, standards, leadership ■ Attend to individual needs ■ Sustain and monitored internally
Develop and test hypotheses	■ Lack of incentives to innovate ■ Reliance on path of least resistance ■ No format for action research ■ Opinions and private information not valued	■ Use data system that promotes pursuit of hunches ■ Give access to simplified action research ■ Allow structured reflection time ■ Recognize and value risk taking and private information in written norms or policies

Without explicit structures that empower people to make the needed changes, including subtraction of obsolete practices, many educators continue to adhere to past expectations. We just assume that others know when they have permission to make changes. Do the teachers you are familiar with have authority (permission) to make these decisions?

- Permission to vary the time given to curriculum content
- Permission to modify or accelerate curriculum based on individual student needs, including permission for students to test out of various units or sections
- Permission to replace grades with scoring guides describing proficiency
- Permission to provide multiple opportunities to demonstrate proficiency, as opposed to only one try on key tests and assessments
- Permission to integrate assessments across curriculum areas
- Permission to work on a team rather than deliver instruction independent of one's peers

This is as true for administrators as it is for teachers. Do the administrators in schools you are familiar with have authority (permission) to make the following decisions?

- Permission to reassign staff at midyear
- Permission to hire staff from those who meet all district criteria
- Permission to change teacher assignments based on student achievement data
- Permission to require side-by-side analyses of standards, assessments, curriculum, and lesson plans
- Permission to direct resources to create additional time and opportunity
- Permission to replace textbooks with laptops, or to use textbooks as supplemental materials while relying primarily on standards-based performance assessments

These examples illustrate that many times educators have very limited authority or permission to subtract ineffective practices.

It is difficult to stop doing anything in schools, simply because permission to stop something is much harder to come by than permission to start something. This is especially true if the innovation was widely adopted throughout the school or district. If a significant investment was made in the program, it is very unlikely that the program will be dismissed now as being of little value. To do so would be to dismiss those who bought into the program as making a grave error in judgment, something educators avoid at almost all costs. Exhibit 5.4 delineates questions to help determine whether and when to subtract obsolete or ineffective practices.

Exhibit 5.4		
Subtracting Obsolete or Ineffective Practices		

Subtraction

	Yes	No
1. Does the practice/resource yield data about teaching or learning?	Yes	No
2. Does the practice/resource address specific content standards?	Yes	No
3. Does the practice/resource provide diagnostic data about student achievement?	Yes	No
4. Does the practice invite collaboration with colleagues?	Yes	No
5. Is there data supporting the need for or value of the practice/resource to improve student achievement in my classroom?	Yes	No
6. Is there a corresponding or competing practice/resource that accomplishes the same end/result?	Yes	No

Yes to three or fewer questions: The practice or resource should be subtracted in some measure.
Yes to four or more questions: The practice or resource should be retained or possibly replicated.

Replacement

	Yes	No
1. Can the same practice/resource be accomplished through other means, such as improved technology?	Yes	No
2. Can the practice/resource be omitted and still achieve the same result?	Yes	No
3. Can the same result be accomplished in less instructional time?	Yes	No
4. Can the same result be accomplished in less preparation time?	Yes	No
5. Can the same result be accomplished with less expense in time, talent, and resources?	Yes	No

Yes to three or fewer questions: The practice or resource should be replaced at some time.
Yes to four or more questions: The practice or resource should be replaced as soon as possible.

A profession committed to encouraging, developing, and nurturing finds it much easier to choose the path of least resistance than to "confront the brutal facts" about past decisions. Yet, Jim Collins, in his bestseller *Good to Great*, describes the ability of people in an organization to do just that—"confront the brutal facts"—as a major characteristic of greatness (2001, p. 69). Collins views this inherent humility as the ingredient that allows people within any organization to learn from the successes of others and from their own mistakes. Unfortunately, schools, as collegial institutions, are often more concerned about avoiding offense than becoming collaborative institutions committed to improving student achievement. In Chapter 4, we defined collaboration in terms of improving student achievement and offered suggestions to increase one's capacity to express diverse opinions and ideas without giving or taking offense. Subtraction requires an ability to face the hard facts and the humility to learn as much from our poor decisions as from our successful ones.

In the midst of Colson ISD's effort to embrace the appearance and trappings of data-driven decision making, was anything subtracted? The superintendent, school board, principals, and teachers all fell victim to bureaucratic creep, adding activities, meetings, and methods to gather data that added demands to their work load. Principals were unable to meet their obligation of classroom visits; the district spent inordinate amounts of time collecting data but very little adjusting instruction to improve student achievement. The result, in a high-stakes and tension-filled atmosphere, was a demoralized and exhausted workforce. Rather than creating a culture of learning without blame or excuses, Colson ISD, without any formal communication or intent, created a culture of no excuses, but lots of blame.

For accountability in data analysis to work, permission to subtract practices and redirect resources, time, and energy must be given to schools and to classroom teachers. Without this authority, data will not drive real-time responses to needs in the classrooms, but will be relegated to annual modifications of plans that have little impact on what happens every day in the classrooms. Knowing what to subtract requires an ability to examine data regarding what works and what doesn't. It requires identifying and monitoring daily routines and behaviors, the work habits of change.

WORK HABITS AND CHANGE

Colson ISD's teachers, principals, central administrators, and school board meant well. Each applied themselves diligently to all the changes with the intent to improve student achievement, and their behavior and strategies embody responses to accountability that can be observed in districts and schools across the country. Nevertheless, their approach was doomed to failure from the outset. Rather than focusing on antecedents of excellence, the district pursued greater parent involvement, more data collection, increased "accountability" in terms of responsibility for results, and lots and lots of monitoring. Little, if any, attention was given to effective teaching strategies or to research about collaboration, and no effort was made to understand how things get done at Colson—or, more accurately, how things fail to get done. As to the seven schools on probation for AYP, one would have to characterize them on the L^2 Matrix (Exhibit 3.2) as "losing," because there was no apparent understanding of what produced low student achievement and the school's inability to close the gap for identified subgroups. Note how teaching faculty looked to deficits in students and their parents, factors that have some influence on student achievement, while neglecting factors that have much greater influence. A powerful study by Howard Wenglinsky (2002) found that professional development, teacher qualifications and content preparation, and classroom practices all have dramatic effects on student achievement. In fact, classroom practices had a greater effect than professional development or teacher quality, and classroom practices (teaching practices) have a greater effect than any demographic variable, including race, income, or educational level of parents. In other words, the primary influence on student achievement is, and has been, those classroom practices or work habits by which things get done.

The processes for accomplishing tasks, procedures, and daily routines are all work habits. Examples are a teacher's bell-to-bell process to optimize on-task time, or another teacher's transition from language arts to science, or a kindergarten teacher's process of opening every school day by checking for understanding and asking students to connect the previous day with planned events for the current day. Work habits also include questioning strategies or peer review of written work. Anything that can be reduced to a series of steps or depicted in a flowchart constitutes a work habit.

Work habits are also antecedents. They define the conditions, structures, and strategies employed to effect learning. Work habits may never change their function, but they can always be improved and enhanced. Because work habits are routine components of each job description, they are easily monitored quantitatively as counts or percentages, or monitored qualitatively as measures of completion, implementation, or adoption of a specific process. Exhibit 5.5 provides examples from various job descriptions for educators.

Exhibit 5.5 — **Examples of Work Habits**

Teacher	Principal	Specialist	Central Administrator
▪ **Develops** lesson plans	▪ **Creates** master schedule	▪ **Aligns** curriculum with standards	▪ **Communicates** vision
▪ **Designs** unit assessment	▪ **Monitors** curriculum alignment	▪ **Monitors** textbook adoptions	▪ **Establishes** accountability system
▪ **Establishes** learning groups	▪ **Observes** teaching strategies	▪ **Designs** professional development based on student achievement results	▪ **Sets** direction with goals and vision
▪ **Collaborates** around student work	▪ **Develops** feedback systems for students, parents, teachers		▪ **Implements** policies
▪ **Analyzes** data			▪ **Reports** assessment results
			▪ **Establishes, implements, and evaluates** budgets

In the exhibit, every example of a work habit begins with an action [**bold**], and every example can be reduced to a sequence of events or depicted in a flowchart. Perhaps most important, every work habit can be improved by streamlining its process or processes, calibrating its execution to achieve greater consistency, or increasing the predictability of the process. Budget development is a work habit that has to be as predictable as possible, whereas classroom analysis of data requires increased precision and accuracy.

The most effective way to measure a work habit is to determine its primary function and measure its essential parts. Developing lesson plans is not nearly as important as the capacity of lesson plans to address content standards, engage students, facilitate higher-order thinking, and provide evidence of learning. Measuring the number of lesson plans developed would have little value, but monitoring the degree to which they engaged students cognitively with quality work products would have great value. Teacher teams could observe and monitor implementation, share and model strategies and applications, and modify lesson plans to reflect best practice. Best of all, they could assess their success or progress with both qualitative and quantitative measures.

The discussion of work habits is equally applicable to the central office administrator, who identifies the steps employed to communicate the goals and vision of the entire district. The central office team could examine their work habits for redundancy and duplication of effort, cost/benefit, and effectiveness in terms of students and staff understanding the school's vision, being able to describe it, or even relating it to their own daily work. Work habits are key antecedents: Our understanding of what we do every day allows us to change, sometimes incrementally, what we do and make enormous strides that improve student achievement.

Exhibit 5.6 depicts a student-developed work habit that became the standard for every project at a large and comprehensive technical school. Students employed this simple but powerful process at San Fernando High School in Los Angeles Unified School District, one of the largest urban high schools in the nation, and one with a predominantly Latino student body. The process was first employed within the San Fernando Education Technology Team (SFETT), but eventually it was extended to all students. The work habit required a public presentation—skills every student would be able to benefit from. The process assumed that an embedded and authentic assessment would be provided, and that every student would be able to identify how each project could be improved. As a result of this single work habit innovation, standards and expectations were clarified, and the connection to employment opportunities and real life was a motivating factor for students within the 500-student technology team. Following implementation of this process, graduation rates and placements from career and technical programs into employment more than doubled. By including the essentials of key work habits as part of our data system, we can determine the interaction and effect of that work habit on student achievement.

SUMMARY

Authority to act, permission to subtract, and responsibility for results have been presented as the underlying elements of accountability, especially of accountability in data analysis. Accountability is not merely collecting and reporting student achievement results. It encompasses taking action based on those results and understanding

Exhibit 5.6

Project Management for Students

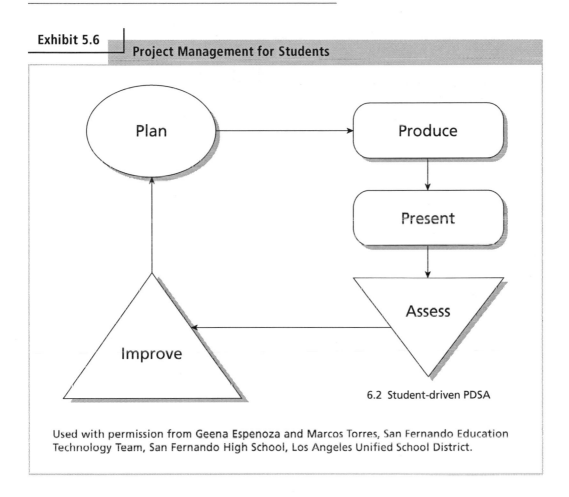

6.2 Student-driven PDSA

Used with permission from Geena Espenoza and Marcos Torres, San Fernando Education Technology Team, San Fernando High School, Los Angeles Unified School District.

the factors that yield the results. This means that every professional educator needs to have sufficient authority to commit resources to intervene on behalf of students, whether they are students who need to be challenged to achieve exemplary status on student assessments or students who need to close the learning gap between themselves and their peers.

We next examined the notion of being able to subtract, discontinue, or deemphasize practices that are no longer productive or that have proven ineffective. This level of authority is as essential to real accountability as the other three elements. We examined work habits, which were defined as those routine daily procedures and protocols that affect instruction, and discussed ways to begin to gather data without overwhelming oneself in the data. In all of these applications, we again stressed the need for collaboration and the need to maintain data on the antecedents that are perceived to have the greatest impact. As educators, we can take responsibility for student achievement results when we have sufficient data on both antecedents and results, if we collectively apply the wisdom we discover through analysis and take decisive action.

DISCUSSION

BIG IDEA

Accountability determines our ability to deliver quality to those we serve.

QUESTIONS

1. *Why is the authority to act so important to accountability, to taking responsibility for results? Describe areas in your work situation where that authority should be given or clarified.*

2. *Do you or your colleagues have sufficient authority (permission) to subtract obsolete practices? Can you identify one such practice that ought to be discontinued or deemphasized?*

3. *Have the most important work habits in your position been captured in a flowchart or sequence of steps? Identify one that should be reduced to writing.*

4. *What did Colson Independent School District fail to do in its attempt to improve student achievement and close the gap for students?*

6

Canaries in the Coal Mine: Get There Before the Results Do!

Even if you are on the right track, you'll get run over if you just sit there.

—WILL ROGERS

Canaries were used for centuries as an early warning signal of gas leaks and accumulations in underground mines. If the canaries stopped singing, or keeled over, miners knew it was time to get out—and get out fast! The rearview-mirror effect will continue to plague educators until they and their schools develop their own "canaries in the coal mine." What "canaries" will allow schools and teachers to make adjustments quickly and respond with agility based on student needs? Data teams provide a very versatile framework within which to probe and monitor student performance in ways that facilitate rapid and focused response. Performance assessments that rely on scoring guides as blueprints to proficiency offer a very sound approach to learning that informs teachers, students, and even parents of a student's progress along the way. Performance assessments that are designed to include interim performance-task indicators, like that taught by The Leadership and Learning Center, act as even more certain "canaries" that allow educators to respond to student needs. Routine, corrective, and instructive feedback as a work habit assists teachers to make adjustments almost immediately, and liberal use of self-assessment efforts constitutes yet another approach that allows the professional educator to make midcourse corrections. Let us examine several "canaries" applicable to today's schools.

The idea of interim assessments is nothing new. Grading systems over the past fifteen years have increasingly relied on progress reports distributed every three weeks to parents and students. Unit tests long ago took away the sting of historical reliance on end-of-course final exams for the bulk of a student's grades. The difference in this era of standards is the expectation that all students, or at least the vast majority, will demonstrate proficiency on rigorous standards that add to content knowledge the ability to apply that knowledge through discrete skills in various contexts.

Most improvement efforts in education assume that changes in student performance take time, and lots of it. However, technology has enhanced our ability to communicate data to all stakeholders, and it is becoming very common for schools to have in place a student data management system that allows parents and teachers to communicate "24/7" about individual student grades, assignments, discipline referrals, and attendance. A society that expects everything to be available instantly, or at least very quickly, also expects its schools to make modifications quickly and routinely. Let us turn to those proven strategies.

DATA TEAMS

Data teams are collaborative, structured, scheduled team meetings that focus on teaching and learning (The Leadership and Learning Center, 2004b). They bring together the components of a professional learning community (Hord, 1997) to answer practical questions such as: "Which students are reading and comprehending at grade level proficiency?" or "Which students will need additional assistance to perform the skills in the next unit of study?" Data teams can consist of entire faculties, but are more apt to be small grade-level or department-level teams that can examine individual student work and analyze antecedent and effect data down to the classroom level.

Teachers bring specific student data to each meeting. This student-specific data is a very powerful tool because a persistent problem for one student is frequently very similar to that experienced by several other students, and by assisting a colleague to address the problem identified, teachers help themselves address the needs of other students. The data team structure adheres to a continuous improvement cycle similar to those reviewed in Exhibit 2.3; examines patterns and trends; and sets forth specific timelines, roles, and responsibilities to facilitate analysis that results in action.

A powerful component of any comprehensive accountability plan, effective data teams serve as a very practical "canary in the coal mine" because of the frequency of meetings, use of mini-lessons, and focus on actual students with names and faces. It engages teams to take collective responsibility for student achievement results; communicates simple, clear, and useful meeting guidelines; and provides a proven process for improvement. The Leadership and Learning Center seminar on data teams (2004b) provides an excellent three-part format for setting up data team meetings, defining the purpose of meetings before any instructional modifications are made, during the instructional intervention and data-gathering period; and following up on intervention to review the success of any changes made.

1. The first meeting examines student work and assessments to plan mini-lessons and changes that will be implemented immediately. A powerful aspect of this process is that it examines both student work and assessments and also provides evidence of teaching. Teams identify exactly what teaching strategies have been employed to equip the students whose work is being reviewed for demonstrated proficiency on the standards. The data team also examines obstacles, challenges, and misconceptions about curriculum, instruction, and student behavior.

2. The second meeting, in the midst of mini-lessons and planned interventions, occurs to determine how well the process is unfolding and to examine unforeseen changes that have occurred.

3. A third meeting determines whether the team was successful in achieving its goal, what the next essential standard will be for a new group of students, or what should be done differently if the goal was not reached.

This cycle typically occurs in bimonthly meetings, meaning that the goals and interventions are scheduled to occur within four to five weeks. The process will work with monthly meetings as well; in both cases, action that produces changes and facilitates improved student achievement occurs much quicker than the average referral process for services for students at risk, let alone interventions to help them in the classroom. Exhibit 6.1 combines the well-known SWOT (strengths, weaknesses, opportunities, threats) analysis framework with the data team emphasis on student performance and evidence of teaching as an example of data needed for the first data team meeting.

Examination of both student performance and evidence of teaching enriches the data available to teachers because it draws from student behaviors, teacher routines, and strategies that address specific needs of students. Mini-lessons from data team decisions are excellent examples of embedded interventions and powerful use of data to drive classroom decisions.

SCORING GUIDES

Scoring guides provide early warning to students, teachers, and parents by informing all involved of what is expected to demonstrate proficiency. They describe not only the desired outcome, but also the pathway to that outcome through the level descriptions: not meeting standards, progressing, proficient, or advanced. Student-generated scoring guides (Ainsworth & Christinson, 1997) add another dimension by asking students to describe the levels of proficiency in their own terms. When students have the ability to self-assess their progress, they not only understand the knowledge and

Exhibit 6.1

	Strengths	Weaknesses	Opportunities	Threats
SWOT Analysis for Data Teams				
Student performance	Students grasp concept of biosphere per quizzes 85%+ Classification, vocabulary demonstrated	Unit test failure, 62% average Problem solving, inventing, and determining cause/effect relationships re biosphere Weak performance on extended response assessments Has yet to demonstrate writing with problem-solving strategies	Projects that call for operations on a higher level of Bloom's taxonomy Explicit problem-solving strategies More writing opportunities Unit lends itself to wide range of activities and projects	Time is limited before state assessment (90 days) Sense of efficacy is weak History of poor academic performance Struggles with activity transitions Easily distracted by noise, social opportunity
Evidence of teaching	Ticket-out-the-door writing activity (daily) Characteristics, types of living organisms, and interaction in biospheres introduced with vocabulary	Essential questions and planned transitions not observed Questioning is primarily single response, yes-no, true-false	Introduce unit and essential questions Establish cooperative learning groups Use Cornell Notes to summarize daily lessons Use open-ended questions	Number of students at risk in classrooms Difficulty finding time to collaborate with and observe colleagues Training in Bloom's taxonomy not scheduled until next fall

skill requirements, but can measure performance as they demonstrate it, making adjustments as they pursue proficiency.

PERFORMANCE ASSESSMENTS

Quality performance assessments address big ideas, essential questions, power standards, the unwrapping or analysis of those standards, engaging scenarios, scoring guides, and well-designed culminating assessments that include multiple interim performance indicators or performance tasks. In this way, performance assessments act as at least two major "canaries": scoring guides that inform instruction and learning, and interim performance tasks that indicate a progressive acquisition of proficiency through increasingly rigorous and challenging performance tasks. Exhibit 6.2 illustrates.

Exhibit 6.2	High School Literature Performance Task Scoring Guide		
Exemplary	**Proficient**	**Progressing**	**Not Yet**
All "proficient" criteria met PLUS: Classifications include methods not discussed in class lecture T-bars show unique thought (outside the box) when generating pros/cons Graphic organizer branches and leaves reflect depth and breadth of knowledge of literature and cultural history of the 1990s Other	Journal-entry style of writing is used Writing reflects standard English conventions, including spelling, grammar, punctuation, and mechanics At least ten methods of classification are used T bars are included for four classification methods T-bars accurately reflect pros/cons for classification Chosen method for project is reasoned and appropriate Graphic organizer is included for the chosen classification method Chosen graphic organizer is appropriate to the classification Graphic organizer includes at least five branches and three leaves for each branch	Standard English conventions are applied inconsistently Fewer than ten, but more than six methods of classification are included T-bars are included for two or three methods T-bar pros and cons are not accurately classified Chosen method for project is limited or inappropriate Graphic organizer is not appropriate to classification method Graphic organizer includes fewer than five branches and three leaves for each branch	Fewer than six methods of classification are included Only one T-bar is included Graphic organizer is not included Other

Used with permission from Laurie Graack, Righetti High School, Santa Maria Joint Union High School District.

CORRECTIVE FEEDBACK

Early warning or early "affirming" indicators of performance need not be limited to formal structures such as those suggested so far. Individual teachers who are proficient at providing feedback that is accurate, timely, and corrective are able to describe where individual students are at any given time in terms of proficiency. Students are also cognizant of their level of proficiency because they are given useful feedback from the instructor before they apply faulty reasoning to their tasks. This is the essence of early warning systems: corrective, timely, and accurate feedback. Corrective feedback has been viewed for years as absolutely critical when acquiring a second language (Lyster, 1998; Mackey, Gass, & McDonough, 2000). It also has been identified as "the most powerful single modification that enhances achievement" (Marzano, Pickering, & Pollock, 2001a, p. 96). Corrective feedback, by definition, serves as a "canary in a coal mine."

DATA IN A DAY

Data in a Day (NREL, 1997) is a collaborative approach to data analysis developed by the Northwest Regional Education Laboratory (NREL) whereby teams of educators and students select a data focus area, collect and analyze the data, and present findings with recommendations within twenty-four hours. This technique, with immediate feedback, collaborative process, and intensive focus, uses available data to identify a problem, craft a solution, and put in motion actions that change the learning dynamic to make a difference. Data in a Day attempts to develop recommendations to improve a wide range of issues within twenty-four hours. Data in a Day could be used as an extension of the critical-incident data analysis tool introduced in Exhibit 4.1, for observing, analyzing, and, most importantly, applying information to make improvements. Exhibit 6.3 illustrates.

Exhibit 6.3

Data in a Day

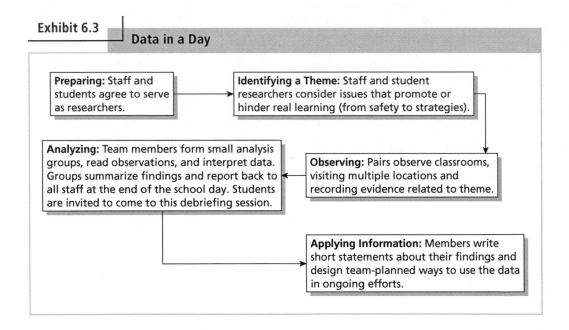

The success of Data in a Day hinges on a clear understanding of the three principles of data-driven decision making reviewed in the last three chapters: antecedents, collaboration, and accountability. It requires a team of educators to understand the different types of antecedents and have the authority to act on the lessons of the data available to them. As we reviewed earlier, this authority to act also means they have permission to subtract practices and redirect resources when the data indicates a need for a change. Lastly, Data in a Day requires team members to understand their responsibility in the learning process and their capacity to improve achievement results for all their students. The public nature of the process invites students and the public in as partners in making improvements and helps build a culture that embraces account-ability in action: where a team is empowered by data, authorized to commit resources and implement changes, and shares responsibility to effect results and improve student achievement.

SUMMARY

This chapter introduced five strategies for developing early warning indicators that contribute to a data-driven culture where evidence is valued, and where professional educators recognize their importance and capacity to make a difference quickly. The strategies of using data teams, scoring guides and powerful performance assessments, embedded and corrective feedback, and rapid-response Data in a Day are analogous to medical teams of experts in hospital intensive care units across the country. Relentless about the data, relentless about securing solutions, candid with one another, and advocating for the patient, intensive care teams are just what we need to be with the data available to us in schools today.

The medical model offers numerous analogies and applications, none of which has to do with how we teach or even how students learn. *Educators* are the experts at education—not legislators, not skilled physicians, not even concerned parents. The public may know what it expects and be able to establish a threshold for what it requires from us, but only educators can determine the solutions to challenges faced by students. If we allow the medical model to instruct us on how to use data effectively, infusing the power of collaboration and a sense of urgency, we will not only be accountable, we will also achieve extraordinary results.

DISCUSSION

BIG IDEA

Data is only as valuable as our ability to respond to the needs it reveals.

QUESTIONS

1. *What is meant by "canaries in the coal mine"? Reflect on any that exist in your workplace, and try to identify one area where your work team needs its own "canary."*

2. *Discuss the benefits of using data teams and why data teams qualify as a "canaries in the coal mine."*

3. *How does corrective feedback in the classroom serve as an early warning system? What does feedback prevent?*

4. *What would have to be in place in your work setting to make Data in a Day a reality? Discuss with a colleague whether it is worth the investment of time and effort.*

Triangulation

*We can't solve problems by using the same kind
of thinking we used when we created them.*

—ALBERT EINSTEIN (1879–1955)

This chapter introduces the reader to *triangulation,* an approach which ensures that the principles of collaboration, antecedent identification and monitoring, and accountability are addressed in data analysis. This approach draws extensively on various data analysis tools, but ultimately relies on the judgment of professionals to make their best decision given limited data. Triangulation is critical to using data to "make visible the invisible" and it is necessary if educators are to benefit fully from the methods and tools of data analysis discussed in the following chapters.

What, then, is triangulation? What is needed to apply it effectively?

THE MARINER AND THE SURVEYOR

Triangulation is well known to architects, engineers, and surveyors as a simple tool, widely used for centuries. To the architect, *triangulation* means discerning with precision key load factors and points in space and time from other reliable and predictable data; to the engineer and surveyor, *triangulation* means calibrating unknown points with precision in space and time on the basis of existing data and irregularly distributed samples of data. For both professions, triangulation uses a variety of forms of existing data—the more the better—to find a desired and unknown reference point. When the surveyor needs to estimate the height of a point on the land surface, she utilizes samples of soil composition, density variation, contours, weather patterns, and a host of other data. A sextant (a triangulation tool used by mariners) allowed explorers to plot the globe by triangulating the stars with each other and the horizon to ascertain longitude and latitude at sea.

Thus, triangulation is a means of determining precise targets with limited information. Do we as educators need tools to read the horizon, determine our location, and chart our paths from limited information? Triangulation is a method of extrapolating meaning from raw data; a means to find the critical information, see the big picture, and identify key components (angles). The term *triangulation* is used frequently these days in education circles to describe efforts to determine needs or targets from diverse types of data garnered from such data-gathering efforts as focus groups, surveys, site visits, and one-to-one interviews (Report to the Commonwealth of Virginia, 2001; Miami Public Schools, 1999). In both the Virginia and Florida cases, data from three different ways to assess perceptions were examined (triangulated) to discover similarities that advocated for reform.

Triangulation can be applied to the data-driven decisionmaking process by examining the interaction of antecedent data, collaboration data, and accountability data. Each set lends itself to trend tracking and pattern identification. Exhibit 7.1 provides examples of data triangulated by principles of data-driven decision making to reveal influences on student performance.

Exhibit 7.1

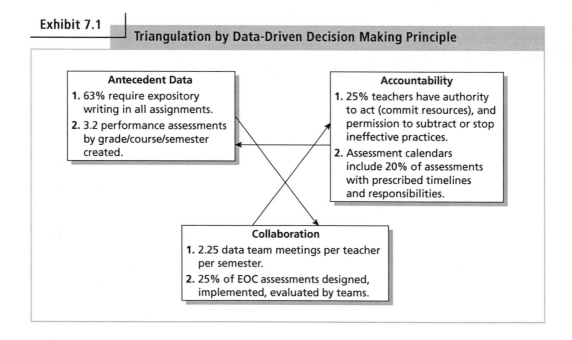

Triangulation by Data-Driven Decision Making Principle

Antecedent Data
1. 63% require expository writing in all assignments.
2. 3.2 performance assessments by grade/course/semester created.

Accountability
1. 25% teachers have authority to act (commit resources), and permission to subtract or stop ineffective practices.
2. Assessment calendars include 20% of assessments with prescribed timelines and responsibilities.

Collaboration
1. 2.25 data team meetings per teacher per semester.
2. 25% of EOC assessments designed, implemented, evaluated by teams.

What can we glean from the interaction of these factors? To answer that, we must first acknowledge that collaboration is an essential part of any triangulation—indeed, of any data analysis tool. Professional judgment (i.e., private information or data in the heads) is absolutely essential for a thorough analysis to take place, especially with limited data. Let us consider the limits of the example data. Only one measure of student achievement is provided in Exhibit 7.1, and that is an annual assessment far removed from the classroom; that is, the kind of data that tends to bait the trap of the rearview-mirror effect. James Popham, perhaps one of the most respected educational statisticians and experts on assessment, stressed the importance of professional judgment when he noted: "What teachers and administrators need to know about testing, at least for purposes of educational accountability, relies on common sense more than statistical exotica" (2004, p. 83). The data is also limited as to effective teaching strategies, as we are made aware of only the expository writing requirement that 63 percent of the faculty have instituted. We do have several antecedent measures, but on balance, one would have to say our data is limited.

Some observations can be made from this triangulation. Although almost two-thirds of teachers understand the value of expository writing in promoting thinking, reasoning, and summarizing, little support in terms of explicit collaboration or accountability measures has been implemented to improve student achievement. A concerted effort to introduce performance assessments was made to improve student achievement (3.2 performance assessments per teacher). A good-faith effort was also made as far as antecedents. The effort falls apart, however, with regard to collaboration and accountability, which appear to be voluntary at best. Data teams meet roughly every quarter, and assessment calendars are used for very few assessments, so it is unlikely that much reflection and analysis are going on. Finally, when three of four teachers do not have the authority to make emphasis or resource adjustments in their classrooms, how can we expect to see improvements in student achievement? They lack the accountability capacity.

Can we glean anything from this exercise? One can surmise that it is not enough to implement quality instructional changes (antecedents), unless there is a corresponding quality change in collaboration around the data, and unless there is sufficient accountability for all faculty members to align efforts to achieve desired results. The second benefit is evident from the numbers for this group; the percent of students passing is comparable (34 percent to 25 percent) to the percentage of teachers practicing effective accountability with data. Assessments are not sufficiently calibrated to ensure quality analysis, reflection, and action. At the very least, we should not be surprised that two of three students were not proficient on the state math assessment.

The sample triangulation would be strengthened with the insights and perspective of teams. I am certain groups of readers would identify recommendations and discover meaning individual readers would not be able to discern. Nonetheless, even this simple triangulation offers still more. It leads us to dig deeper inside the data to see how students in classes of teachers with the authority to be accountable performed on the state assessment. If they outperformed those who lacked such authority, we will have a very valuable finding. Likewise, we would want to correlate student performance with those teachers who collaboratively developed the single EOC assessment (one of four core subject possibilities or 25 percent).

The quick sample triangulation provided direction for further data analysis. In Exhibit 7.2, the same data is presented across four teams at the school, offering a different slice of data to triangulate. Complete the exercise by recording one insight you observe and one recommendation for the future when this data is added to what was learned from Exhibit 7.1.

Exhibit 7.2
Triangulation of Data by Teams

	Team A	Team B	Team C	Team D
Proficient math assessment	60%	20%	40%	16%
Data team meetings per semester	4	1	3	1
Expository writing required daily	Yes	No	Yes	No
EOC assessments developed collaboratively	Yes	No	No	No
Assessment calendars applied to assessments	80%	No	No	No
Teachers have authority to be accountable	Yes	No	No	No

Observation from Exhibit 7.2? _____

_____

_____

Recommendation? _____

_____

_____

The preceding example allows a number of conclusions to be drawn—to improve performance of teams C, B, and D, especially—even though data seldom provides such direct and powerful correlations. Nonetheless, triangulation examines data that are unrelated statistically, but are extremely valuable in identifying practices that work and those that don't. Quite simply, triangulation extrapolates meaning from raw data. As useful as it is to triangulate student achievement data with evidence about antecedents, collaboration, and accountability structures, triangulation need not be limited to three types of data. Returning to data from Timberline Middle School (see Chapter 2, Exhibits 2.1, 2.4–2.6), we find that at first glance, not much is changing in terms of overall school averages. When we examined antecedent training programs that address instructional strategies, however, we discovered that students in classrooms where teachers received training outperformed their peers dramatically. The data was sufficiently compelling to at least warrant continuing the training practices and perhaps mandating training in the three interventions over time. Let us see whether a three-way intersection or triangulation adds value in any way.

We know that Team A developed end-of-course (EOC) assessments collaboratively, whereas the other teams did not. We determined in Chapter 2 that students in classrooms where teachers received training in various instructional strategies outperformed students in classrooms where teachers did not receive training. We know that Timberline had so many assessments that we had to be concerned about the effect of testing itself on student motivation and effort. Examine Exhibit 7.3 to determine whether the triangulation process can help us understand the interaction of these variables: professional development and EOC assessment development by teachers, and test taking.

We used the average unit scores for fall and spring trimesters for all core subjects as our dependent variable. As expected, students whose teachers had been trained in one or more instructional strategies did better on the unit tests than students whose teachers had not received the training. The data also indicates that students whose teachers had developed EOC assessments collaboratively did better than their counterparts, if teachers received training in instructional strategies. If teachers participated in

Exhibit 7.3

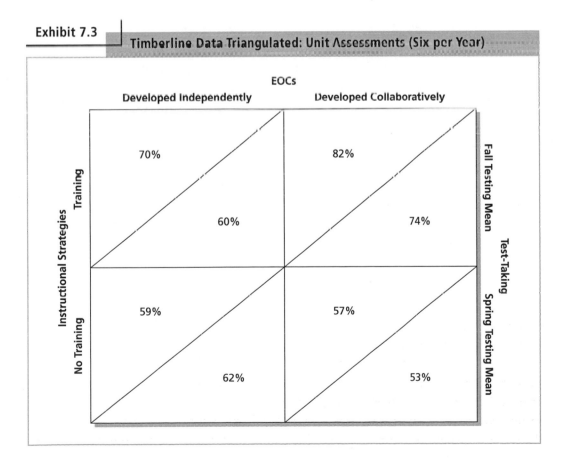

Timberline Data Triangulated: Unit Assessments (Six per Year)

collaborative design of EOCs but did not receive training, there was virtually no difference. The final point from this triangulation is that students generally scored lower on the spring unit assessments than on fall assessments. The purpose of this design is to illustrate how almost any form of triangulation can be quite instructive, even with limited data. We found out two useful pieces of information: instructional strategy training for teachers added value, and students did suffer from testing fatigue, as indicated by lower scores for every group between fall and spring.

Victoria Bernhardt (2000, p. 34) referred to a similar process as "intersecting of data," recommending dual measure intersection, three-way intersection, and four-way intersection. This approach not only looks at the full range of antecedents, from the results of EOC assessments to instructional strategies, but also triangulates data by framing questions that represent a variety of hypotheses. Intersecting practical questions about the classroom and school focuses data analysis to identify the root causes of student achievement results. Exhibit 7.4 provides examples of two-, three-, and four-way data intersections, sorting them by the three principles of data-driven decision making.

Each added intersection digs deeper in the analysis process, providing more precise information. Monitoring the two-way example may establish a relationship between improved achievement and collaboration of teachers on EOCs; another may determine the relationship of activity participation to achievement. The three-way intersections dig deeper by examining the impact of teaching strategies on the EOCs for all students while drilling deeper still to determine which subgroup benefits the most from such strategies, and by examining whether activities apply to subgroups with historically high performance. The four-way intersection digs deeper still by examining the relationship of grades to both assessments and activity participation. At this point, we have revealed important insights about collaboration of teachers, impact of instructional strategies, and school antecedents with much more precision than mere examination of student achievement data could offer. A valuable aspect of triangulation is the way it sets the stage for each of us to check our assumptions at the door when it comes to data analysis.

THE MYTH OF APPLES AND ORANGES

Statisticians go to great lengths to convince laypeople of the errors of mixing and matching data types, and the need to avoid compromising our sampling and test designs to ensure reliability and validity. We are frequently warned that you cannot mix apples and oranges. Triangulation, however, necessitates discovery of insights from often unrelated data: hence the importance of applying this process to educational data that is varied, often unrelated, and collected at different times for different purposes. Can we mix parametric and nonparametric data? How can we use classroom assessment

Exhibit 7.4

Intersection of Data	Antecedent	Collaboration	Accountability
Two-Way Intersection			
■ Do students in activities do better on state assessments?	✔		✔
■ Do students with better grades also do better on writing assessments?		✔✔	
■ Do students of teachers who collaboratively design, implement, and evaluate EOCs do better on EOCs than students of teachers who do not?		✔	✔
Three-Way Intersection			
■ Do Asian students in activities do better on state assessments than Asian students who do not participate in activities, and do their grades correlate with activities or state assessments?	✔✔		✔
■ What teaching strategy has the greatest effect on EOCs for students with less than a 15% learning gap, and what subgroup (ethnic/gender) has shown the greatest progress on EOC assessments?	✔✔		✔
Four-Way Intersection			
■ Do students in activities do better on state assessments than students who do not participate in activities, and do grades correlate with activities or state assessments? How do the correlations of subgroups (ethnic and gender) differ as to grades, state assessments, and activity participation?	✔✔		✔✔

data when sufficient rigor has not been applied to test design and item analysis? The problem of data in the public schools (and probably in any application other than wheat yields) is the fact that the data available is seldom perfect. However, the triangulation process has been employed for centuries for the very purpose of gleaning meaning from imperfect and incomplete data. Though there are certainly instances in which data should not be compared in a statistical sense, the complexity of education compels us to look for patterns and trends in a practical sense that lead us to decisions that improve student achievement, regardless of the type of data.

Triangulation is a messy process. It requires teams to make assumptions, draw inferences, and come to conclusions without total certainty. When data is triangulated, each point serves as a check on the other dimension, with the desired outcome from use of the various data points (and types) always being the realization of new insights that are not available from examining only one type of data or one perspective.

Triangulation requires us to look beyond the numbers by examining data from various perspectives. The following exercise reexamines Timberline Middle School, a school with a reputation for high performance and excellence that finds itself caught in a vise between changing demographics on one side, and what seems to be an onslaught of accountability to the state, the federal government, and the public on the other.

Timberline Middle School has sufficient enrollment to compare all NCLB subgroups, and the principal is committed to extensive data analysis. Twelve types of student achievement results, requiring 180 assessments during the school year, are collected and monitored. Timberline offers after-school and Saturday opportunities, and alignment of curriculum, instruction, and assessments with standards is its hallmark. Even though the school is long on collection of achievement data and short on identification of antecedents, we can at least triangulate the data available to Timberline in search of deeper understanding. Examine Exhibit 7.5 to help Timberline Middle School and offer them insights you glean from the process of triangulation. Effects, causes, and antecedent conditions/structures have a plus (+) or minus (−) sign preceding them, or no designation for items that could have an effect in either direction. After examining for patterns, complete the reflection questions that follow.

What does the data about class schedules indicate? How about the difference in design of EOC assignments by grade level, or the distinction between those who took advantage of the ETS training and those who didn't? What if you knew which teachers applied what strategies or which teachers relied on rubrics or scoring guides? The list is endless as to the types of additional data that could be very helpful, and the process is designed to elicit questions as well as greater awareness. Even without additional data, however, triangulation focuses our data analysis to help us discover serious gaps in terms of teacher practices and structural antecedents. Although we have yet to discover the causes of the growing gender gap or issues with subgroups of students, one can see the immediate benefit of triangulation—a benefit that multiplies when professionals triangulate through a collaborative process, even if the collaborative groups are as small as two or three people. Finally, it doesn't matter whether the data is parametric or nonparametric. You can mix and match all types of data, even observations and opinions. Just use the process to verify those opinions and hunches with direct and indirect indicators.

THE WAGON WHEEL

This section introduces a data analysis tool that enables teachers and principals to conduct multivariate analyses without having to be experts in statistical analysis. Modern statistics relies on bread-and-butter multivariate methods such as multiple regression, analysis of variance, and analysis of covariance. Each of these statistics allows the researcher to control for variability and enables her to determine the relative

Triangulation for Timberline Middle School

Effects (performance results +/−)

+ Gap closed for Hispanic students each year, all subjects.
− Gap opened for African-American boys from −25% to −35%
+ Gap closed for African-American girls each of last 3 years
− ESA gaps doubled from −15 to −30%

	Rdg	Wrtg	Math
03	67%	48%	62%
04	63%	49%	67%
05	72%	57%	70%

(Related data from Exhibits 2.4 to 2.7 and Exhibits 7.1, 7.2, and 7.4)

Cause Data (teacher behaviors +/−)

% volunteering for effective teaching strategies (ETS) training: 86% (31/36)

% using 2 or more performance assessments
- 6th grade: 25% (3/12)
- 7th grade: 0% (0/12)
- 8th grade: 33% (5/12)

Teacher experience & ETS
- 0–5 years: 8/12
- 6–10 years: 12/12
- 10+ years: 1/12

All departments and teachers provide letter or percentage grades; no evidence of rubric use in grading

Antecedents (structures and conditions)

+ 100% of courses have EOCs
+ 100% of classrooms use at least one performance assessment

EOCs designed by Volunteer teacher/Teacher teams
- 6th grade: 25%/75%
- 7th grade: 100%/0%
- 8th grade: 0%/100%

− 90 classes interrupted for tests
− Classes divided between core academics and electives; students have a.m. or p.m. core classes
+ Excelling classrooms are recognized monthly (based on assessment data)
+ Writing assessment improvement recognized on principal's data wall
+ Faculty meetings devoted to data analysis

Students falling behind are monitored, with report sent to principal

Reflect about the insights and awareness you discovered and list recommendations you might provide the principal at Timberline as a result of this triangulation exercise:

1.

2.

3.

4.

effects of variables as they interact with and counteract each other. Undoubtedly, these methods provide the most precise means of ascertaining cause and effect in the complex study of human beings. The wagon wheel is a simple but effective way to investigate multiple variables at once, and determine with confidence (against predetermined performance standards) which variables warrant a focused response. The wagon wheel (also known as a *spider chart*) allows users to compare differences between schools, classrooms, or teachers, and differences within the same entity. Exhibit 7.6 depicts the wagon wheel and the process for employing it.

To illustrate the capacity of this wonderful tool for triangulation, we selected eight very different variables, and we will compare three classrooms on each of the eight

Exhibit 7.6

The Wagon Wheel Data Analysis Tool and Graphic Organizer

Steps in using wagon wheels:
1. Assign key variables to each spoke on wheel (10).
2. Collect data across key variables.
3. Establish scale for each spoke, with highest performance on outer rim of circle. Label each individual spoke with its own scale.
4. Plot performance data along spokes, color-coding to distinguish units being compared (classrooms, schools, departments, grade levels, budgets, certification areas, etc.).
5. Connect lines for each unit if comparisons are made between units.
6. Identify the pattern of performance against selected performance standards.

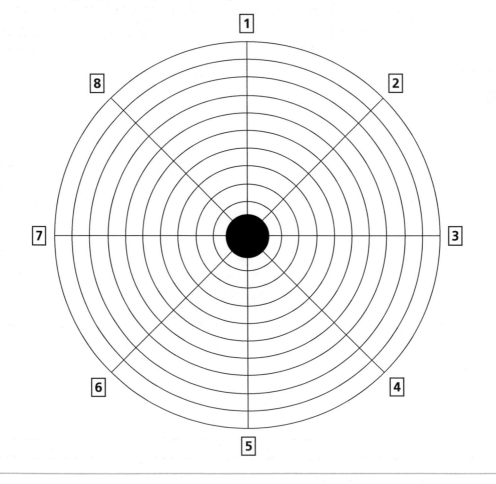

variables. A wagon wheel could have more spokes, but the sheer volume makes it difficult to extend much beyond the example. Examination of more than eight to ten variables is awkward at best and not recommended. Note the ten concentric circles in Exhibit 7.6, a figure that lends itself to metric scales such as percent or currency. The beauty of the wagon wheel is that one can use different scales and still retain integrity in the analysis.

Step 1: Assign Variables

Assign key variables to each spoke on the wheel. The wagon wheel is a graphic representation that facilitates comparison of several variables and several entities. Analysis may examine classrooms, students, and the entire school on the same wagon wheel. It might be used to analyze assessment results with textbook purchases and collaborative planning. It might examine professional development and its impact on student achievement, as we did with Timberline's data, and it might examine the degree to which a teacher adheres to a defined teaching process used in a specific lesson plan. Some have used the wagon wheel to monitor progress against performance standards for individual personnel evaluations or improvement goals. To illustrate the robust capacity of this simple tool, the following diverse variables were selected for wagon-wheel spokes:

1. Budget projections. Budgeted-to-actual expenditures reveal degree of precision and accuracy for administrators, with 100 percent standard for excellence.

2. Use of technology. Degree of variability within entities in terms of fluency and application of end-user technologies, such as software applications. Measurement will be percentage used proficiently, based on seven Microsoft Office Suite applications (i.e., Microsoft Word, Excel, Publisher, etc.).

3. Percent of total student assessments subject to assessment calendars at school.

4. Reduction of classroom interruptions (e.g., intercom announcements per day), measured in raw numbers (range 0–10).

5. Classroom checklist for standards implementation (see Exhibit 3.6) measured in terms of percent of fourteen items monitored by teacher.

6. Percent proficient on the state writing assessment.

7. Teacher absence rates, measured by average number of days out of classroom per teacher for any reason for the last twelve-month period.

8. Time lag between special education referral and delivery of specialized instructional services, measured by total referrals/school days between referral and first day of service (range 1–100).

Step 2: Collect Data

The versatility of the wagon wheel becomes evident in step 2, as professionals can create the wagon wheel after the fact, or respond to triangulation activities by creating wagon wheels to address the issues raised. The benefit of front-end planning ensures that the data is available, thorough, and accurate. Still, teams can benefit from the wagon-wheel tool simply by identifying criteria important to those engaging in analysis and re-creating the data as accurately as possible, or beginning a wagon wheel for future review. Administrators have astutely used all eight or ten spokes as elements of evaluation criteria delineated in quality scoring guide rubrics.

Step 3: Establish Scale

Establish a scale for each spoke, with highest performance on the outer rim of the circle. This is necessary to provide the visual understanding of which entities (schools, teachers, districts, departments) are most consistently performing at or near the desired standards. Teams may want to use the bull's-eye or hub of the wheel as the targeted performance level; this is an individual preference, but the important factor is to have the standard be obvious, uniform, and consistent across the variables being measured.

Step 4: Plot Performance Data

Plot performance data along spokes, color-coding to distinguish units being compared (classrooms, schools, departments, grade levels, budgets, certification areas, etc.). If you prefer, you can use black-and-white geometric shapes and patterns to distinguish units, rather than color-coding. This step advocates for a manageable number of variables and units (spokes and entities being compared).

Step 5: Make Connections

Connect the lines for each unit if comparisons are made between or among units.

Step 6: Identify Patterns

Identify the pattern of performance against the selected performance standards. This final step is really the beginning of analysis. The wagon wheel is really a form of triangulation, although the data for each variable is quantitative rather than completely unknown. It is the interaction of the data that produces the "ah-hahs"—the insights —associated with triangulation and for that reason the tool has been included here.

Exhibit 7.7 illustrates the visual power of the wagon wheel to reveal discrepancies, strengths, and weaknesses. For the purpose of simplicity, three classrooms have been selected as units of comparison, even though spokes 1, 7, and perhaps 8 are administrative indicators that are unlikely to be selected as variables by teachers. The other variables,

Exhibit 7.7

Wagon Wheel Illustrated

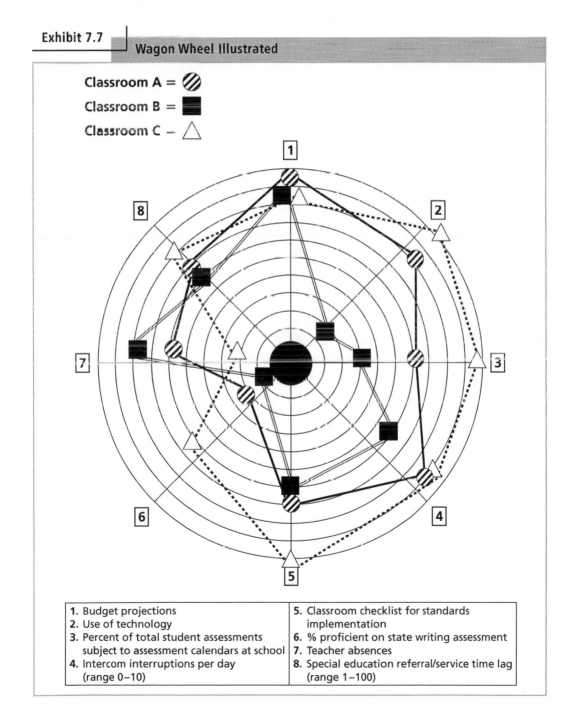

1. Budget projections
2. Use of technology
3. Percent of total student assessments subject to assessment calendars at school
4. Intercom interruptions per day (range 0–10)
5. Classroom checklist for standards implementation
6. % proficient on state writing assessment
7. Teacher absences
8. Special education referral/service time lag (range 1–100)

however, provide both administrators and teachers with valuable information that can help in setting priorities, identifying antecedents, and initiating improvements.

The wagon-wheel data reveals areas of strength and weakness for all three classrooms. In terms of budget projections, all three classrooms ranged from 80+ percent to 95 percent, usually a positive indicator of good planning and careful expenditures. There was also very little variation in lag time (#8) between referral to special education and delivery of services. This is probably attributable to district procedures to comply with federal law, but the range from twenty to forty days is not unusual, alas. There was considerable discrepancy when it came to standards, however, as Classroom C performed much closer to the standard in proficiency on the writing assessment, antecedents for a standards-based classroom, and adherence to an assessment calendar for almost all its assessments. Classroom B, unfortunately, was furthest away from the desired performance on all but teacher absences, and had the lowest percent proficient on the state writing assessment. Classroom B was also the furthest from the standards in technology literacy; though there is room for all classrooms to improve, Classroom B needs immediate assistance to reach the desired levels. This example intentionally included measures that counted both from the bulls'-eye out and the outer rim in (time lag for services, #4; and intercom interruptions, #7) because the outer rim was the performance standard, illustrating how even the scales can be varied to provide the most complete picture of proficiency or achievement of desired targets. Schools, departments, teams, and dimensions can be compared in this way, and the possibilities for triangulating data are unlimited and very user-friendly. Appendix D provides a template of the wagon-wheel data analysis tool.

SUMMARY

Triangulation is a process of discovering the unknown by looking at things from different angles. It necessitates diversity of ideas, experiences, and perspectives, and therefore requires a healthy dose of collaboration. It also requires solid data points to triangulate from, whether the data describes results in student achievement, compliance with policies and procedures, or monitoring of the quality and degree with which proven instructional strategies are deployed. It therefore requires a healthy dose of accountability, where people are empowered to take responsibility not only for their actions but also for results. Accountability requires authority to take action on the basis of data, as well as permission to clean house and sweep away obsolete and counterproductive practices and programs when needed.

Triangulation reveals understanding that mere data, standing alone, cannot, as we discovered in the wagon-wheel exercise. As educators, we must be prepared to respond to such discoveries as a moral imperative to make a difference for the students we serve. That requires leadership and accountability, and the capacity to create a sense of

Exhibit 7.8

Scoring Guide for Triangulation 7.0

Analysis Dimension	Meeting the Standard	Progressing Toward the Standard	Not Meeting the Standard
7.0 Triangulation	The educator applies at least two data tools to every triangulation, triangulating student achievement data effectively with supporting student achievement data, antecedent data (conditions and structure), accountability data (responsibilities, reporting, SMART measures), or collaboration data (various team formats, lesson logs, instructional calendars, etc.). The educator monitors staff triangulation of achievement data to ensure inclusion of related and unrelated data points (e.g., instructional strategies, allocation of time, professional development, side-by-side curriculum analysis, standards, and assessments).	The educator applies at least one data tool to every triangulation effort, and is beginning to triangulate student achievement data with antecedents, collaboration data, or accountability structures (principles of DDDM).	The educator is unaware of the principle of triangulation of data, and instead focuses his or her efforts on compliance with district and state reports.
7.1 Low Inference Insights	The educator leverages triangulation to engage teachers in self-discovery of insights, new learning, and recommendations for changes in the educational process. The educator triangulates data effectively, with each point serving as a check on the other dimensions; the desired outcome is the realization of new insights from the various data points (and types) that are not available from examining one type of data or one perspective in isolation.	The educator understands that triangulation requires teams to make assumptions, draw inferences, and come to conclusions without total certainty. The educator recognizes that triangulation necessitates discovery of a center point from other, often unrelated data, and the educator triangulates student assessment data with antecedents and cause data wherever possible.	The educator is directive in interactions with teachers, and does not engage teachers in triangulation of data.

(continues)

Exhibit 7.8

Scoring Guide for Triangulation 7.0 (Continued)

Analysis Dimension	Meeting the Standard	Progressing Toward the Standard	Not Meeting the Standard
7.2 Triangulation Conversations	The educator models triangulation in formal and informal settings, and asks teachers to add value to their analysis of all data by triangulating data with colleagues. Triangulation is an expected exercise for all grade, department, and data team meetings, and the leader routinely includes cause data and administrative antecedents in triangulation. The educator applies triangulation to encourage innovative teaching strategies and facilitate new approaches to instruction through action research. Data is specifically analyzed to engage staff in conversations about assessments.	The educator uses the triangulation process to coach teachers in making assumptions, drawing inferences, and developing hunches that can help identify replicable practices, verified through action research.	The educator views data as numbers and does not engage faculty or staff in making inferences or reaching for assumptions, believing that none of the school staff is a statistician and shouldn't claim to be.

urgency when the data indicates the need for decisive and courageous actions. Triangulation is also about introducing antecedents of all kinds into the analysis of data, as we did in Exhibit 7.3 to examine unit test scores in light of teacher training and collaborative development of EOCs.

Triangulation requires a healthy dose of antecedents and a willingness to recognize their influence. The remaining chapters will assist us in getting beyond the numbers to make a difference in our schools, leveraging the principle of subtraction, and establishing a thorough process for gathering information and insights from systems and a changing environment. We will develop ways to replicate those brilliant teacher practices that are so often confined to a single teacher rather than shared with the field. Lastly, we close with Chapter 10, "The Teacher as Expert." Triangulation equips us to move into that arena, where the expertise of the profession is applied to data analysis to create solutions beyond the numbers. Exhibit 7.8 (see pages 121–122) delineates a standard for triangulation to support current and future triangulation efforts.

DISCUSSION

BIG IDEA

Triangulation identifies possibilities beyond the numbers.

QUESTIONS

1. *Describe a principle of triangulation as it relates to mixing apples and oranges.*

2. *What is the relationship between triangulation and accountability in data analysis? Between triangulation and collaboration?*

3. *What is the benefit of developing triangulations to examine effects data, antecedent data, and measures of accountability?*

4. *Consider designing your own wagon wheel with another colleague who is familiar with your school or position. Collaborate to identify the variables that are most important to your work.*

The Environmental Scan

*You cannot depend on your eyes when your
imagination is out of focus.*

—MARK TWAIN (1835 1910)

We have seen how triangulation helps extrapolate meaning from raw data and how it can be an effective means of finding critical information and seeing the big picture when we have limited information. In the same way, an environmental scan helps us extrapolate meaning from the changes that are occurring in our classrooms, schools, systems, and communities. The best environmental scans require us to examine areas we otherwise would ignore or avoid. It is an important component of the "treasure hunt" because it ensures that we include changes in data analysis—that is, if we are to avoid scenarios like that of Apple Blossom Unified School District.

CASE STUDY

Apple Blossom USD prided itself on being on the cutting edge of curriculum design, professional development, and instructional technology. The community it served was a reflection of that pride: well-educated, affluent, with a large proportion of the community employed in networking, Internet, or wireless technologies. As a result, when the school rolled out its bold move to make Apple Blossom the first district in the state to have fiber-optic cable installed throughout the district, the board and advisory councils were excited and the local press portrayed Apple Blossom as the darling of public education. Apple Blossom had a history of very commendable test scores, and to the outside observer, this was *the* place to live and work. Because average test scores ranged between the seventieth and ninetieth percentiles on the norm-referenced test, and the pattern had been consistent for more than twenty years, there was considerable pride in the curriculum and the broad range of course offerings in the high schools.

(continues)

CASE STUDY

Some teachers periodically questioned the range of course offerings that qualified for the same credit and ultimately, the same diploma. Other staff, supported by a growing number of parents, inquired about starting a school of choice, but most criticisms and calls for change were summarily dismissed by a reference to "our fine schools being the envy of the state." During the campaign for fiber-optics, the district's graduation rate was reported as 95 percent (another attractive feature), so when the mill levy passed to build the fiber-optic network, it appeared that the sky was the limit and the district had nowhere to go but up.

Within a year, the investment in fiber-optics had fallen into disrepute; the curriculum was being lambasted in the press for not being aligned to the new and challenging state standards; parents had picketed the school board for being unresponsive to student needs and subscribing to a one-size-fits-all mentality; and various advocacy groups had Apple Blossom in their sights as a district that had misled the public and failed, through indifference and prejudice, to address the needs of students characterized as transient, low-income, and of color.

What happened? How can one year make such a difference?

Apple Blossom rested on its laurels and made a number of strategic errors, not the least of which was its failure to have quality listening systems in place. Listening systems would have revealed that a large investment in fiber-optics was premature in light of the move toward DSL solutions, high-speed cable, and Web-based information management through the Internet. Listening systems would also have seen the movement toward standards and accountability building for years, as well as the movement toward choice and charter options. The district's data analysis was fixated on the use of averages, which did indeed mask serious problems for a minority of its students, and the reporting system for graduation rate was calibrated on an annual basis; hence it reported 95 percent graduation, instead of the more accurate 76 percent that would have emerged when those enrolled as fall-semester freshmen were compared with those listed in the graduation program four years later. Some of these issues remain today, although other issues have been addressed while dealing with the requirements for NCLB and state accountability. Apple Blossom, almost overnight, saw its reputation plummet from being the "darling" and "visionary" school system to being at best a run-of-the-mill organization that had to react to change rather than lead it.

ENVIRONMENTAL SCANS: AN INTRODUCTION

An *environmental scan* is a process to examine changes: mandatory changes, such as contained in the NCLB Act; chosen changes, such as the desire to build a fiber-optic system; and external changes, such as the movement toward choice that has built so rapidly (by 2005, more than forty states had passed charter school legislation). Apple Blossom USD is not entirely a fantasy, because each component of the preceding scenario is an illustration of actual events that have stopped well-intentioned and dedicated educators in their tracks. Completion of an environmental scan facilitates a more thorough understanding of change factors and resource needs.

An environmental scan examines seven characteristics of organizations that are present whether the organization is effective or ineffective. A scan can be employed by a classroom teacher, a principal and her faculty, or a school system. It is based on systems analysis, a process designed to clarify the purpose, parts, and functions of an organization to reveal its degree of interdependence and to discover any unintended consequences of that interdependence. If we look only to Timberline Middle School (see Chapter 2), for example, we can safely conjecture that the emphasis on collecting data produced an unintended (and unhelpful) reaction from staff against data and against data analysis. The same is true with Apple Blossom USD; its leaders had no idea of the effect reporting a 95 percent graduation rate would have on its reputation, even when the state probably employed the same faulty methodology. Similarly, Dennis (see Chapter 3) did not see how his leadership in creating collaborative opportunities and aligning effort to promote literacy influenced student achievement—but it did. Superintendent Ellison's attempt to implement too many initiatives at once (Chapter 1), and her reliance on the past to predict the future, also had consequences that distracted from efforts to improve teaching and learning—something that was hardly intended.

Our environmental scan will examine two types of changes across three dimensions: external and internal changes across programmatic, instructional, and organizational dimensions. *External changes* are simply changes that are outside of one's control. To the state officials, NCLB is most definitely an external change, and though it affects both the organization and instruction, it is a *programmatic change*. To a school system, legislative action that requires an individual learning plan for every student who is not proficient is also an external programmatic change, as is growth or decline in enrollment. The fact that a school has three years to meet adequate yearly progress goals for all subgroups, or face the possibility of reconstitution as a charter school, is an external change reality facing schools right now in twelve states. This change will require a response across all three dimensions. Finally, the requirement that every teacher be prepared, on demand, to articulate where each student is in terms of becoming proficient on key standards, is also an external requirement, though it will necessitate an instructional response. None of these are particularly pleasant challenges facing educators at any of these levels. Nevertheless, they are realities and can be ignored only at one's professional peril.

PLANNING AREAS

The first area to be scanned for changes is leadership. Changes in leadership include personnel changes; changes affecting accountability issues, such as authority to act or permission to subtract; and the leadership impact of collaborative structures such as data teams. An external change would be assignment of a new administrator. An internal change would be the opportunity to be involved in the selection of that new administrator. An organizational change would be the reconstitution noted earlier, significant changes in policy, a change in superintendent, or a change in the makeup and philosophy of the board of education. An example of a programmatic change that is also a leadership change is the creation of data teams with authority to commit resources for materials, teacher training, or additional time and opportunity to assist certain students to close their learning gaps. An example of instructional change regarding leadership would be a change in actions of leadership within the classroom as to how performances are monitored, expectations communicated, feedback provided, feedback elicited, and decisions made. Though seldom associated with leadership, these actions of teachers in the classroom are demonstrations of leadership, and lesson planning provides a framework for intentional response to changes (external) or for initiation of changes (internal) to improve student achievement.

The second area is planning of strategies. Strategies have been discussed almost exclusively in terms of classroom teaching strategies, but planning certainly extends to programs and organizations as well. External planning strategies include how a classroom responds to a principal's requirement to demonstrate the relation of each lesson to specific content standards. The method for creating an effective response to that requirement is the teacher's planning strategy (such as backward curriculum mapping that leads to an effective instructional calendar). An internal planning strategy for the principal might be the way in which she intends to increase the quality of a note-taking and summarizing strategy in all classrooms. That planning process might include an introduction containing a compelling argument from the research, warnings on common pitfalls, and ready-to-use suggestions for teachers following the introduction. It might include a planned modeling of lessons by the principal or a teacher who is accomplished in note taking and summarizing. The planning process might stipulate how teams are expected to work together and produce a model, with timelines and accountability expectations delineated. Finally, an effective planning strategy would complete the cycle by monitoring implementation and providing a method to evaluate success of the strategy.

This internal planning example addresses instructional issues (note taking) as well as programmatic issues (modeling, teamwork, monitoring, and evaluation). An obvious example of an organizational planning strategy is the challenge facing schools everywhere to develop an improvement plan that achieves dramatic results. Principals, teachers, central office administrators, and specialists must consider what works well in their particular work environments and intentionally plan strategies to make a difference.

The third area is the quality and effectiveness of listening systems. I have chosen this term to include surveys, stakeholder feedback, the method by which complaints are addressed, and collective input of the community in a way that does not stop after the completion of a survey or a focus group. Listening systems must be pervasive, ongoing, and embedded, and must be accountable enough to produce action that improves student achievement. External listening systems are ways to communicate with and listen to patrons and parents in the community. Internal listening systems ensure that we hear from staff and students. Data in a Day (see Chapter 6) is an example of a listening system component.

The fourth element of a comprehensive environmental scan is information and data. Not only should we gather and analyze data on each component of the environmental scan, but we also need to understand how well our data system works, and what external and internal changes advise us to do in terms of our data system. The Timberline Middle School prided itself on its range of student assessments, yet its data and information system failed to help people manage information well enough to make informed decisions. An internal data scan examines the work habits associated with analysis, and might reveal that our collection system is cumbersome and uneven, or that assessments lack consistency and reliability, or the need for EOC assessments for every course and grade.

Before the advent of external state accountability systems and NCLB, many considered it sufficient to use classroom-developed internal assessments, and perhaps one NRT assessment administered every three years. If a school had been using the environmental scan wisely, though, it would have been able to recognize that accountability systems were coming; even the details of NCLB were discernable with specificity at least a year before the requirements were formally instituted. Schools and districts that recognized the importance of content standards early are now glad they did.

The fifth area is the work environment, where we examine the impact that districts with higher salaries have on the ability to recruit and retain the best teachers possible. There may be factors between schools that make one school a more desirable place to work; for example, as part of School B's environmental scan, an attempt to determine the characteristics that make School A more desirable would be helpful to School B's effort to retain and recruit teachers. Many factors influence the work environment, from common planning, to facilities, to resources, to quality and availability of meeting rooms, to salaries and insurance packages, to size of classrooms. A quality environmental scan will examine all changes that affect those working in the subject environment.

Earlier chapters introduced work habits as antecedents that describe how things get done. External changes frequently include additional paperwork and compliance requirements, whereas internal changes may come in the form of new systems to monitor performance or introduce lessons, or asking students to take greater responsibility for assessing and monitoring their own performance in the classroom. The need to include work habits in a comprehensive environmental scan arises from the purpose of the scan: simply, to examine what is done now, to determine what should be done, and to consider a range of improvements for greater efficiency and effectiveness.

The final component of an environmental scan is consideration of the results that are being pursued. Again, external changes may require a different reporting system or inclusion of new subgroups. A thorough environmental scan will be helpful in establishing the format for reporting, aggregating, and presenting results that provide meaningful information on an ongoing basis.

KWL AS A FILTER FOR ENVIRONMENTAL SCANS

KWL is familiar to educators as a reading strategy (Carr & Ogle, 1987). It is most closely associated with nonfiction reading comprehension and summarizing, and has seen wide application to classroom instruction across content areas and grade levels. Its simplicity accounts for its widespread adoption and adaptation:

- K represents "What do I *K*now about _____?"
- W represents "What do I *W*ant to learn about _____?"
- L represents "What have I *L*earned about _____?"

The KWL strategy is recommended here as a filter to answer questions regarding each component of the environmental scan. For example, what do I know about leadership? What do I want to learn about planning strategies? What have I learned about work environments? When these questions are posed to educators, particularly in a collaborative setting, much important data is gleaned that can inform planning and help teams proactively prepare for the future. The process also enables educators to better understand all the influences that are affecting their schools, classrooms, or districts. Exhibit 8.1 provides a template for a thorough environmental scan, capturing programmatic, instructional, and organizational factors; addressing external and internal changes; and applying the KWL filter to increase understanding of existing data at all levels. The environmental scan depicted in Exhibit 8.1 combines the systems approach across seven organizational variables with the KWL filter to deepen our ability to examine the impact of changes, both mandatory (e.g., NCLB) and voluntary (e.g., "Making Standards Work").

The template provides no fewer than twenty-one possible ways to scan the learning and organizational environment of a classroom, school, or district (see checked items). Each of these areas is then scrutinized to determine what we now know about that organizational component, what the organization wants or needs to find out, and what we anticipate might be learned from the data analysis. Exhibit 8.2 shows a completed environmental scan example that demonstrates how a simple KWL method can

Exhibit 8.1

Environmental Scan Template

	Leadership	Planning Strategies	Listening Systems	Information and Data	Work Environment	Work Habits	Results—Performance and Process
Programmatic	✔	✔	✔	✔	✔	✔	✔
Know							
Want							
Learn							
Instructional	✔	✔	✔	✔	✔	✔	✔
Know							
Want							
Learn							
Organizational	✔	✔	✔	✔	✔	✔	✔
Know							
Want							
Learn							

✔ = changes initiated

Exhibit 8.2 | Environmental Scan for Data Analysis

	Leadership	Planning Strategies	Listening Systems	Information and Data	Work Environment	Work Habits	Results—Performance and Process
Programmatic	Reading recovery	School Improvement Process (SIP)	Satisfaction surveys	Data: Student achievement tracking	Negotiated work day/hours	Barriers to professional development to improve instruction	State assessment AYP; EOC assessment requirements
Know (current knowledge)	1.0 FTE staff assigned to each school	Requirements, expectations, and deadlines	Data is inconclusive	Expectation to report results to community	Policies and terms of negotiated agreement	Programs, policies, traditions	Trends and patterns; dates when subgroup gaps must be closed
Want (to know)	Program effectiveness?	Possibility of midyear changes and process to add antecedent data indicators?	What do students, parents, teachers really think?	How to include qualitative and antecedents to student achievement data?	How much latitude to accommodate with flexible hours, waivers, compensation?	What is needed to align with standards, increase agility, and improve instruction?	Impact of investment in professional development, curriculum alignment with standards, and triangulation of data?
Learn (evidence)	Percent proficient in reading within 6 months. *Discontinued—* cost/benefit $	Specific process for midcourse changes and use of antecedents	Creation of alternate data collection systems	Evidence of gaps in achievement closing; obsolete subtracted	Areas where principals can leverage incentives to achieve results	Specify policies, traditions, and barriers; actions needed when?	What is working? Actions to replicate practices that work and eliminate existing barriers
Instructional	Expectations re standards and assessments	Effective teaching strategies	Student view of classroom instruction	Data-tracking practices to replicate	Ability-grouping, secondary; elementary departmentalization	Opening classroom activities	Cohort improvement by subgroup and gaps opening or closing

(continues)

Exhibit 8.2 Environmental Scan for Data Analysis *(Continued)*

	Leadership	Planning Strategies	Listening Systems	Information and Data	Work Environment	Work Habits	Results—Performance and Process
Know	Standards are aligned with daily lessons	Teachers employ one or more daily	Students have no means to register concerns	No system is currently in place	Wide variation; little training; no clear expectations	Wide variation; little training; no clear expectations	3 years of cohort data by subgroup on state assessments only
Want	Quality of implementation?	Which strategies, and why chosen?	What are student preferences for teaching?	How to recognize replicable practices early?	Impact on student achievement by subgroups?	Openings promote engagement or reduce disruption?	Early-warning EOCs and performance indicators ("canaries")?
Learn	Gap between observed lesson plans and declared	ETS integrated, declared by teacher, observed by others	Strategies, antecedents that will engage students	Correlation between teachers and achievement	What works for all students, and what groupings close gap?	Need for training, cost, anticipated student gains	Where resources and opportunities have to be created and when?
Organizational	Site-based management	Policies promoting ETS	Community aware-standards?	Need assessment calendar mandate	Relation of experience to achievement	Duplication of effort, related cost	Accountability and authority to act
Know	District policy that decisions will be made at sites	Policies exist; principals to monitor ETS use	Accountability new to schools—misinformation	Lots of data never analyzed properly—all levels, sites	Historically positive correlation, no data since 1990	Budgets tighter every year; some processes lengthy	All staff have limitations on authority to act
Want	Discretion for staff transfers, budget carryover?	Degree monitored; "when" and "how" data?	Process to communicate re standards	Correlation of achievement to testing calendars?	What is relationship between experience and achievement?	How to streamline for efficiency and effectiveness?	What artificial barriers inhibit bold, effective leadership?
Learn	Link all decisions to school goals	To disaggregate by ETS usage	Type and frequency of communication	Need for training, time, requirements	Importance of teacher longevity	Value of speed to responsiveness	How to promote creativity, risk-taking

be applied to secure answers to persistent and challenging questions, not only about student achievement but also about the health of the organization.

SEEING THE FOREST FROM THE TREES

Throughout this book, we have stressed the need to simplify things, the ability to reflect on what we do well and what we need to do to get better, and the need for teachers to trust their collective wisdom. Despite dramatic improvements in recent years, education is still characterized by bureaucratic structures (Darling-Hammond, 1997). The typical response when challenges go unmet in bureaucratic organizations is to "create new offices, job titles, and programs that seek to compensate for the effects of an ill-defined system" (p. 202). Once again, the experience of most educators will ring true with this observation, even in an era of tight budgets and increased scrutiny and accountability. The standards movement and the accountability of NCLB have created positions like assessment coordinator, director of research and evaluation, executive director for learning services, instructional data manager, assistant for assessment and continuous improvement. It isn't that those job functions aren't necessary; the point is that our profession struggles with finding alternate ways to respond to the challenges that come our way.

This section briefly addresses the need to keep things simple. Society in the twenty-first century uses platitudes that were not common a generation ago: "Work smarter, not harder," " Less is more," and of course, the definition of insanity. Exhibit 8.3 provides an opportunity to identify all the kinds of data collected in your work situation, reports you must file, information you must process. Check all that you believe are

Exhibit 8.3

Data, Reports, and Information at Work

	Analyzed Y/N		Analyzed Y/N
1.		9.	
2.		10.	
3.		11.	
4.		12.	
5.		13.	
6.		14.	
7.		15.	
8.		16.	

never analyzed for improvement. If you are uncertain, check no, and make a commitment to yourself to find out what happens to the information.

The next step in seeing the forest from the trees is to stop collecting data that is never analyzed. Confer with a colleague about your discoveries from Exhibit 8.3. If you do not have the authority to subtract, agree to go to those who can give it to you and get it. Few can argue with a request to stop doing something that is producing no value, and everyone will be relieved to find out that such a radical idea is even possible.

SYSTEMS ANALYSIS

Systems analysis is a method of analyzing data that focuses on two things only: revealing areas of interdependence and discovering unintended consequences. When we conduct a thorough environmental scan, we need to look for these characteristics of systems.

Our scenarios throughout this book have depicted smart, dedicated professionals who were all intent on improving student performance. Whereas Dennis was successful and did not know why, Dr. Ellison, the staff at Timberline Middle School, the teachers at Maple High School, and those at Colson ISD shared a proclivity to make things worse in their efforts to make things better. How did that happen? They all failed to recognize the fundamental laws of systems: They exist whether we create them or not; they are by definition connected and interdependent; and finally, a change in one area will most certainly affect another area, whether the consequence is intended or not. That is why an environmental scan is so important, and why the seven components are so universal.

Leadership is a factor, whether present or absent, and every classroom in the United States has leaders who set the standard for quality and have enormous influence. Thankfully, most classroom leaders are also teachers, but unless we recognize how an action in one aspect of an environment affects another, we will not be as effective in data analysis as we otherwise could. Classrooms have information and data, and they have a work environment for teachers and for students. They also host numerous work habits, both collective and individual, that have a dramatic impact on student achievement. Systems are not just about districts, states, and nations. They are present in families, and, yes, in classrooms.

LISTENING DATA

Listening data has been referenced several times, not the least of which as a component of a quality environmental scan. Few schools in the twenty-first century are without some method of gathering input from its stakeholders, and the most common form is the satisfaction survey. This format is often a requirement of school improvement planning, and many schools utilize sophisticated surveys that have been validated by national organizations (which are usually more than happy to analyze the results . . . for a fee). Schools also are much more prone in this generation than the last to take these surveys seriously, to analyze the results internally, and to use the results to drive school improvement planning, at least in part. I applaud these listening systems as far as they go, but believe they seldom go far enough.

In Chapter 4, we discussed at length the importance of collaboration and the reality of a collective wisdom that emerges when groups of people apply their common sense to solve a problem. In Chapter 6, we discussed briefly the importance of corrective feedback in improving student achievement and in avoiding the learning of things that will have to be unlearned later. In the context of a thorough environmental scan, designed to provide a wealth of data that we need to make better decisions about our current reality and to respond to demands of the future, listening systems must be designed to provide both collective wisdom and corrective feedback. They must do so efficiently, routinely, and certainly not just annually. Can you see that the rearview-mirror effect is indeed alive and well? For these reasons, a single satisfaction survey just will not suffice. In fact, not even several satisfaction surveys—one for teachers, one for parents, and one for students—will suffice if excellence is what we desire.

An effective listening system will have multiple dimensions and perspectives that allow us to see things from all the angles and triangulate the information with precision and wisdom. An effective listening system will have numerous probes throughout the school year, working similarly to a comprehensive assessment system that is monitored and directed by an effective assessment calendar (see Chapter 2). Finally, an effective listening system will insist that action be taken on the basis of data gathered from it. Many educators resign themselves to using satisfaction surveys because they understand that few parents and fewer students know what they really need. The argument goes that if physicians did everything we told them to, they would be taking unnecessary and reckless liberties with our health. The argument continues that educators would be equally unwise to take the advice of those they serve. Students are not customers, after all. I couldn't agree more: they are *not* customers, they are children during a period in their lives with great potential for growth and inspiration. So the argument is persuasive, if flawed.

Let us return to the medical model once more. Though it is true that physicians would be very unwise to allow us to self-medicate and self-diagnose, it is also true that physicians have learned to listen well to their patients, involve them in understanding the data, and ask for their feedback frequently and continuously. Listening systems do not dictate how we as a profession will respond to the needs of our "clients" (our students and their families), but they are a means to collect meaningful data for analysis, just as teacher behaviors are important pieces of data. And like the physician's patients, many of our students and parents have extraordinary insights: If we listen to them, we can avoid "surgery" and get them on the path of educational health and learning.

The Data in a Day program, designed by the Northwest Educational Laboratory (see Chapter 6), included a debriefing session with the entire staff. One recommendation was that the assessment calendar include consistent public communication with all those involved in data management, even when no changes are implemented as a result of the data collected and analyzed. As noted earlier, one reason for doing so is to communicate to all involved that their work has been taken seriously. Data in a Day does the same. Data teams, discussed in Chapter 6 and refined by The Leadership and Learning Center, insist on wide dissemination of data team minutes as a means to hold one another accountable and as a means of creating a history, a narrative, a Tier 3 form of data. By conducting the business of public education in public, we introduce the principle of *audience* that always calls participants to their highest standard. Listening systems, like the assessment calendar, demand a response from those analyzing the data. Educators who communicate the data of listening system probes to all concerned will be seen immediately as both transparent and inclusive. More importantly, the insights gained from a comprehensive listening system should inform planning strategies and help shape an unfolding vision of the future based on reality.

Exhibit 8.4 presents a framework for an effective listening system that continues to value satisfaction survey data, but supplements it with Website and electronic feedback systems, and with focus groups and interview data, which contain qualitative assessments of the values, experiences, perspectives, and needs of those we serve. There undoubtedly are other listening frameworks. My own experience included an office visit feedback card to monitor my ability to meet the needs of those who took the time and effort to visit me in my office. Let us look, however, at the listening system template in Exhibit 8.4. A sample listening system is shown in Exhibit 8.5, and Appendix F offers a black-line master.

The most obvious part of the listening system is the expectation that it will gather data on multiple fronts simultaneously. At a minimum, it should have the capacity to triangulate data from surveys, in-person focus groups and interviews, and electronically through Web sites, email, and student information systems that are available and distinct depending on the agency.

The second feature is the expectation that a rationale exists justifying current practice for each component of the listening system. This ensures a means to revisit each component to determine whether it is still useful or whether it should be changed or subtracted.

A third feature is found in the columns marked P, I, and E. Is the component in the proposal stage, has it been introduced, or is it established? This is an important

Exhibit 8.4 — Listening Data

School: _____ Principal: _____ Date: _____ Email: _____

Types of Data	Parents	Teachers and Administrators	Staff	Students	Patrons	P	I	E	Rationale: Current Practice
Satisfaction Surveys									
What do we currently do with the data?									
Authority to act? (commit resources)									
Who?/When?									
How?									
Focus Groups, Interviews									
What do we currently do with the data?									
Authority to act? (commit resources)									

(continues)

Exhibit 8.4

Listening Data (Continued)

School: Principal: Date: Email:

Types of Data	Parents	Teachers and Administrators	Staff	Students	Patrons	P	I	E	Rationale: Current Practice
Who?/When?									
How?									
Website Comments									
What do we currently do with the data?									
Authority to act? (commit resources)									
Who?/When?									
How?									

Proposed = P   Introduced = I   Established = E

Guidelines for Listening Systems: Cyclical, predictable, public (open, transparent), user-friendly

Exhibit 8.5 | Sample Listening Data (Milford School District)

School: Principal: Date: Email:

Satisfaction Surveys	Parents	Teachers and Administrators	Staff	Students	Patrons	P	I	E	Rationale: Current Practice
What do we currently do with the data?	Look at it; address top-concern area as one SIP goal	Gather; tabulate, publish, discuss with faculty; address in SIP	Gather; tabulate; publish report to all staff	Student council coordinates survey; published in school newspaper	Surveys limited to bond issue and mill levy campaigns; election team review			✓	Satisfaction surveys have been in place for 11 years. Few changes implemented as a result; survey results vary little from year to year; emphasis/ monitoring on % responding.
Authority to act? (commit resources)	Established through SIP process	Not defined	Not defined	Student council may propose recommended changes to principal through advisor	Primarily to assess level of community support; action related to campaigns	✓			Authority to act has always been assumed. Only parent and faculty satisfaction surveys result in action; even then, may be limited to an activity or objective in the SIP. Very limited patron and community efforts other than Website communications.

(continues)

Exhibit 8.5 Sample Listening Data (Milford School District) *(Continued)*

School: Principal: Date: Email:

Satisfaction Surveys	Parents	Teachers and Administrators	Staff	Students	Patrons	P	I	E	Rationale: Current Practice
Who?/When?	SIP leadership team; May of each year	Principal holds key; annually in May	Principal; annually in May	Advisor coordinates, facilitates review; as needed	No other process to act on patron concerns		✔		Administrative function; some cooperation with teacher representatives; rare to collaborate or insist on action to follow. All data examined at end of year, with numerous competing priorities.
How?	Team reviews results, discusses outcomes	Presentation at faculty meeting; Q&A held to clarify and explain status quo; changes rarely made	Written report distributed	Council forwards to advisor, who forwards to administration	N/A. No process exists outside of efforts to secure votes	✔			Action is generally discussion or completion of a report. Wide variability in terms of structure that connects results to action. Format for action often misses key opportunities.

Summary of Satisfaction Listening System:

Satisfaction is the most established listening format for Milford, with routine inclusion in school improvement plans for parents and teachers.
Student feedback is obscured through organizational layers; little evidence exists of a predictable and viable cycle; action on the basis of satisfaction data is taken randomly at best.

(continues)

Exhibit 8.5

Sample Listening Data (Milford School District) *(Continued)*

School: Principal: Date: Email:

Focus Groups, Interviews	Parents	Teachers and Administrators	Staff	Students	Patrons	P	I	E	Rationale: Current Practice
What do we currently do with the data?	No data	Faculty meeting minutes; no process to gather open-ended data from faculty	No data	Topic-driven focus groups (e.g., dress code, open campus)	Superintendent conducts quarterly town meetings		✓		Few elements in place; need to make sure current data is analyzed and responded to.
Authority to act? (commit resources)	N/A	Not defined	N/A	Not defined	Superintendent has authority, limited by policy	✓			Ambiguous format for taking action; totally situational.
Who?/When?	N/A	No systematic process in place; as needed	N/A	Principal directs actions	Superintendent responds to situations	✓			Little assurance that action will follow input.
How?	N/A	Principal assesses need and responds	N/A	Direct, by delegate, or consensus	Varied responses to concerns	✓			Administrative prerogative.

Website	Parents	Teachers and Administrators	Staff	Students	Patrons	P	I	E	Rationale: Current Practice
What do we currently do with the data?	Complaint review by leadership team; acts on select complaints	Teachers and administrators have individual Web sites for communication	Discretion to create and respond to Web site	Same chance to respond as parents with school officials	Same chance to respond as parents with school officials	✓			Plan to respond to complaint/concern next year based on technology.

(continues)

Exhibit 8.5

Sample Listening Data (Milford School District) *(Continued)*

School: | Principal: | Date: | Email:

Website	Parents	Teachers and Administrators	Staff	Students	Patrons	P	I	E	Rationale: Current Practice
Authority to act? (commit resources)	Leadership team grants authority to act if complaint is viewed as having merit	All have authority to respond to concerns or suggestions within job description or sphere of influence	Staff are expected to respond to all concerns	No format for response to students	No format for response to patrons, except phone policy of 48 hours	✓			No standards currently in place; action taken varies by administrator's discretion; reactive.
Who?/When?	Administrators, department chairs, counselors; no response standard	Response based on concern raised and time constraints; no response standard	Staff respond as with phone policy (48 hours)	No requirement or timeframe standard exists	No requirement or timeframe standard exists	✓			No systematic connection from process for input to action taken.
How?	Principal assigns responsibility	Collaboration; modify instruction, materials, time. and opportunity	Email, involve others	N/A	N/A	✓			Wide discretion to administrators; no standard for action.

Summary of Focus Group/Interview and Website Listening Systems:
Focus groups and Website listening systems are neither systematic nor reliable; response standards nonexistent; need for standards, processes, accountability. Systems fail to adhere to guidelines, even though capacity exists for transparency and user-friendly technology is available.

Proposed = P   Introduced = I   Established = E
Guidelines for Listening Systems: Cyclical, predictable, public (open, transparent), user-friendly

factor, not because it recognizes the ebb and flow of any service provided, but because it requires respondents to consider the quality of implementation and whether more or less time should be given to it.

Sets of four questions are posed for every component to ensure that action is taken as to the data collected and analyzed; that accountability is associated with action in terms of authority to commit resources; and that there are specific accountability provisions in terms of how, when, and by whom any action will be initiated.

The listening system template also offers four concise guidelines. Examine the sample listening system described in Exhibit 8.5 to determine whether Milford School District's system is cyclical, predictable, transparent, and user-friendly. Listening systems have to be *cyclical* to be of the greatest utility and value. By gathering the same type of information at various junctures throughout the year, schools can monitor the ebb and flow of each school year, not only in terms of opinion but also in terms of perspective and meaningful feedback. If, for example, the teacher found that parent satisfaction peaked every year following parent conferences in November, and reached its low point in May, perhaps there might be a problem in terms of communication, or even in terms of integrity or student achievement.

Is the listening system *predictable?* Do stakeholders have confidence that when they provide input, that input will be analyzed, and action taken (if warranted)? Does the school or district value this information sufficiently to make it public in some way or report to stakeholders what was done with the data? Finally, is there a flow to the listening system that makes the benefit of information gained worth the effort expended to provide, collect, and respond to the data? In a predictable listening system, the opportunity to be heard is reliable and consistent for stakeholders. When such a system is in place, professionals have greater confidence in the results and the likelihood that constituent groups will participate again is greater. The template assumes that not only parents and students will be surveyed, but also staff, teachers, administrators, and patrons. The category of "patrons" often consists largely of a retired community that determines whether a bond issue or mill levy passes or fails. It may also include alumni or former employees, but in today's society, where parents and grandparents seldom make up 33 percent of the electorate, this is a key group to hear from—and hear from often.

Listening systems must be *transparent,* as noted earlier. That alone inspires confidence and builds trust with constituents. It communicates a willingness to listen, the courage to share results, and a commitment to learn from the feedback the community provides. Such transparency is hardly restricted to the school board and superintendent; principals, teachers, and staff can all benefit from this characteristic, especially in terms of relationships with respondent groups. Just as an effective assessment calendar mandates a written rationale for action taken (or the decision to take no action) to everyone involved in the process, a quality listening system communicates in some way that educators listened carefully to the input provided.

The final guideline asks users to ensure that each component is *user-friendly*. A number of validated parent surveys constructed by reputable educational organizations are nonetheless lengthy and laborious. Some survey parents with questions containing sixty words of two and three syllables, and do it again and again for more than seventy questions. How many respondents will take the time needed to complete such a survey? Will the results be representative when only the most supportive or least supportive take the time to complete the survey? Educators often excuse a poor response by comparing the results to a political poll and relying on the standard error of measurement. We are not polling strangers! Though the return may be statistically valid, does a small response offer the rich insights that a more user-friendly (yes, that means shorter) survey or interview might provide? Listening systems are essential to effective data analysis. They are not student achievement results, but, like teaching strategies, conditions for learning, and administrative structures that correlate with improved student achievement, the data is essential for thorough analysis and a comprehensive environmental scan of our educational communities.

SUMMARY

Apple Blossom USD was ambitious, proud, and committed to excellence. The district was also shortsighted and failed to see the educational change coming its way. An environmental scan is designed to lessen the possibility of that sorry eventuality. It scans the horizon for insights, examining the internal workings of a classroom, school, or district in terms of external changes and internal initiatives. It examines these influences in terms of seven components of every organization, and it drills deeper by using the well-known KWL process to determine what is known and what is needed programmatically, instructionally, and organizationally. The environmental scan example in Exhibit 8.2 described how quality data gathering can help improve the school for all stakeholders, and especially improve student achievement. The template is a tool to assure a broad yet focused effort to get better.

We then turned our attention to the need to keep things simple and to periodically examine what we are most fond of, to determine whether something can be abandoned or subtracted. Systems analysis was introduced as a construct to reveal interdependence and to discover unintended consequences. Like listening systems, systems analysis is a way of looking at things that assists us in understanding the environment we find ourselves in. We live in an age unique to all of human history in its accelerated pace of change, and we need to do everything necessary to understand our circumstances and utilize the full range of data available to us to make informed, wise decisions and choices. Chapter 9 examines the challenge of replicating best practices.

BIG IDEA

Environmental scanning identifies current needs and anticipates future challenges.

QUESTIONS

1. *What does the KWL reading strategy have to do with analysis of data?*

2. *True or false? The most effective environmental scans examine organizations on the basis of finance, personnel, special education, textbooks, and logistics. Explain why you responded as you did.*

3. *Shouldn't we just focus on internal changes in our own organization? Why or why not?*

4. *In your own words, describe the key elements of a listening system. What changes do you envision making in your work environment this year?*

Replication:
Sharing the Wealth

Just do it!

— NIKE

The Nike slogan immediately resonates. It speaks of making the most of our opportunities, and it applies to replication. Teachers and teaching are treasure chests of innovation and inspiration, and we need a means to capture, expand, and apply those practices that work best to as many settings as possible, to reach as many students as possible. Replicating good ideas should be the reason we analyze data in the first place, to extend what works as quickly and efficiently as possible. Replication and subtraction are nothing less than the evidence of a dynamic and effective data management system. If schools fail to replicate best practices or to eliminate ineffective practices, where is the improvement?

FOUNDATION FOR REPLICATION

Fortunately, there is ample evidence in the literature and numerous blueprints about how to implement and sustain program replications. Very few educational programs are formally adopted or replicated without application of a rigorous validation process. In fact, thirty-eight comprehensive school reform models have been identified as "research-based" innovations, including familiar programs such as Core Knowledge, Direct Instruction, Success for All, Accelerated Schools, Onward to Excellence, High Schools that Work, and the School Development Program (National Clearinghouse for Comprehensive School Reform, 2004). A rigorous evaluation process has been created for professional development that insists on the capacity to generalize to new settings (Shaha, Lewis, O'Donnell, & Brown, 2004). Commercial publishers of textbooks and educational materials (including McGraw-Hill; Addison-Wesley;

Silver-Burdett; Sage; Holt, Rinehart, & Winston; and others) subject themselves to very rigorous validation methods.

Successful programs, such as those designated "research-based" for comprehensive school reform purposes (part of the No Child Left Behind Act), have a number of characteristics in common. By statute, they must:

- Employ a systematic approach to schoolwide improvement that incorporates every aspect of a school, from curriculum and instruction to school management.

- Employ a program and a process that are designed to enable all students to meet challenging academic content and performance goals.

- Employ a framework for using research to move from multiple, fragmented educational programs to a unified plan with the single focus of academic achievement.

- Be a product of the long-term, collaborative efforts of school staff, parents, and district staff.

These characteristics are valuable guidelines for replication. They require an effective data system that monitors growth and addresses all the key factors and elements of a school setting, examining the role and function of instructional strategies and other antecedents to design a program to meet challenging academic and performance goals. Lucy Steiner (2000) conducted a meta-analysis of replication in education and identified six elements of successful "scale-up" or replication efforts: (1) program design, (2) buy-in at the school level, (3) supports that include resources and freedom from restrictive regulations, (4) leadership, (5) quality assurance, and (6) conscious effort to build constituencies that support necessary changes. These elements describe how effective replications warrant understanding of antecedents; collaborative analysis, including the insights of triangulation; and a clearly delineated accountability structure in which individuals are responsible for specific actions at specific times for specific purposes. Educators should be leaders in replicating best practices and taking advantage of the rich incubators of innovation we call schools, but the evidence suggests that the reality is otherwise.

The "knowing–doing gap" (Reeves, 2004a, p. 2) is a problem everyone in education can recognize. Graham and colleagues (Graham, Harris, Fink-Chorzempa, & MacArthur, 2003, p. 279) note that only 42 percent of teachers, when presented with compelling evidence about the power of nonfiction writing (with editing and revision) to improve achievement in all areas, made any adaptations at all for poor writers. Only 10 percent utilized the strategies of mini-lessons, tutoring, and revised instruction that were presented as the very antecedents that led to improved achievement. As a profession, we struggle with applying the lessons from the research that shout at us about leveraging numerous antecedents of excellence.

Steiner (2000) referred to replication as "scaling up," in a review that recognizes the problem is not unique to education. Unfortunately, according to Steiner, the problem of replicating good ideas is particularly severe within public education. Several reasons are given to explain this phenomenon. One is the need for large groups of educators to "unlearn" the assumptions that underlie our current work—work designed for a different era and a time when data was a necessary inconvenience, not a central component of reform and school improvement. Linda Darling-Hammond described schools as bureaucratic structures that have changed very little in the past century (Darling-Hammond, 1997, pp. 199–204). Some may blame the structures of schools for this reality, or teachers themselves, but Reeves argues that the knowing–doing gap is not the result of indifference, indolence, or a lack of knowledge, or even a lack of will (2004a, pp. 1–2). The problem is that we are looking in the wrong place for answers to replication. Replication that is agile enough to help students when they need it is personal. Surowiecki (2004, p. 61) tells the story about farmers who were convinced that a new seed would increase yields dramatically, but did nothing to change their planting regimens. Even when their neighbors had success with the new seed, most farmers only tested the seed in a small part of one field. Not until each farmer experienced personal success did anything approximating a program adoption take place. The analogy to our classrooms is striking: teachers must first see the benefit that replicating the practice will yield to their classroom and their students.

Data analysis is the parent of action research and replication. One reason best practices in schools have not been replicated sufficiently is because there were few vehicles to validate successful programs, and because the antecedents for success were (and are) rarely monitored to produce evidence that warrants replication. This chapter attempts to ensure that replication of best practices becomes the norm for successful practices rather than the exception it has been for so long. We begin by comparing two actual schools of comparable demographics within the same school system, using more than a decade of data depicted in discrepancy charts.

A *discrepancy chart* establishes a standard of performance and depicts performance along a horizontal line. Performances exceeding the standard are represented by bars or data points above the line; performances not yet at the desired standard are represented by data points or bars below the line. An excellent tool for identifying relative strengths and weaknesses in terms of academic content standards, discrepancy charts are useful in any area where a standard can be established. Discrepancy charts are great for measuring progress toward universal compliance, such as the number of teachers who have conducted side-by-side analyses of their curriculum with state standards or of their assessments with state assessments. Discrepancy charts also depict success in achieving zero tolerance, as in achieving zero expulsions or zero gun incidents at school, or percent of expenditures against budgets. In this case, we will compare actual student performance against predicted performance. Exhibits 9.1 and 9.2 illustrate

Exhibit 9.1

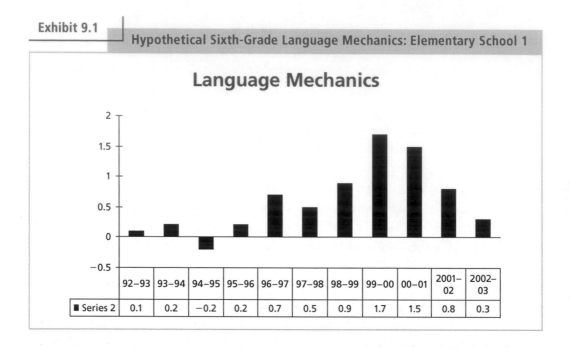

Hypothetical Sixth-Grade Language Mechanics: Elementary School 1

Language Mechanics

	92–93	93–94	94–95	95–96	96–97	97–98	98–99	99–00	00–01	2001–02	2002–03
■ Series 2	0.1	0.2	−0.2	0.2	0.7	0.5	0.9	1.7	1.5	0.8	0.3

Exhibit 9.2

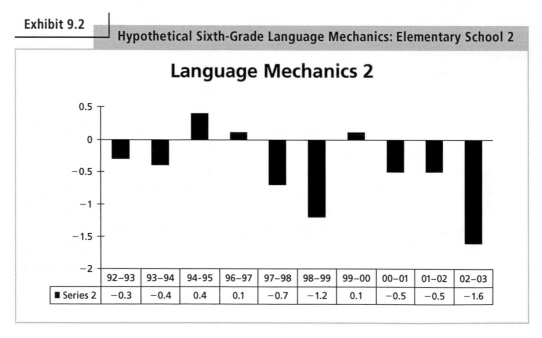

Hypothetical Sixth-Grade Language Mechanics: Elementary School 2

Language Mechanics 2

	92–93	93–94	94-95	96–97	97–98	98–99	99–00	00–01	01–02	02–03
■ Series 2	−0.3	−0.4	0.4	0.1	−0.7	−1.2	0.1	−0.5	−0.5	−1.6

the difference between achievement test scores for two elementary schools and the scores predicted for them. In these data, a value of zero means that the actual score was the same as the predicted score. A positive value means that, on average, the students in that school scored higher than predicted. Achievement test scores were predicted from cognitive ability and socioeconomic status. The amounts above or below the predicted scores are expressed in standard deviations, showing actual trend data and school performance against expected performance.

By 2000, students in Elementary School 1 were outperforming their demographics by almost 1.7 standard deviations. Scrutinize the data for the same time period for Elementary School 2. Because both schools have very similar student-body demographics, and because both schools are part of the same school system and enjoy the same resources, reasonable people should be able to agree that School 2 needs some help. In contrast, at School 1 students have outperformed their demographics in ten out of eleven years.

The real question, however, is when was the most opportune time to begin looking for replicable practices? In 1994–95, School 2 looked like the successful school, at least in terms of gains in language mechanics. In 1995–96, differences were negligible, and 1997–98 was the first year in which School 2 scores showed a serious decline. If teams waited until the millennium to look for patterns, they would have seen that both schools had begun to decline from previous years' scores. It would have been easy, in small increments, to explain away the differences between these schools, and to miss the opportunity to learn from the distinctions that warrant a second look. Nevertheless, after waiting several years, attuned professionals who were attentive to the data could have called for a closer look, and found antecedents at School 1 that could help School 2. Unfortunately, in this era of standards and accountability, we need to ask ourselves whether we really have several years to wait.

Replication in teaching practice will not happen by adopting a new program that was proven effective elsewhere, especially when other "proven" practices are not subtracted from a very full plate first. Some educators, who are quick to call for "pilots" to scrutinize an innovation for statistically significant differences, are perfectly content with the status quo, even though current practice has no more validity or evidence of effectiveness than the new, and sometimes less. Others are willing to require a supermajority of faculty buy-in before replicating an instructional strategy, in the name of collaboration. Unfortunately, neither approach serves improved student achievement well. We need to find ways for practices that are true antecedents of excellence to be replicated in earnest, to take stock of lessons learned, and to make adjustments to improve student achievement. In short, we need a recipe for replication.

RECIPE FOR REPLICATION

Replication is very personal, even when the data tells us otherwise. *Recipes* are rapidly disseminated ideas when they are replicated. They are only replicated, however, when another cook sees and experiences the benefit of that recipe; when one takes a personal interest and recognizes personal value in its ingredients. It is not enough for someone just to enjoy the recipe; only those who both understand and enjoy the benefits will replicate it. Stephen Covey describes a process he refers to as "third person learning" (1996, p. 60), a process that also occurs routinely and effortlessly with one's favorite casserole recipe. The first person shares knowledge with a second person. The cook explains the recipe to the learner, demonstrating the steps, pacing, and tricks of the recipe. The second cook then shares the recipe with a third person, teaching and modeling the proper use of the recipe and offering corrective feedback as needed. The third person thus receives added-value knowledge.

Recipes are replicated because participants are able to experience the benefits of a best practice at first hand. They are personal, as in the illustration of the farmers' fields, and they epitomize replication because they represent step-by-step innovations that are reproduced and multiplied through third-person learning. Thus, recipes serve as a useful illustration for replication of practices at the classroom level. Exhibit 9.3 reminds us of the salient features of recipe-style replication.

Exhibit 9.3

Informal Recipe-Style Replication

- Benefit is obvious to person(s) planning to replicate

- Replication is user-friendly

- Replication occurs informally through third-person learning

- Replication is rarely undertaken just on the basis of external success stories, research reports, or other data

- Replication is more likely to occur if the practice is successfully implemented internally

- Replication is most likely to occur if the teacher experiences the benefit of the strategy or innovation

It is a fair question for busy professionals to ask how replicating any practice will benefit them, or more accurately, benefit their students. Teachers have every reason to be skeptical, because far too many magic bullets have been promised: questioning strategies, lesson openings, summarizing strategies, and so on. It is also fair to remind busy professionals that teaching and learning are interdependent, so that every bit of our profession should be collaborative. A primary consequence of interdependence is a collective responsibility for results, a common accountability for the learning and achievement of every student we have the privilege to serve.

Remember Mary Ann and Georgia at Maple High School (Chapter 4)? Mary Ann was talented and dedicated, but assumed no responsibility for the growth of her peers; she was willing to be collaborative, but never delivered. Reflect on the previous discussion about data teams, where mini-lessons, reflection, and essential questions were put into action. The closeness to the classroom meant that data teams were able to affect instruction directly with instructional strategies, novel transitions, and other changes—as long as they didn't involve changing practices Mary Ann had grown accustomed to. Georgia, in contrast, needed help and was highly open to change.

Charlotte Danielson's "Framework for Teaching" (1996) is a highly regarded and frequently replicated framework for supervising and evaluating teachers. In "Domain 4: Contributing to the School and District," Danielson's four-point rubric defines *proficiency* as teachers having relationships with colleagues that are characterized by support and cooperation (p. 114). A distinguished designation would include taking a leadership role among colleagues. Mary Ann, on this continuum, would be at least proficient and possibly distinguished. Still, Georgia needed more from Mary Ann than the opportunity to observe her class. Professionalism should compel us to recognize that our best work gets better only when collaboration is allowed to generate the collective wisdom needed in the complex business of teaching and learning. Exhibit 9.4 suggests a few of the many strategies that can be employed to help institutionalize replication.

Early replication signals are the other side of the coin of "canaries in the coal mine." Many times, I hear the statement: "We just implemented that program. Give it time to succeed." How much time? If you are not seeing progress from new programs almost immediately, there are only three possible explanations: (1) teacher training is required, and more time for the teacher to demonstrate the desired level of proficiency; (2) clarification is needed to make sure the program is being implemented consistently across teachers and settings; or (3) there are local contextual characteristics that inhibit its success, including student readiness, alignment with other work habits, and alignment with local curriculum expectations. Otherwise, the practice being replicated should demonstrate improvements almost immediately.

But wait: improvement in student achievement on the EOC or state-level assessment will not be evident, so how can improvements occur immediately? "Have you lost your mind?," the reader may be thinking. No, I haven't, and yes, improvements can and should be evident from day one. The indicators that should accompany something worthy of replication are student (or teacher) enthusiasm, levels of engagement, understanding of what is expected, participation, improvement ideas from students, time on task, fun, and all of the indicators of effectiveness teachers keep in their heads every day. This is the "data in their heads" referred to earlier (see Chapter 7). It is important, valuable, and valid when we can observe it in an objective way.

Meeting the expectations in Exhibit 9.4 will require data collection and monitoring of antecedent teacher and antecedent student behaviors. Typically, there will be no need to add one more measure of student achievement. If additional recordkeeping is required to monitor teacher and student antecedents, such as what students would like repeated, it is recommended that a data collection and analysis structure be included in the listening system for students. The data about saving time and ideas borrowed and given away also lend themselves to a listening system. In this way, teachers and teacher teams can structure any data collection in a deliberate, user-friendly, and

Exhibit 9.4

Strategies to Promote Replication

External (between schools, across districts)	Internal (within schools, departments, grades)
School and District	
■ Disseminate results of data team minutes to colleagues/peers at other schools via Web sites, email; omit student names and other confidential data. ■ Quarterly, disseminate or present school data charts/graphs of ideas borrowed, ideas given away, and results to other schools. ■ Develop a question-and-answer communiqué that invites ideas, strategies, and structures to address real student and teacher needs in real time. Rotate responsibility for developing answers from school to school. ■ Establish an electronic "We Made a Difference" data wall. ■ Define a preponderance of evidence that will suffice to initiate external, school-to-school or district-wide replication.	■ Establish a "We Made a Difference" data wall (electronic or physical) that monitors the number and type of interventions that have been implemented, with accompanying results. ■ Principal establishes expectation of receiving weekly reports of "ideas I borrowed," "ideas I gave away," and results from ideas. ■ Add a column to the "We Made a Difference" data wall labeled "Learning Opportunities" where results were less than immediate. ■ Create standing agenda items for meetings: What works well for whom, why, and how do you know? ■ Define a preponderance of evidence that will suffice to initiate internal replication.
Classroom	
■ Identify students whose behavior or performance have turned around; verify with data. ■ Value observation data as much as numbers data. ■ Disseminate classroom practices that save time (Q&A or "We Made a Difference" data walls). ■ Disseminate classroom practices that students would like repeated (Q&A or "We Made a Difference" data walls). ■ Disseminate classroom practices that increased collaboration (Q&A or "We Made a Difference" data walls).	■ Create and institutionalize "What's Working" meetings with recorders and group responsibility (verify preponderance of evidence, what works well for whom, and why). ■ Each week, all teachers submit to principal a list of "ideas I borrowed this week" and "ideas I gave away." ■ Early replication signals include evidence of changes, enthusiasm, indicators, students outperforming their demographics. ■ Identify classroom practices that: □ Save time □ Students would like repeated □ Increase collaboration

achievable fashion, complete with time for reflection and time for action. The principle of subtraction is critical at this point, but my observation has been that teachers, given the opportunity to improve a process or structure, are more than capable of finding ways to save time, given the permission to subtract and become accountable. Exhibit 9.5 identifies structural questions whose answers build a foundation for replication. Like power standards, they are best developed at the school level, but require

---

Exhibit 9.5

Establishing a Foundation for Replication

1. How would you identify home-grown successes?
2. What is needed in a data system to ensure that such successes are:
   a. defined?
   b. recognized?
   c. validated for replication?
3. What is reasonable to consider as a preponderance of evidence and best practices?
4. Define preponderance of evidence.
5. Define an internal best practice.
6. What high-performing schools' practices do we know we want to replicate?
7. What is necessary before a decision is made to replicate a practice?
8. Should replicable practices be tested through action research? When? Why?

---

buy-in from faculty to guide implementation of local, personal strategies and responses to early replication signals.

The lesson of recipe-style replication is that it is personal, and that smart people need to see the benefit. It would behoove those committed to serious reform efforts and breakthrough improvements to structure any effort to replicate around the personal nature of replication.

WHERE SHOULD WE START?

The ideas that Exhibit 9.4 will generate will be as varied as students, as varied as the experience and background of teachers, and as varied as the context and history of the work habits at each school. The ideas may become as universal as writing every day in every subject, and have enormous impact on education for years. The ideas also may become "learning opportunities" that will not be repeated, but serve to warn faculty of a path to avoid in the future. These are not necessarily strategies or antecedents that we know have great potential to improve student achievement. Exhibit 9.6 offers nineteen of them.

QUICK, GET THE CAMERA!

The "third-person learning" process (Covey, 1996) described earlier offered three basic steps for replication: capture, expand, and apply. Like use of a digital camera, we need to develop a work habit to capture evidence of success, even incremental, qualitative evidence like a smile or a raised hand or on-time attendance for the high school junior who lets everyone in class know every day that she doesn't like being there. All of these

Exhibit 9.6

Antecedents of Excellence: Replicable Practices Right Now

Structures, Conditions, and Teacher Behaviors Worth Replicating	Categories of Effective Teaching Strategies
1. More writing, thinking, analysis, and reading, in every content area.	11. Identifying similarities and differences.
2. Collaborative scoring of student work.	12. Summarizing and note taking.
3. Flexible schedules and greater investment of time in basic sources; associated with lower failure rates.	13. Reinforcing effort and providing recognition.
4. More frequent feedback; associated with improved student work ethic, motivation, and performance (1 through 4, see Reeves, 2004b, pp. 97–98).	14. Homework and practice.
	15. Nonlinguistic representations.
	16. Cooperative learning.
5. Collaboration structures for analysis of data (Surowiecki, 2004, p. 39).	17. Setting objectives and providing feedback.
6. Creation of data teams; increases the presence of effective teaching strategies and increases student achievement (Leadership and Learning Center, 2004b).	18. Generating and testing hypotheses.
7. Discussion, review, and focus on actual student work; closes the learning gap for all cohort groups (see Schlecty, 2000, pp. 134–139; Heacox, 2002, pp. 27–41; Reeves, 2004c, pp. 201–207; Singham, 2003, pp. 586–591).	19. Questions, cues, and advance organizers to increase student cognition and engagement (11 through 19, see Marzano, Pickering, & Pollock, 2001a, pp. 6–10; Schlecty, 2000, pp. 147–153; Reeves, 2004c); Fredricks, Blumenfeld, & Paris, 2004, pp. 59–109; Intrator, 2004, pp. 20–26).
8. Learning logs to collaboratively monitor student progress (Schmoker, 2001, pp. 13–15).	
9. Mandatory department teams with responsibility and authority for selecting effective strategies, development and evaluation of EOCs (DuFour, 2003, pp. 63–64).	20. Differentiation of instruction (Heacox, 2002, pp. 91–111).
10. Relentless focus on student achievement; protection of time, and deep professional development (NSDC, 2001).	

can be objectively measured and monitored and provide meaningful Tier 3 data about student performance. Such data contributes to a robust capacity to recognize replicable practices early, rather than reacting only to changes in achievement data (as our example showed with Schools 1 and 2).

The camera analogy goes further than this snapshot application, however. Digital cameras are, first and foremost, easy—so easy that major camera companies are abandoning film photographs completely, recognizing that the future is digital. Data has to be user-friendly to reduce its costs. There are many benefits to a robust data system, but, as we found with Timberline Middle School and Colson ISD, the value of robust data that takes too much time is badly compromised. "Catch them doing something good" is a great strategy. Recording the good they were doing is even better.

ACTION RESEARCH

Action research is simply a proactive hunt for a better way. After analyzing data for patterns, teachers develop hunches about relationships between instructional strategies, antecedent conditions such as materials or programs, and student achievement. Sadly, many of these hunches become either folklore or legend, or are lost to the profession altogether simply because we fail to do anything about them.

Witness the story of Flora Flagg, who single-handedly gave the profession a simple and effective tool to engage students in thinking and reasoning every day, in every classroom. Ms. Flagg is the Milwaukee principal who introduced the notion of gathering writing samples from each teacher and scoring them herself weekly. The school became a 90/90/90 school. Had this pioneer failed to engage in a form of action research (which she did with assistance from The Leadership and Learning Center), only hundreds of students would have benefited rather than millions.

Emily Calhoun recommended three levels of action research that continue to advocate for action and replication: teacher as individual researcher, collaborative action research, and school-wide action research: Our discussion has focused on her first two levels, places where action research is relatively easy to implement. Consistent with a theme of this book—that individual teachers and small teams are fully capable of sophisticated data analysis—those who apply the lessons here will be well on their way to practicing action research. Calhoun defined *action research* in five steps: (1) select an area to research, (2) collect data, (3) organize data, (4) analyze and interpret data, and (5) take action (1994, p. 2). Once again, we observe an improvement cycle similar to those discussed in Chapter 2. Calhoun cites Kurt Lewin, who created the term *action research*, who defined it as a three-step process: (1) planning that involves reconnaissance or fact-finding, (2) taking actions, and (3) fact-finding about the results of the actions (p. 16). The process offered here has six self-explanatory steps, illustrated in Exhibit 9.7: (1) observe, (2) hypothesize, (3) predict, (4) test hypothesis, (5) gather data, and (6) explain (draw inferences, conclusions, applications).

Action research is the kind of analysis warranted when there is a desire to replicate externally. It is the process of verifying results achieved using the same problems and variables but with variations as to who, when, and where. A general rule of thumb for action research is:

> *Use action research when patterns emerging from the data*
> *suggest that something new is happening that should be verified,*
> *clarified, or discovered.*

Exhibit 9.7

Steps of Action Research

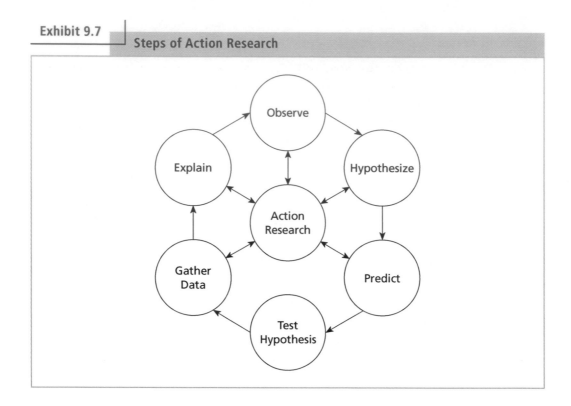

The outer circles denote a linear, step-by-step process, whereas arrows connecting steps to the action research process denote a dynamic at work that informs practice during action research. Action research can change midcourse if it improves student achievement. For instance, if students in the treatment group are experiencing dramatic improvement in their ability to achieve rigorous standards, and students in the control group are not, it is advisable to make a midcourse adjustment and include both groups in the treatment. But won't that invalidate the research? Yes, just as ceasing to administer placebos to advanced-state cancer patients midstream when the treatment is proving successful for the treatment group does. Action research is first and foremost about action, not research for the sake of research. Although allowing a study to continue for the entire planned term is preferred, there may be times when, like the cancer patients, we take action midcourse on behalf of student achievement. The inner-circle connections may also point out the need to modify data-gathering procedures because the original plan was too cumbersome, or discoveries midcourse may add to the original hypothesis or hunch.

As a proactive hunt for a better way, action research is as simple as examining independent variables (causes and antecedents) to determine their influence on dependent variables (student achievement and other results indicators). Five suggestions are provided here to facilitate quality replication in schools, using Schools 1 and 2 for illustration.

Respond to Data Patterns

Use action research when patterns emerging from the data suggest that something new is happening that should be verified, clarified, or discovered. Rather than relying on schoolwide achievement data for language mechanics, perhaps two intermediate-level teachers acted on professional development they received in a "Writing Excellence" seminar (The Leadership and Learning Center, 2002b), agreeing to focus on nonfiction writing and the writing process, with consistent and challenging editing and revision techniques, such as explicit corrective feedback for writing conventions and posting of writing standards in both classrooms. When these teachers' peers noted how engaged students were; how students from their classrooms were self-editing written work in other classes; and how the quality of written work was neater, more complete, and more consistent, they asked for assistance. Within the first year, unbeknownst to the principal, four of the nine intermediate-level teachers had joined the two pioneers, and their students' achievement was showing less variability and higher scores on EOC assessments, on the district writing assessment, and on the state language-arts assessment for those classes.

By then, they had the principal's attention, and she wanted to replicate schoolwide what had been happening in their classrooms. Primary teachers were resistant, however, citing demands on their time and the need for students to learn to read rather than expecting them to read to learn. The principal, however, was convinced that the methods that improved scores in language mechanics could be applied, at least in part, to improve reading comprehension scores, distinction between fact and opinion, and vocabulary for intermediate students.

She met with all teachers, indicated that they needed to pay attention to the data, introduced external research that validated the writing emphasis, and asked for ways to study this strategy to verify whether it was something that could help everyone in the school. Primary teachers took the lead in designing a study that followed cohorts of students with low and high reading performance on the state assessment. A third-grade teacher suggested that the school also monitor whether introduction of this new focus on nonfiction reading and writing was having a desirable impact on discipline referrals and tardies. Two intermediate classes were selected for the control group. One was a teacher volunteer who was interested in possible differences, but who had a very busy personal schedule the coming year due to her daughter's wedding and caring for an elderly father. She knew she could continue doing a great job, but was not sure she could give the new approach the focus it might deserve. The second classroom selected was not quite as clean as a control group, because the volunteer teacher was scheduled for a student teacher throughout the year. Nonetheless, the entire faculty agreed that if the treatment group were teachers other than those who had brought the innovation to the school, everyone could have confidence that the results were meaningful, especially if the differences were significant.

Determine the Number of Variables

The faculty completed a detailed Hishakawa Fishbone to isolate the variables they believed would be most important to monitor, and agreed to study the following independent variables or antecedents:

1. Daily nonfiction writing across core areas for the treatment group; nonfiction was to be used only as one of several language-arts genres with the control group, and no effort was to be made to institutionalize it across the core subjects.

2. Use of discrete editing and revision of writing assignments in all four core subjects, with a minimal standard for conventions (complete sentences) and use of writing assessments to substitute for select responses at least weekly.

The variables dependent on those antecedents were limited to (1) EOC assessments, because everyone took the same assessments, and every grade utilized them in all four core areas; and (2) the number of discipline referrals and tardies. Everyone realized that the study had some limitations and that other factors might influence the results, but with effective facilitation by the principal, every single teacher spoke up to support the study and agree to modify his or her work if the results warranted. There was no interest in the interaction between subjects or between discipline and tardies, or even between editing, revision, or the types of assessment.

KISS

The third suggestion for the school was to "keep it short and simple" (KISS). This was well received, as the faculty recognized from the selection of variables how easy it would be to become complicated. For the dependent variables, they decided to use pre/post measures on state language mechanics assessment scores, and to monitor changes in reading comprehension. They struggled with using pre/post measures on the EOCs, because each grade had constructed the assessments with a different emphasis and the content and focus changed considerably from grade to grade. Some wondered whether the school should commission a team to address the leveling and alignment issues, but once again, cooler heads prevailed to keep it short and simple. "Great idea," the principal added, "but this study is going to take a lot of our energies. Let's allow the process and the data to guide our next steps."

Independent variables would be monitored for implementation according to a ten-part checklist developed by the school innovators. Everyone agreed that those implementing the changes needed access to the innovators and sufficient training from them prior to the start of school. Because this involved only four teachers, the principal would also monitor progress with the same observation checklist; data would be tabulated and monitored monthly. Finally, the behavior data was the easiest, as the discipline incidents and tardies prior to the intervention were already in the computer. After some discussion, the faculty agreed to measure improvement on this variable rather than raw score or percent of classroom referrals.

Select Analysis Tools

The principal recommended the use of a couple of analysis tools to help reveal progress or lack thereof throughout the year at faculty meetings. The team decided to use a 2 × 2 matrix and a scatter gram as they tracked the data. These tools would reveal three basic constructs behind statistical analysis: measure of central tendency (examination of means, modes, medians), measure of relationship, and analysis of differences (including analysis of variance). They also requested that the principal involve the district assessment coordinator and ask her to run the statistics at the end of the study and report back to the faculty. In this way, everyone was satisfied that their action research study was solid, balanced, and fair, and that results would be both reliable and valid.

Select Proven Antecedents

The final suggestion is to select from those antecedents that have been proven to make a difference to date (e.g., those in Exhibit 9.6), especially for an initial study. Our example team selected those characteristics of writing that have been shown to have a profound influence on student reasoning, thinking, summarizing, and achievement.

Here is a recap of suggestions to enhance action research efforts:

1. Let existing data determine what direction your study will take you, focusing on things you want to verify, clarify, or discover. In this scenario, the study was designed to verify the effectiveness of the approach several teachers had already replicated on their own.

2. Keep the number of variables to a minimum, especially the dependent variable measure of success (typically student achievement). If your team wants to examine several antecedents at once, treat them as components of one or two variables.

3. Keep action research studies as short and simple as possible. Research studies gravitate toward the complex, so explicit efforts to keep things simple will pay dividends.

4. Use data analysis tools that use pictures to tell the story of what is happening, and that provide both trend and pattern data, if possible.

5. Begin with powerful antecedents that are associated in multiple settings with improved student achievement, such as those in Exhibit 9.6.

Exhibit 9.8

Scoring Guide for Replication 9.0

Analysis Dimension	Meeting the Standard	Progressing Toward the Standard	Not Meeting the Standard
9.0 Replication	The educator has a system in place to identify home-grown successes that includes a common definition, a process to recognize successes, and a method to validate and replicate the successful practice. The educator has defined a preponderance of evidence as sufficient data to answer the questions: **What works well for whom, why, and how do you know?**	The educator promotes replication of best practices from current educational research and has a system in place to recognize teachers for improved student achievement. At least one replication is discussed and teachers are encouraged to observe each other for best practices.	The educator resists efforts to formally replicate practices, viewing the process as divisive and as singling out one teacher over another.
9.1 Decision to Replicate	The educator follows up on hunches associated with data patterns by initiating a process for replication with teachers when student performance patterns correlate with specific strategies or antecedent structures and conditions for learning. The educator employs a specific decisionmaking process at key intervals with affected teachers to determine how, when, and whether to replicate a practice.	The educator communicates frequently with teachers to identify patterns and trends in student performance that correlate with specific instructional strategies or the presence of antecedent structures and conditions for learning. The leader initiates a discussion about possible replication with affected teachers and staff.	The educator views differences in classroom performance as inherent differences in teaching personality and student demographics.

Exhibit 9.8

Scoring Guide for Replication 9.0 (Continued)

Analysis Dimension	Meeting the Standard	Progressing Toward the Standard	Not Meeting the Standard
9.2 Action Research	The educator is fluent in the six steps of action research, and is quick to translate hunches about patterns into action research hypotheses, engaging teachers and staff in a common action research approach characterized by: ■ Simple relationship design between one independent variable (cause data) and one dependent variable (effect) or 2 × 2 variable matrix if necessary ■ Simple pre/post assessments ■ Use of same course/grade classrooms as control group ■ Recommended use of meta-analysis categories of effective teaching strategies as independent variables ■ Data collection embedded into instruction ■ Prescribed time period, format	The educator is fluent in the six steps of action research: 1. Observe 2. Explain 3. Predict 4. Test hypothesis 5. Gather data 6. Explain The educator examines data for patterns and trends associated with specific classrooms and instructional strategies.	The educator shows no interest in action research, viewing the time and effort required to implement it as disruptive to the learning process.

SUMMARY

Replication is probably the best indicator of a high-quality and effective system of data analysis. It represents efforts by educators to multiply what works and epitomizes continuous improvement. It is intensely personal, and will seldom occur at the classroom level in earnest if teachers do not experience the benefit of adopting the practice firsthand. Replication has traditionally been associated with large-scale change efforts, programmatic changes, and even professional development models. It must become much more pervasive and much more automatic if it is to build the capacity we need to respond to student needs. Several suggestions were provided to facilitate a functional and dynamic system for replication. "What's working?" meetings and "We made a difference" data walls can go a long way toward encouraging work habits that result in the everyday replication that is as common as sharing a favorite recipe. Exhibit 9.8 (see pages 162–163) provides a scoring guide to monitor and measure one's familiarity with and application of replication and action research.

DISCUSSION

BIG IDEA

Replication is simply making sure that what works very well for a few students is available to as many students as possible.

QUESTIONS

1. *Are there early indicators for replication in your current position? What could be done to make sure they are operating?*

2. *What kinds of things must be defined to establish a foundation for replication?*

3. *Why do educators have such a difficult time replicating best practices? What strategies are needed to make replication a central component of your data analysis system?*

4. *Discuss with a colleague the relative advantages of replicating "proven" practices versus a great idea that emerges at your school. (Hint: There is no right answer.)*

CHAPTER

The Teacher as Expert

Learning is finding out what you already know.

—RICHARD BACH

Previous chapters described a foundation for data analysis that was collaborative, leveraged antecedents for excellence, and defined and established accountability structures. We then described ways to make data work through effective triangulation, replication of best practices, implementation of environmental scans to diagnose and respond to needs, and establishment of early warning signals (education's "canaries in the coal mine"). All these efforts require those closest to students to be actively engaged in every stage of data analysis. Teachers are not only in a position to offer insights and apply strategies that make a difference, they are also in the *best* position to do so. This chapter emphasizes how important it is for teachers to understand the inherent expertise they alone can bring to data analysis. The following scenario illustrates the need to examine data from a new perspective, and shows why teachers are best served when we help them find out what they already know.

CASE STUDY

"In general, less variance in a range trading in the higher score possibilities produces the highest *F* score. Multiple regression, on the other hand, studies the magnitude of the effects of multiple independent variables on one dependent variable using principles of correlation and regression. ANOVA looks for deviations from the mean, while regression analysis looks for relationship. Both examine the interaction of the variables, and respective contributions to the treatment variable(s)." The instructor noticed the two students in the back who were not paying attention.

Todd and Liz wanted to increase their expertise in data analysis. Liz had always been interested in data, as evidenced by the faculty's reliance on her to create all

(continues)

the charts and graphs during the past two years. Todd taught math at the middle school, and colleagues brought their data problems to him, expecting his math background to carry the day with data.

"Does content validity measure the subject content that's intended, as long as it's corroborated by face validity and sampling integrity?" Liz whispered. "I think construct validity is similar, but it's the degree to which a test measures traits like honesty or intelligence that can't be measured precisely, as opposed to subject content or areas of knowledge. Todd, is that right?"

"I think so. Try this one. I'm constructing my final exam with ten multiple-choice items per standard, and since we are addressing all six math standards, I'll need sixty items plus a written component where students describe how to solve a problem for algebra, geometry, and measurement. I'm thinking about splitting the ten questions between best answer from alternatives and questions requiring one correct answer response. What do you think?"

The instructor had been patient, and caught Liz by surprise with his question: "Liz, assume you are designing a research project. Describe the threat a pretest poses to external validity."

"Uh, if students respond differently to the treatment as a result of pretest learning, external validity can be compromised, I think."

"All right," Dr. Smith replied, albeit slightly disappointed. "Is there a volunteer who can describe the four characteristics of normal distributions?"

Both Todd and Liz began to page through their notes, relieved.

Returning to school in August, these two teachers were certainly better equipped to understand educational research, testing, and very basic data analysis. Unfortunately, they had forgotten as much as they remembered. The content seemed to have little relevance to the challenges they faced, despite all the expectations for results. They appreciated their greater capacity to read the results of the district norm-referenced test, but they were hardly experts in data analysis.

Few teachers enter the profession to become either famous or wealthy, and my own observations have been of a profession so self-effacing that it fails to recognize the complexity of its craft or the skill and expertise teachers demonstrate every day. After all, the need and expectation to make decisions based on data is a relatively new phenomenon in education, one that current accountability systems have elevated in importance. Data continues to be associated more with Statistics 101 than with practical management of teaching practices to improve student achievement. Data analysis continues to be a topic that engenders feelings like thoughts of root canals or fingernails on a chalkboard. Educators, from the board room to the classroom, are reluctant to view themselves as experts, deferring instead to number crunchers and policy wonks who deal with large data sets and macro trends. It is time to celebrate the fact that educators in the field are best equipped to make decisions affecting their practice, especially when collaborative processes provide the benefit of multiple viewpoints and interpretations. It is time to celebrate the teacher as expert in data analysis, and this book is an initial effort to assist educators in finding out what they already know about the data of teaching and learning.

David Berliner has been a staunch defender of our nation's system of public education, and an even stronger advocate of its teachers. Berliner studied expertise across professions (1994) and identified three ways in which experts differ from novices: (1) experts bring knowledge to bear more effectively on problems than do novices; (2) experts solve problems more efficiently, and do more in less time, than do novices; and (3) experts are more likely to arrive at novel and appropriate solutions to problems than are novices. Knowledge, efficiency, and insight are the primary features that distinguish the expert teacher from the novice.

The purpose of this book has been to provide practitioners with the skill and understanding to make insightful decisions based on the data available to them. Although districts and schools across the nation have multiple measures of student achievement, few monitor the antecedent data that contributes to that achievement. Those who understand the pitfalls of traditional data analysis—including the rearview-mirror effect, the challenge of having too much data, and the need for sub-traction—are much more apt to be empowered to apply their talents and contextual understanding, as experts, to avoid the experience of the scenarios highlighted throughout the book.

In Chapter 2, we found that data analysis must be as deliberate as our lesson planning; that data collection, analysis, reflection, and a continuous improvement cycle are critical to the capacity to make sound decisions about data. A data calendar was introduced as a structure to ensure that teams of educators take time to examine data, unwrap assessments to align purpose to standards, and ensure that emphasis for each assessment is well placed and measured. A proven improvement cycle for data analysis offered educators insights into the need for discrete and focused processes that probe to determine the need to intervene, adjust, and generally make midcourse corrections with data.

Chapter 3 introduced the concept of antecedents of excellence: those behaviors, strategies, structures, and learning conditions that can be correlated with improved student achievement. The Leadership-Learning (L^2) Matrix developed by Dr. Douglas Reeves was included to reveal the power in leveraging antecedents to produce improved student achievement, as well as the vulnerability of educators who fail to apply antecedents deliberately and strategically. A checklist for a standards-based classroom was analyzed to illustrate the distinctions between antecedents and key questions, and to add value for those faced with decisions about how to allocate resources. Finally, a Hishakawa Fishbone was modified with guidelines to help identify the causes and antecedents that produce positive results and those that lead to consequences we wish to eliminate or reduce. Educators empowered with an understanding of antecedents, the ability to select strategically from a robust antecedent repertoire, and an ability to determine the relationship between cause and effect are able to more effectively bring knowledge to bear on problems than those who lack such skills and abilities. This is in fact characteristic of experts in every endeavor.

Antecedent structures that capitalize on the power of collaboration were described in Chapter 4, along with methods to develop team thinking and candor. Nine explicit methods were recommended to integrate collaboration into decision making. Collaboration helps educators like Liz and Todd to solve problems more efficiently, to do more in less time, and to arrive at novel and appropriate solutions to problems as experts.

Accountability was reviewed in Chapter 5, to underscore that responsibility for results must be accompanied by both authority to take action and commit resources, and comparable authority to eliminate practices and obstacles to improvement. Ten actions of accountability, common barriers to them, and remedies to equip educators to institute accountability were delineated. Educators who solve problems efficiently reflect the ability of experts, and Chapter 5 offered several concrete strategies and structures for that purpose.

Chapter 6 described the need for early warning indicators that compel us to act on behalf of students and improved achievement. Data teams, Data in a Day, scoring guides, performance tasks in performance assessments, and corrective feedback were presented as "canaries in the coal mine"—effective indicators that enable expert data analysts to respond with agility as needs warrant.

Readers were introduced, in Chapter 7, to triangulation as a means to apply the principles of accountability, collaboration, and antecedents to effective data analysis. Several examples were provided, including the use of a wagon-wheel data analysis tool. The wagon wheel empowers those who use the tool to effectively conduct multivariate analysis of distinct variables in such a way as to reveal patterns and trends that would otherwise remain veiled or unclear. Experts are more likely to arrive at novel and appropriate solutions to problems, and triangulation provides insights and tools that give teachers and administrators in the field the expert's capacity to find creative solutions to the challenges before them.

Environmental scanning was discussed in Chapter 8 to enable readers to plan a thorough and comprehensive analysis of those organizational factors that impact every organization. The framework builds on instructional strategies that are well known and commonly applied by teachers, and an extensive environmental scan in Exhibit 8.1 illustrated how the process could offer educators strategically placed reform efforts that get at the heart of how things work in schools. The discussion of comprehensive listening systems added practical ways to bring knowledge to bear more effectively on problems than the ways available to those whose approach to data analysis is dominated by attention to results alone.

Replication, as delineated in Chapter 9, provides readers with strategies to multiply practices that work quickly, to selectively identify practices that warrant replication, and to institute methods to ensure that replication is valued, promoted, and monitored. A practical teacher-to-teacher view of replication was introduced to jump-start action research and relentlessly pursue replication of local teaching practices as a matter of equity, fairness, and even social justice. Berliner's definition of *expertise* identifies insights, knowledge, and efficiency as measures of expertise in a particular discipline, implying replication and adaptation of strategies that work in as many applications as possible. His study and others represent expertise as something that is continually unfolding, strengthened by practice and experience, but differentiated by insights, knowledge, and efficiency.

The premise of *Beyond the Numbers* is that teachers and hands-on principals all over the nation possess, *right now,* the expertise to make decisions on the basis of sound data. We need to move beyond the numbers of test scores and introduce the insights of experts working collaboratively to discover solutions that make a difference. Educators are savvy learners with extensive experience and expertise, making hundreds of decisions each and every day. Multidimensionality and simultaneity are realities for educators at all levels, and when a group of these people undertake reflection with a commitment to act on the lessons they learn from the data, the potential for creativity and improvement is enormous.

SUMMARY: CREATING A CLIMATE OF EXPERTISE IN DATA ANALYSIS

Several structures have been introduced in this book for the purpose of ensuring that sufficient time and attention are given to collaboration, antecedent management, and precision in accountability. Adoption and adaptation of such structures will assist in creating the climate necessary for teachers to function as experts in data analysis. For example, training in and creation of data teams by departments or grade levels immediately brings data analysis to the classroom level, providing a framework that focuses on the work of students—students with names, faces, smiles, and potential. An assessment calendar focuses attention on the quality as well as quantity of existing assessments. The calendar anticipates action that results from analysis and reflection. It respects all participants in data analysis by advancing transparency and ensuring that an effective improvement cycle is operational. One caveat is that the assessment calendar begs the question of subtracting obsolete or counterproductive assessment practices.

Beyond the Numbers introduced a number of analysis tools, including a modified Hishakawa Fishbone, the wagon wheel, critical-incident analysis, and the triangulation process. Numerous guidelines were provided to identify the most salient antecedents and to ensure that action research is employed to verify the need for replication. Listening systems were recommended as part of a comprehensive environmental scan to assist the expert educator in keeping current with external and internal changes. It is hoped that these strategies and structures will promote the kind of cultural change necessary to make data analysis as routine and efficient as quality lesson planning is, in this era of standards and accountability.

Teachers like Todd and Liz learned in their seminar that they were short on facts and formulas, and therefore unqualified to serve as experts in data analysis. The reality is that teachers who are committed to leveraging antecedents, embracing collaboration that is long on candor and respect, and demonstrating accountability by acting on what is learned are experts in every sense of the word. When professionals apply their insights to triangulate complex issues with divergent data, apply fast-track multivariate analyses without the need for statistical tests, and conduct in-depth and focused environmental scans, they are operating as experts. As actions are systematically driven by their collective wisdom, educators will reclaim the initiative as to data analysis from policy makers and politicians. It is hoped that *Beyond the Numbers* and its companion handbook, *Show Me the Proof!,* will dramatically improve data analysis in schools by providing a standards-based framework for data analysis, practical strategies and processes to build capacity, and specific tools to usher in successful replications and improved student achievement.

DISCUSSION

BIG IDEAS

Expertise in data analysis is the ability to bring information to bear to solve problems and arrive at solutions consistently, efficiently, and effectively.

Teachers who leverage antecedents, engage in candid collaboration, and hold themselves and others accountable for results demonstrate expertise in data analysis.

QUESTIONS

1. *What characteristics uniquely qualify classroom teachers as experts in data analysis?*

2. *What unique knowledge do teachers possess that they can bring to bear to make informed, astute decisions regarding data?*

3. *What must occur in your classroom, school, or school system to promote teacher expertise in data analysis?*

APPENDIX **A**

Scoring Matrix for Analysis of Data

1.0 Data Management

Analysis Dimension	Meeting the Standard	Progressing Toward the Standard	Not Meeting the Standard
1.1 **Data Collection**	The educator makes informed decisions at all levels based on formative assessments of prior learning, embedded assessments during instruction, and summative assessments of results following instruction. Data collection demonstrates understanding of **antecedent** data, including administrative structures and conditions and **cause** data (teacher behaviors that engage students in thinking and learning). Results (**effects**) data includes student performance; pre- and post data; use of longitudinal cohort data for patterns and trends; embedded performance assessment data; and common assessments by department, grade, or discipline. Data provides evidence of antecedents and instructional strategies.	The educator ensures that teachers and support staff collect and monitor data associated with goals, and that data is maintained for both summative and formative purposes. Emphasis is primarily on collection of results (effects) data, with limited evidence of cause data measures or programmatic and administrative antecedents (conditions and structures that correlate with excellence in student achievement). Educator attempts to schedule data collection so it does not interrupt instruction.	The educator's data collection system is limited to external requirements for compliance in annual student assessment results. No evidence of attempts to link cause and effect; institute continuous assessment measures before, during, and after learning; or address timing issues of data collection.

(continues)

1.0 Data Management *(Continued)*

Analysis Dimension	Meeting the Standard	Progressing Toward the Standard	Not Meeting the Standard
1.1 Data Collection *(Continued)*	Data collection minimizes interruption of instruction, with data collected limited to critical variables that lend themselves to triangulation.		
1.2 Improvement Cycles	The educator employs improvement cycles for all major programs and unit teams. Cycles ensure that plans are informed by data, implemented to address gaps and opportunities, analyzed, and routinely and systematically revised for improvement (e.g., 7-step DDDM, PDSA, etc.).	The educator is beginning to apply an improvement cycle to assess student achievement across state or local requirements (e.g., seat time, Carnegie Units, state assessment). Application to adult practices or administrative and programmatic structures has yet to be attempted.	The educator reacts to state or local requirements for data and does not employ improvement cycles that link data to planning and implementation.
1.3 Analysis/ Reflection/ Action	The educator examines test scores for trends within subjects, relationship to grades and state assessments, internal consistency across subjects, unanticipated gains, and outlier performers that score well above and well below standard. Data is routinely triangulated with antecedent, collaboration, and accountability data to reveal insights not available from examining single data points. The educator has formed teams and meeting times to examine data for improved student achievement. The educator sets aside specific times and formats to ensure that collaborative analysis takes place; that quality data tools are applied to facilitate that analysis; that insights from reflection are recorded; and that action is planned, implemented and monitored on the basis of the analysis.	The educator has formed teams and meeting times to examine data for improved student achievement. The educator examines test scores for trends within subjects; relationship to grades and state assessments; and internal consistency across subjects; and to identify students with unanticipated gains.	Data is collected and recorded, but seldom analyzed to improve student achievement.

2.0 Antecedents of Excellence

Analysis Dimension	Meeting the Standard	Progressing Toward the Standard	Not Meeting the Standard
2.1 Cause Data and Instructional Strategies	The educator provides evidence of specific antecedents used in classrooms or school to increase student achievement effects (**results**) through teacher behaviors in the classroom (**causes**), and systematic teaching strategies. The educator modifies and adjusts antecedent cause data (teaching behaviors and practices), and shares with colleagues current research findings describing causes that produce the greatest gains in student achievement for all subgroups; effective cause strategies are implemented in classrooms or the school, and the Hishakawa Fishbone is frequently used to examine current data, determine root causes, and take action through effective intervention plans.	The educator recognizes effective teaching strategies that impact student thinking and reasoning as causes that lead to achievement effects (**results**), and is conversant with current research about the causes most apt to produce the greatest gains in student achievement for all subgroups. The educator recognizes that cause/effect data represents strong correlations, not actual causes. The educator is beginning to identify antecedents to improve student achievement based on available data.	The educator is not able to identify antecedents or leverage them to increase student achievement.
2.2 Administrative Structures and Conditions	The educator leverages a wide range of antecedent conditions and structures to increase student achievement, and monitors their impact with user-friendly data. The leader is adept at creating antecedents that increase student achievement, leveraging time, settings, and resources to align and focus efforts (i.e., technological capacity, time and opportunity issues, staff training, levels of implementation in specific teaching strategies, attendance).	The educator recognizes antecedents in terms of time, technology, training, logistics, and level of implementation, and applies them periodically to improve student achievement based on external research findings and antecedents employed in neighboring or comparable schools.	The educator does not view administrative structures of time, technology, textbooks, or training as possible antecedents for excellence that can be modified for improved student achievement.

(continues)

3.0 Collaboration around Student Work

Analysis Dimension	Meeting the Standard	Progressing Toward the Standard	Not Meeting the Standard
3.1 Planning to Execution	The educator ensures ongoing, reflective, and meaningful collaboration that captures the best thinking of staff to improve student achievement through a variety of methods, such as: (1) **action planning,** including all steps of a continuous improvement cycle; (2) **lesson logs** shared and distributed by departments or grade-level teams; (3) **common assessments** created, evaluated, and revised by teacher teams; (4) **instructional calendars** that align curriculum and instruction with regent examinations; (5) development of **data teams** to monitor outlier student performance and close learning gaps, or (6) establishment of a clearly defined **program evaluation** process. Teacher-developed measures of collaboration complement those initiated by individual educator.	The educator promotes collaboration around student work by examining student work at faculty meetings and asking staff to identify solutions to patterns of lagging student achievement and strategies to replicate evidence of dramatically improving student achievement. The educator promotes collaborative data analysis by establishing one or more ongoing methods to examine student performance and implement strategies to improve that performance: (1) **lesson logs** shared and distributed by departments or grade-level teams; (2) **common assessments** created, evaluated, and revised by teacher teams; or (3) **instructional calendars** that align curriculum and instruction with regent examinations.	The educator looks for the path of least resistance in developing data monitoring systems; she or he frequently avoids collaboration beyond initial consensus to adopt a program or strategy; reflection is nonexistent.
3.2 Team Thinking	Solutions generated by others are valued, especially when generated from within the educator's support group. The leader ensures that team thinking permeates the data analysis process by requiring that: (1) all team members proactively analyze data for discussion in advance of meetings; (2) team processes routinely identify improvements; (3) training is provided and encouraged in mental models, team learning, and cognitive coaching; and (4) training updates on data analysis tools are provided to all teams.	The educator promotes team thinking in data analysis by providing and encouraging: (1) training in mental models, team learning, and cognitive coaching; and (2) training in data analysis tools for interested team members.	There is no evidence of a systematic plan to improve the quality of collaborative thinking in examining student work.

3.0 Collaboration around Student Work *(Continued)*

Analysis Dimension	Meeting the Standard	Progressing Toward the Standard	Not Meeting the Standard
3.3 Integration into Decision Making	The educator integrates collaboration in data analysis into all key decisions through collaborative processes that benefit from the best thinking of classroom teachers. Evidence is demonstrated through a variety of means, such as: (1) recommendations are reviewed only when submitted with peers; (2) collaborative schedules provide common planning, teaming; (3) teacher teams examine student work; leader requests analysis and recommendations for specific students; (4) assessment calendars are required of all department/grade-level teams; (5) early release times are established for collaboration around student work; (6) Time and effort are reallocated to respond to urgent challenges, through collaboration that develops powerful instructional strategies. **Assessment calendars** establish times for collaboration in analysis, reflection, action planning, and implementation.	The educator attempts to integrate collaboration in data analysis into decision making by one or more of the following: (1) requesting that recommendations be submitted with support by two other peers; (2) establishing school schedules with common planning/teaming; or (3) providing data to teacher teams (flexible grouping) and requesting analysis and recommendations for specific students.	The educator views decisions regarding data analysis as the prerogative of administration or as isolated acts of leadership separate from lessons revealed by data.

4.0 Accountability

4.1 Authority to Act	The educator establishes written policies, within his or her direct control and influence, that provide teachers and other staff the authority to implement changes designed to improve student achievement based on a preponderance of the	The educator advocates for written policies, within his or her direct control and influence, that provide teachers and other staff the authority to implement changes designed to improve student achievement. Data provides some evidence to	The educator defers to popular opinion in making changes, with little evidence of efforts to extend authority for program or instructional changes to teachers or staff.

(continues)

4.0 Accountability *(Continued)*

Analysis Dimension	Meeting the Standard	Progressing Toward the Standard	Not Meeting the Standard
4.1 Authority to Act *(Continued)*	evidence revealed from data available at any given time. Preponderance of evidence is determined through triangulation of data and thoughtful, collaboration around actual student performance.	assist teachers and staff in making changes designed to improve student achievement; triangulation and thoughtful collaboration around student performance occur sporadically among teachers and staff.	
4.2 Accountability Structures	The educator integrates accountability into all major decisions by delineating explicit responsibilities for teams and individuals, establishing user-friendly timelines for data, and establishes multiple feedback systems, such as assessment calendars, formal listening systems for student, teacher, parent, and staff stakeholder groups, grade level/department teams, or data teams.	The educator has developed accountability methods that specify responsibilities for teams and individuals, establish timelines for data collection/disaggregation, and provide at least one formal and responsive feedback system to improve student achievement.	Focus is on compliance with external requirements established by supervisor or institutional policy; little evidence exists to demonstrate a commitment or plan to add value with accountability systems.
4.3 Accountability Reports	The educator publicly displays and communicates results of ongoing, monitored accountability measures for Tier 1 data (system-wide indicators), Tier 2 data (school-based indicators), and Tier 3 data (narrative description of school successes and challenges). The educator supplements measures at all levels with performance indicators that add value and focus efforts to improve student achievement.	The educator communicates the results of ongoing, monitored accountability measures that exceed Tier 1 (district-wide indicators) requirements, and supplements such measures with a number of performance indicators that add value and focus efforts to improve student achievement.	The educator communicates only those results mandated by external requirements (Tier 1 or compliance measures). There is no evidence of plans to develop, monitor, or communicate Tier 2 or Tier 3 data to staff, parents, students, or patrons.
4.4 Permission to Subtract	The leader establishes written policies, within his or her direct control and influence, that give teachers and other staff permission to eliminate, reduce, or omit historical practices or instructional strategies that inhibit improved student	The leader has developed a policy giving teachers and staff permission to eliminate, reduce, or omit historical practices or instructional strategies that inhibit improved student achievement, but has yet to establish written policies,	The leader is reluctant to share the authority to eliminate, reduce, or omit existing practices with staff, and is unable to identify current instructional strategies or antecedents (conditions and structures) that inhibit improved

4.0 Accountability *(Continued)*

Analysis Dimension	Meeting the Standard	Progressing Toward the Standard	Not Meeting the Standard
4.4 Permission to Subtract *(Continued)*	achievement, based on a preponderance of the evidence revealed from data available at any given time. Preponderance of evidence is determined through deliberate triangulation of data and thoughtful collaboration around actual student performance.	within his or her direct control and influence, to that effect, and has not yet developed a system to monitor implementation of the policy. Data provides some evidence of assistance to teachers and staff in eliminating obsolete, redundant, or neutral practices that do not contribute to improved student achievement. Triangulation and thoughtful collaboration around student performance occur sporadically among teachers and staff.	student achievement for groups or individuals
4.5 Responsibility for Results	Performance goals are met for student achievement that meet AYP requirements and close the learning gap for all subgroups. Sustained record of improved student achievement on multiple indicators of student success can be verified. Explicit use of previous and interim data indicates a focus on improving performance. Efforts to assist students who demonstrate proficiency to move to the advanced or exemplary level are evident, and new challenges are met by identification of needs from existing data, creation of timely and effective interventions with monitoring data, and selection of meaningful and insightful results indicators.	Staff members report that they should be responsible for student achievement results, but have limited understanding of the factors (antecedents) that effect student achievement. There is evidence of improvement for one or more subgroups, but insufficient evidence of changes in antecedent measures of teaching, curriculum, and leadership to create the improvements necessary to achieve student performance goals for all subgroups.	Indifferent to the data; tendency to blame students, families, and external characteristics. Staff and leaders do not believe that student achievement can improve through their efforts. No evidence of decisive action to change time, teacher assignments, curriculum, leadership practices, or other variables of achievement.

(continues)

5.0 Triangulation

Analysis Dimension	Meeting the Standard	Progressing Toward the Standard	Not Meeting the Standard
5.1 Triangulation	The educator applies at least two data tools to every triangulation, triangulating student achievement data effectively with supporting student achievement data, **antecedent** data (conditions and structure), **accountability** data (responsibilities, reporting, SMART measures), or **collaboration** data (various team formats, lesson logs, instructional calendars, etc.). The educator monitors staff triangulation of achievement data to ensure inclusion of related and unrelated data points (e.g., instructional strategies, allocation of time, professional development, side-by-side curriculum analysis, standards, and assessments).	The educator applies at least one data tool to every triangulation effort, and is beginning to triangulate student achievement data with antecedents, collaboration data, or accountability structures (principles of DDDM).	The educator is unaware of the principle of triangulation of data, and instead focuses his or her efforts on compliance with district and state reports.
5.2 Low Inference Insights	The educator leverages triangulation to engage teachers in self-discovery of insights, new learning, and recommendations for changes in the educational process. The educator triangulates data effectively, with each point serving as a check on the other dimensions; the desired outcome is the realization of new insights from the various data points (and types) that are not available from examining one type of data or one perspective in isolation.	The educator understands that triangulation requires teams to make assumptions, draw inferences, and come to conclusions without total certainty. The educator recognizes that triangulation necessitates discovery of a center point from other, often unrelated data, and the educator triangulates student assessment data with antecedents and cause data wherever possible.	The educator is directive in interactions with teachers, and does not engage teachers in triangulation of data.
5.3 Triangulation Conversations	The educator models triangulation in formal and informal settings, and asks teachers to add value to their analysis of all data by	The educator uses the triangulation process to coach teachers in making assumptions, drawing inferences, and developing	The educator views data as numbers and does not engage faculty or staff in making inferences or reaching for assumptions,

5.0 Triangulation *(Continued)*

Analysis Dimension	Meeting the Standard	Progressing Toward the Standard	Not Meeting the Standard
5.3 Triangulation Conversations *(Continued)*	triangulating data with colleagues. Triangulation is an expected exercise for all grade, department, and data team meetings, and the leader routinely includes cause data and administrative antecedents in triangulation. The educator applies triangulation to encourage innovative teaching strategies and facilitate new approaches to instruction through action research. Data is specifically analyzed to engage staff in conversations about assessments.	hunches that can help identify replicable practices, verified through action research.	believing that none of the school staff is a statistician and shouldn't claim to be.

6.0 Replication

Analysis Dimension	Meeting the Standard	Progressing Toward the Standard	Not Meeting the Standard
6.1 Replication	The educator has a system in place to identify home-grown successes that includes a common definition, a process to recognize successes, and a method to validate and replicate the successful practice. The educator has defined a preponderance of evidence as sufficient data to answer the questions: **What works well for whom, why, and how do you know?**	The educator promotes replication of best practices from current educational research and has a system in place to recognize teachers for improved student achievement. At least one replication is discussed and teachers are encouraged to observe each other for best practices.	The educator resists efforts to formally replicate practices, viewing the process as divisive and as singling out one teacher over another.
6.2 Decision to Replicate	The educator follows up on hunches associated with data patterns by initiating a process for replication with teachers when student performance patterns correlate with specific strategies or antecedent structures and conditions for learning. The educator employs a specific decisionmaking process at key intervals with affected	The educator communicates frequently with teachers to identify patterns and trends in student performance that correlate with specific instructional strategies or the presence of antecedent structures and conditions for learning. The leader initiates a discussion about possible replication with affected teachers and staff.	The educator views differences in classroom performance as inherent differences in teaching personality and student demographics.

(continues)

6.0 Replication *(Continued)*

Analysis Dimension	Meeting the Standard	Progressing Toward the Standard	Not Meeting the Standard
6.2 Decision to Replicate *(Continued)*	teachers to determine how, when, and whether to replicate a practice.		
6.3 Action Research	The educator is fluent in the six steps of action research, and is quick to translate hunches about patterns into action research hypotheses, engaging teachers and staff in a common action research approach characterized by: ■ Simple relationship design between one independent variable (cause data) and one dependent variable (effect) or 2×2 variable matrix if necessary ■ Simple pre/post assessments ■ Use of same course/grade classrooms as control group ■ Recommended use of meta-analysis categories of effective teaching strategies as independent variables ■ Data collection embedded into instruction ■ Prescribed time period, format	The educator is fluent in the six steps of action research: 1. Observe 2. Explain 3. Predict 4. Test hypothesis 5. Gather data 6. Explain The educator examines data for patterns and trends associated with specific classrooms and instructional strategies.	The educator shows no interest in action research, viewing the time and effort required to implement it as disruptive to the learning process.

APPENDIX B

Common Questions about Data Analysis

Classroom- and School-Level Assessment Concerns

Question 1: How can we best utilize test data in regard to common assessment data?

Common EOC assessment data provides the capacity to find patterns related to sub-group performance differences, teacher strategies, curriculum alignment, and time and opportunity to develop proficiency. This data should be particularly powerful for teacher teams in that it allows them a glimpse inside their collective classrooms to determine what is working, what isn't working, and why.

The data will immediately reveal differences among groups, among classrooms, and within the curriculum. These differences and patterns will provide the basis for modifying instruction, focusing curriculum, and adjusting time and opportunity issues.

Presentation ideas. Tell this story in two parts: (1) findings, patterns, and differences; and (2) lessons, modifications, and adjustments planned. Common EOC assessments offer the most agile form of district assessments for modifying professional practice. One or two graphs or charts for the first part of the story and one or two for the second part should be very instructive to any audience, and play well within a three- to five-minute board of education presentation.

Recommended tools. Wagon-wheel/relations diagram to identify such patterns by teacher and by curriculum unit for subgroups.

Questions Regarding Annual State Tests (Both NRTs and CRTs)

Question 2: How can we best utilize test data in regard to norm-referenced data?

Norm-referenced data offers five basic benefits:

1. NRTs allow us to identify patterns and gaps by subject and subscales that reflect local emphasis in curriculum and instruction for all students.

2. NRTs also provide a vehicle to examine the degree to which students are achieving within their expected abilities (NRT relationship between cognitive ability scores on some state assessments).

3. By triangulating NRT data with CRTs, EOC assessments, state assessments, Safety Net performance assessments, and writing assessments, one can determine the degree to which these tests corroborate one another, and identify the types of assessments on which groups of students excel and where performance differs.

4. The NRT data primarily compares our students and our curriculum preparation by subject and subscale with performance of students across the nation. That comparison alone offers insights into how well local schools are preparing students to compete in a larger arena with their peers.

5. NRTs are always indicators of the range of student responses and offer local districts a picture of the degree of variance in student performance. NRTs can be used to monitor that range over time and develop interventions to reduce the variance and close the gap.

Caveat: NRT averages mask gaps within subjects and between subgroups. NRTs also rank students and do little to determine proficiency or provide meaningful comparisons outside their respective NRT sampling pools. NRTs always have 50 percent scoring above the norm and 50 percent below, although reducing the variance in benefit #5 can provide a very strong external measure of success.

Presentation ideas

- Present NRT scores in the context of being one of many valid assessments rather than *the* primary measure of achievement or student ability.
- Describe briefly how NRTs differ from CRTs and standards-based assessments, and frame NRTs in terms of the value they offer you locally, stressing your intent to close the gap by reducing variance over time.

Recommended tools. Slides of:

1. Bell curve, in context of desire to reduce variance
2. Patterns suggesting strengths and weaknesses of current curriculum

3. Chart/table comparison with other assessments

4. Caveats, especially as to masking and inability to measure proficiency in terms of knowledge and application

5. Trend data for local performance by subgroup on the NRT

If combined with other assessments in presentation, choose one or two slides from these five. Stand-alone should allow for a BOE presentation of five minutes or less.

Question 3: I'd also like to know more about interpreting ability scores; for example, when do they show we are working above anticipated abilities and achieving beyond what was predicted?

Ability scores are scaled in a way similar to traditional IQ tests, but they are not IQ scores. They reflect only the ranked performance on a scale where 50 percent of students score below the scale of 100 and 50 percent score above. Standard deviations have been calibrated at 16 points, again reflective of many IQ tests (WISC-IV, etc.), but ability scores should not be substituted for the individually administered cognitive IQ exams. The value of the ability score is its thumbnail look at cognitive ability, and the comparisons one might draw in terms of students exceeding expected performance. Comparing a cognitive ability score to the normal curve equivalent (NCE) scores provides a convenient correlation for this issue.

How can we reflect this in our success stories?

Presentation ideas. Present patterns comparing cognitive ability measures where scores "beat the odds" or where ability scores mirror actual performance. Limit your presentation to one or two slides.

Question 4: How can we best utilize test data in regard to criterion-referenced data?

CRT data offers important information about student performance against certain criteria or standards. Like a quality performance assessment addressing a Safety Net standard, CRTs allow us to determine whether students have met the criterion, with this caveat: Unlike a performance assessment, we may have to assume that performance on a select-response CRT actually reflects the student's knowledge of the criterion and his or her ability to demonstrate and apply that knowledge with the appropriate skill in various applications. Benefits of CRTs include:

- Test data reflects student proficiency in terms of knowledge of the criterion.
- CRT test data give detailed information about how well a student has performed on each of the educational goals or outcomes included on that test. For instance,

a CRT score might describe which arithmetic operations a student can perform or the level of reading difficulty he or she can comprehend.

■ As long as the content of the test matches the content that is considered important to learn, the CRT gives the student, the teacher, and the parent more information about how much of the valued content has been learned than does an NRT.

■ All students can "pass" a CRT test, whereas only 50 percent can meet or exceed the mean NRT score.

■ Most state academic content standard assessments are CRT tests, in that "cut" scores are identified to indicate a level of proficiency.

Question 5: How can we best utilize test data in regard to NCE scores, national percentiles, and scale scores?

NCE scores are equal-interval scores used to compare achievement across subject areas over time. They provide you with information that is more precise regarding raw score performance than the national percentile score, but, absent subscale information, offer little to help in diagnosing student performance or designing interventions.

National percentile (NP) scores represent the percentage of students in the norm group whose scores fall below a given level. A student whose NP is 65 scored higher than 65 percent of students in the norm group. NPs compare the achievement of students in a local group with that of students in the nation as a whole.

Grade equivalent (GE) scores indicate the year and month of school for which a student's score is typical. A GE of 6.2, for example, shows that the student is achieving at a level typical of students who have completed the second month of grade 6 at the time the test was standardized. Interpret GEs with caution. A student in grade 3 may attain a GE of 6.2—this does not mean that the student is capable of doing sixth-grade work, only that the student is scoring well above average for grade 3.

Scale scores are similar to NCE scores in that they provide a common scale to compare variability in student performance from grade to grade or subject to subject. On the NAEP, scale scores are used almost exclusively to ascertain the degree to which performance is improving and to determine whether the variability in scores is tightening. Scale scores on the state assessment can provide similar helpful information.

Presentation ideas. Present patterns in terms of scale scores. Whereas school and district averages may move only slightly, scale-score results can indicate movement toward higher achievement by indicating reduced variance in scores and consistency across subjects. Scale scores also can help drill down to areas of need, when discrepancies are evident. For board of education presentations, omit this information, or use one slide to tell the story in one to two minutes.

Question 6: How can we best utilize test data in regard to quartile growth?

Examining test results in light of students most apt to move up to the next quartile is instructive in that it helps us see how relatively easy it is to make pretty significant growth when we concentrate on individual students with names and faces. A second benefit of examining performance by quartiles is that it is a quick and easy way to identify how cohorts compare from grade to grade or school to school, to determine how effective curriculum is by grade and how effective teaching practices are by school.

Question 7: How can we best utilize test data in regard to fall-to-spring comparisons?

Fall and spring data points are wonderful opportunities to update data walls, celebrate improvements, and revise goals. This question underscores the importance of maintaining and growing a comprehensive and multifaceted assessment battery, because there are cohort survival changes between fall and spring and because the snapshot exams within the testing window will always be influenced by illness and other personal factors. Performance assessments that are embedded and address power standards with leverage are essential components of any assessment battery.

Fall-to-spring comparisons should always anticipate gains, and the test data can be utilized to inform curriculum planning, especially instructional calendars that emphasize safety-net standards at specific junctures within a school or department during prescribed months or weeks.

Presentation Concerns

Question 8: I think we still need some DDDM skills in presentation graphics and longitudinal data interpretation.

Training in presentation graphics, such as Excel and PowerPoint applications, is always valuable. The ability to interpret longitudinal data improves as more data points are added. This may seem self-evident, but one problem with longitudinal data is the need to start over as data sets change. Find a quality measure, something you are confident will be just as important a decade from now as it is today, and stay with it (antecedents as well as results indicators). Advanced presentations for data-driven decision making will require practice in Excel at higher levels and knowledge of general principles of presentations, including colors, clutter, charts, graphs, data scales, and so on.

Question 9: I would like information on the most effective way to scale
graphs. I think some of the differences on data points may have
been overly exaggerated by using too small a scale on the Y-axis.

This is a common complaint and legitimate criticism of data presented for almost every purpose. If the gains are minimal, conventional wisdom suggests that we shrink the Y-axis scale; if scores have shown significant decline, we enlarge the Y-axis scale to minimize that decline. To stop this practice, we need common standards for presenting data graphically, just as we promote common EOC assessments for students. I suggest that the Y-axis always span the range of possible outcomes. If percentile scores are compared, a scale from 0 to 100 is warranted. If raw scores or scale scores are used, every possible score should be accommodated by the Y-axis. Some educators improve even on this basic expectation for data presentation by using logarithmic scales that increase geometrically as the number value increases. In other words, the Y-axis distance between number 1 and 10 is equivalent to the distance between 10 and 100, which is equivalent to the distance between 100 and 1,000. Microsoft Excel accommodates this format, a scale widely used in medicine, agriculture, and finance for its accuracy in establishing trend lines for growth and contraction. This tool is addressed in a brief exercise within the "Advanced DDDM" seminar by The Leadership and Learning Center (2004a).

Question 10: I would like to look at some nontraditional ways of
displaying large numbers of data points. Usually large
amounts of data are summed or averaged for display.
Unfortunately, this also results in loss of data. Are there
other ways to display all the pertinent information?

The Indiana Academic Content Standards group has a wonderful Web site that examines data in several different ways. One of the most useful methods is its "Drilldown" graphs, which examine by subgroup and test the difference between a school's average score and the minimum passing score for that standard—a school's performance (average skill score) is compared to the passing skill score. With the zero line representing the passing skill score, the graph displays how far above or below the school performed on a specific standard.

Another method for examining issues is the wagon wheel, which offers graphical representations to compare performance of several entities (classrooms, students, schools) across multiple variables (up to eight). Its primary purposes are to (1) determine which issue is most critical, and (2) compare performance across multiple dimensions. An equally powerful tool is a simple graph of the range of student performances on particular assessments; this is an important measure because we always want to reduce the variability in student performance and at the same time see achievement increase. These two measures and others provide insightful ways of displaying data without resorting to totals or averages in such a way as to mask important patterns and discoveries. They provide very interesting alternatives to traditional line and bar graphs of average scores for presentations.

Question 11: What data can you compare, and how do you accurately represent data when interpreting and sharing with others?

Comparisons are useful with almost all data when a benchmark exists for excellence or high performance, given similar demographics and resources. "Comparing apples to oranges" is such a common metaphor that the phrase is used for almost any comparison, but the lesson is a valid one. Comparing a school with other schools that are performing below standard seldom yields meaningful information for improvement. Comparing one's school with the most successful school in the district or state, by subgroups and subscales on specific tests, can yield very important information when we drill down to identify antecedents (adult behaviors) that led to higher achievement.

Certainly, assessment data lends itself to comparisons. Other process data are better assessed by examining the integrity of internal factors, such as redundancy, duplication of effort, consistency, and timeliness in delivery of the process. The previous question inquired about alternative ways to gather and represent data in presentations. Data is best represented when a number of guiding principles are applied:

- **Describe data in its context** by separating anecdotal information in your presentation and labeling it as such. (Anecdotal data is extremely important to tell the story, but if it can't be presented in terms of data, present it separately.)

- **Describe data with integrity,** using scales representing the full range of possible responses or scores (e.g., 0 to 100 for percentiles or percent).

- **Interpret data conservatively and avoid conjecture.** Let the data tell the story (explaining differences by saying that you have "a different group of kids this year" insults your audience). Offering subsequent graphs and charts to describe those differences with deeper analysis (e.g., correlations for certain subgroups based on teaching methods, attendance, behavior) strengthens the story you are telling and adds credibility.

- **Never present data that depends on anecdotal narrative to tell the story.** If the data does not reveal patterns or trends, let it tell its message of the null hypothesis (assumption that changes will be miniscule). Lessons can be learned when no changes are evident, especially lessons for examining at deeper levels and identifying alternative measures.

- **Use graphic organizers liberally** to interpret data and share with others. Graphic organizers are "thinking tools" that lend themselves to group processing and data analysis.

- Remember that data should make visible what is otherwise invisible.
- **Know your data so well** that you can tell the story behind the numbers without apology, conjecture, or embellishment.

Question 12: *How do we improve the process of communicating data? It is the prelude to determining its meaning for future action.*

This question gets at the heart of effective data analysis: pervasive, ubiquitous, user-friendly communication of data that promotes a data-driven culture. How is that accomplished? All data systems, whether classroom, school, or district, should include:

- Scheduled dates and times for collection, aggregation, and disaggregation of data
- Reserved, required time for analysis, reflection, and recommendations for changes
- Mandatory written rationales for decisions to proceed with no changes or to implement recommendations
- Dissemination of the data-driven decision to all affected parties, including parents and the public

District and school data are different from classroom data in that district data is almost exclusively results or effects data; schools engage and monitor both cause and effect measures, and classrooms engage with antecedent and cause data as well.

Question 13: *Principals need to learn how to present data well, so that it tells the true picture. What guidelines can you offer to assist in this process?*

This question is an excellent illustration of the desire of many educators to add precision to our craft, especially when we present findings to a broader audience. The seven guidelines provided in the answer to question 11 address the telling of the "true picture" by, among other things, insisting on a common scale or principle for Y-axis scales. Present only what is important and adhere to Schmoker's mandate to "make visible the invisible." Four additional recommendations for presentations include:

1. **Present the story you are telling in terms of comparisons, relationships, or trends.** Without these connections, data has very little meaning.
2. **Limit the content of presentation slides** to seven lines of type, and no more than three comparisons per chart or table (2 × 2 matrices have only two dimensions per axis).
3. **Avoid charts or tables with more than seven variables.** More than that is not only cluttered, but also difficult to interpret.
4. **Let the data breathe and speak.** Never use color or templates that draw attention away from the message of the data presented.

Analysis Concerns

Question 14: How can I better read the subskills portion of our data to know what is the most important skill to focus on? What should I do to get the most bang for our buck and time?

Subskill data tells a story about strengths and weaknesses, both of which can inform our decisions and help us prioritize skills to focus on. In math, the building-block skills of basic operations may be compelling enough to stay with that instructional focus even though students show a weakness in statistics or geometry. In language arts, a reading subskill weakness in sentence fluency can guide how you design and monitor the writing process and how writing is integrated in all other content areas. As a general rule of thumb, however, ask the following questions:

- How do the subskills interact?
- Are some subskills prerequisite to proficiency in another skill or subscale?
- Is there a subskill that offers greater leverage opportunities?
- Do students consistently show higher performance in one subskill than another?
- Have classroom teachers conducted a side-by-side analysis of curriculum with test data?
- Have you analyzed where time and resources are allocated in the subject area tested?

You will determine what is most important by examining the number of classrooms and students with the same common pattern, applying the power of the research regarding effective teaching strategies to deepen areas of strengths, and reallocating time to make sure sufficient attention is given to areas of general weakness. Subskill performance data for each school can be analyzed with several advanced DDDM tools, including the wagon wheel.

Question 15: Schools are still comparing state assessment scores among noncohort groups. Because we are held accountable each year for state assessment results, what can be done to help us focus on longitudinal progress of cohort groups?

Comparison of different groups of students from year to year is a legitimate and pervasive criticism of standardized testing from educators. Maintenance of this practice is built on the assumption that though individual students will differ, the cohort as a whole will be representative of the previous year's cohort (same neighborhoods; same racial, economic, ethnic, and educational backgrounds). Hence the assumption that improved scores indicate improved practices, and that declining scores indicate less-than-stellar teaching practices. In fact, with very large schools and large samples (e.g.,

100 or more students per grade), the data will reflect many common characteristics from year to year. This satisfies the null hypothesis, and given a sufficient sample size, we have every right to expect similar results. The problem, of course, is that *similar* results are no longer acceptable. The very reason that annual comparisons have so little value for analyzing individual student performance is what makes them so useful in analyzing curriculum. If subscales indicate strong number sense and geometry skills accompanied by weak performance in measurement and problem solving, we can confidently attribute the pattern to the emphasis we place on various aspects of the curriculum, not to student differences.

NCLB's emphasis on all subgroups showing sustained improvement in reaching proficiency is consistent with standards-based education. NCLB's requirement for annual testing, grades 3 through 10, will soon push states to begin reporting by cohort, even though historical practice examines the test (third-grade reading, fourth-grade math, fifth-grade writing, etc.).

What can be done? Begin today to track performance by cohorts and to take advantage of the rich data that tracking will provide about teaching quality, about articulation across levels, and about the need to vary time, interventions, and opportunity to ensure that all students achieve proficiency. Longitudinal measures shift the focus from specific tests to the ability of the district or school to show continuous improvement. Don't forget to include antecedents that correlate positively with excellence as measures and a liberal proportion of cause data. The result will be a data framework that allows you (and others) to see clearly what is occurring with any learning gaps by cohort groups, and to monitor individual performance.

Caveat: Be careful in selecting indicators for longitudinal tracking. Far too often in public education, the target shifts with new tests that require at least a trend line distinguishing prior test results from current. This question underscores once again the need for a comprehensive, multifaceted assessment program that includes embedded performance assessments, common EOC assessments, assessments for power standards, CRTs, writing assessments, and NRTs, *or* the blended efforts in most state assessments that attempt to measure performance against fixed criteria (standards) using a multiple-choice, select-response framework common to NRTs, with shifting cut scores based on percentiles rather than adhering strictly to a proficiency standard.

Presentation ideas. Compare prior-year performance on specific assessments for the most recent two or three years to describe the annual testing paradigm still in place. Point out, with a second slide, key patterns that emerged in terms of subscale scores, with a description of plans to address the discrepancies and bolster the curriculum. Finally, use one or two slides to present the longitudinal gains made by the cohorts referenced in your first slide. Again, this analysis could be completed for most boards of education in three to five minutes (excluding question times).

Question 16: How do we determine the most critical data and conduct comparative analyses of CRA and standardized test data?

Many schools and school systems examine their state assessment data to identify the area of greatest weakness and proceed to target that weakness as their top priority for the coming year. Frequently, school improvement plans establish annual goals on the same basis, only to shift emphasis the following year when scores for a different cohort of students improve in one area and lag in another. So, the question itself is critical. How do we develop priorities based on the data, including not only classroom assessments, EOC assessments, and state assessments, but also lessons from the research?

Several tools lend themselves to this process, including the Hishakawa Fishbone, by which we analyze data in terms of cause and effect. A decisionmaking matrix with weighted factors is a very useful tool to establish priorities based on current realities. A less-known process, which is equally collaborative and enlists our best thinking, is the use of critical-incident analysis, a process that examines events related to the data to help us understand with greater precision what we can do to solve the problem the data indicates. Low scores in reading are not a problem, but an indicator. Critical-incident analysis allows us to take the data, reveal the root cause of low performance, and prioritize what will be done differently to achieve a different result. For example, assume that the assessment data consistently points out that students struggle with the writing process, as measured by a holistic analytic writing process or 6+1 Trait rubrics. Critical-incident investigation shifts our thinking from the effect data (resulting writing scores) to their causes, asking questions such as, "Which aspect of the writing process is most difficult to handle? Is there a point in the process/in the use of prompts/in submission of final products where students are most apt to shut down, express resistance, or generally perform below their ability?" Critical-incident analysis examines root causes for very specific data deficits, linking our allocation of time, resources, and teaching strategies as we develop priorities that lead to action.

Finally, a process of triangulation, widely used in construction and by mariners, is a very helpful tool in determining the most critical point from diverse assessment data. Most educators are faced with multiple forms of data, all from tests administered at different junctures, ranging from classroom performance assessments, EOC assessments, unit tests, projects, CRTs, state assessments, to independent NRTs such as SAT or ACT scores. We need to be able to triangulate with confidence, and "Advanced DDDM" (Leadership and Learning Center, 2004a) provides exercises to apply these tools and procedures to go deeper with greater precision and focus.

Question 17: How do we process through the drill-down data by subskills and by breakout groups (identifying needs)?

Another insightful question. The seven-step DDDM process takes us to the point where we not only identify needs by subskills for subgroups, but we also begin to identify effective teaching strategies to address the needs of very diverse learners. "Advanced Data Analysis" takes the lessons from DDDM further by providing numerous analysis tools and the ability to triangulate (see question 16) data from multiple sources.

I would also suggest adoption of a list of common expected teacher behaviors, to ensure that school leaders and classroom teachers have a very deep understanding of expectations from the state assessment, content standards, district curriculum, and each of their students. Here are a few:

- Teachers know what concepts and skills are tested on district/state assessments for their particular grade levels.

- Teachers know the district standards and English Language Development (ELD) standards for each grade level.

- Teachers have studied a side-by-side content analysis of standards, assessments curriculum, and textbooks.

- Teachers at each grade level calendar what they are going to teach each month based on the assessments and standards.

- Teachers have selected target students, by name, to whom they give extra attention and help based on assessment data.

- The principal knows—at least monthly—which students have recently reached grade level.

Be explicit enough about professional expectations that each and every teacher knows as much as possible about her or his own curriculum, assessments, standards, and teaching materials.

Question 18: How do we select approaches to address weaknesses once drill-down data has been analyzed?

This question underscores the need for advanced data analysis by pointing out the importance of establishing strategic priorities based on best practices in teaching strategies and data analysis. It is critical to sustain key principles from DDDM in all we do, especially reliance on the power of collaboration, use of antecedents in planning and execution, and accountability. In "Advanced Data Analysis," we employ a framework to remind us to address each of these issues when selecting from a wide variety of approaches in a data-driven environment in which questioning and positing hypotheses is the rule rather than the exception.

Data Systems Concerns

Question 19: *Can you suggest books or other resources for teacher leaders who are responsible for promoting data-driven decision making at the school level?*

Absolutely! Schmoker's *Results* (1999) and *Results Fieldbook* (2001) continue to offer exceptional insights into managing data. In addition, other authors, such as Guskey, Reeves, and Popham, offer excellent resources in educational leadership, as does The Leadership and Learning Center's *Holistic Accountability* (Reeves, 2002a) and *Accountability in Action*, 2d ed. (Reeves, 2004b). "It would also be advisable for any teacher leaders who are serious about making the data work for their schools to become fluent in the use of Excel and its many functions; they will assist you not only in crunching numbers, but also in analyzing to the third or fourth probe or "drill-down" levels.

Question 20: *How do we organize and track consistent data? Each year we add new data sources, such as STAR. Which do we keep and what do we eliminate?*

A very important part of the "Advanced Data Analysis" workshop is a section on managing the data calendar. This is no less critical for schools and classrooms than for the central office; all staff need a process to spread out important data points; reduce the crunch in December, April, June (or any other months that may be data bottlenecks); and ensure that data is verified, collected, examined, analyzed, evaluated, and acted upon, to improve decision making. This question raises a compelling concern that is also central to our workshop approach in "Advanced Data Analysis": How do we eliminate anything? What process(es) will allow us to routinely make good decisions about aggregating certain data and eliminating other data? Who has the authority to give permission to eliminate certain data points, and how can that be established within a comprehensive school system? For all of these concerns, a concise and helpful process is provided to all participants in "Advanced Data Analysis."

Concerns about DDDM for Instructional Improvement

Question 21: *What is the most effective way to correlate the successful strategies with the improvements? Are we as successful as we might be in determining our antecedents of success?*

In the new "Advanced Data Analysis" workshop, The Leadership and Learning Center takes great care to make sure the key principles from "Data-Driven Decision Making" are extended and refined. Key strategies that are highly correlated with effective teaching are aligned with these principles in such a way as to deepen participant application of both data-driven decision making and effective teaching strategies, while learning new tools to apply local data in their own districts, schools, and classrooms. An extensive "Hypothesis Matrix" provides each participant with a process to incorporate the principles of "Data-Driven Decision Making" with the most effective teaching strategies and apply data analysis to close the learning gap and improve student achievement for all with confidence. This matrix addresses the first half of your question by ensuring that participants include antecedents for success, collaboration, and accountability in each and every effort to address the needs revealed by thoughtful and focused data analysis. As educators, we seldom are as successful as we might be, but The Leadership and Learning Center offers practical tools that advance our efforts to a new level of precision, clarity, and focus in data analysis that works.

APPENDIX

Template for
Triangulation of Data

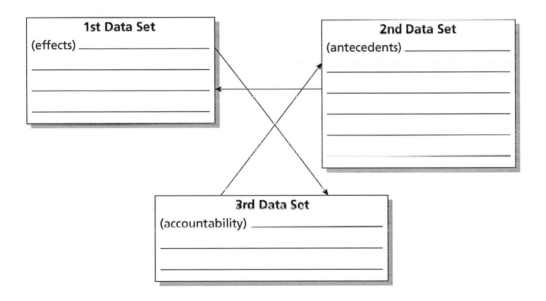

What do we **Know** from these data (patterns, trends, similarities, differences, outliers)?

_____

_____

_____

What do we **Want** to find out? (decide on purpose of analysis)

_____

_____

_____

195

What do we need to **Learn,** and how will we know we learned it? (choose analysis method)

_____

_____

_____

Purpose of Analysis	Analysis Method Selected	Tools

APPENDIX **D**

Template for Wagon-Wheel Tool for Data Analysis

Steps in Using Wagon Wheels

1. Assign key variables to each spoke on wheel (10).
2. Collect data across key variables.
3. Establish scale for each spoke, with highest performance on outer rim of circle. Label each individual spokes with its own scale.
4. Plot performance data along spokes, color-coding to distinguish units being compared (classrooms, schools, departments, grade levels, budgets, certification areas, etc.).
5. Connect lines for each unit if comparisons are made between units.
6. Identify the pattern of performance against selected performance standards.

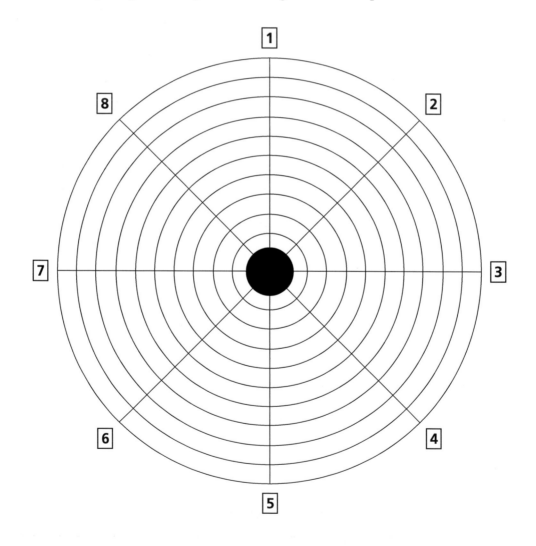

Wagon-Wheel Tool for Data Analysis

School: _____   Date: _____

Department/Team: _____

_____

Team Members: _____

_____

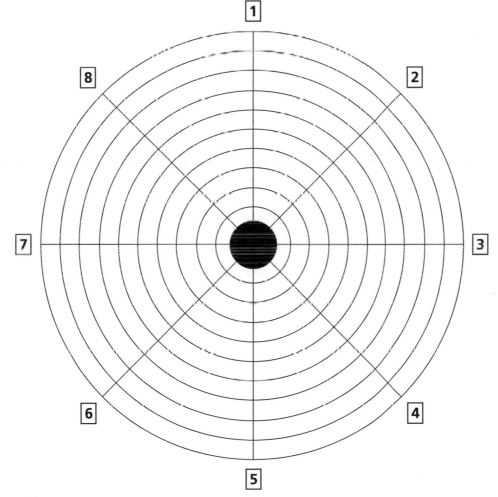

Variables:

1. _____   5. _____
2. _____   6. _____
3. _____   7. _____
4. _____   8. _____

Source: Adapted from Andersen & Fagerhaug (2000) with permission.

The Hishakawa Fishbone: A Cause-and-Effect Diagram

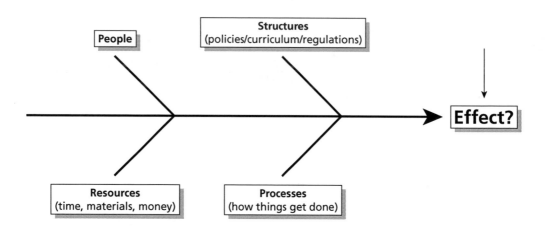

Tips for Cause–Effect Analyses

1. Brainstorm for possible causes of the effect or problem.
2. Assign possible causes to basic categories.
3. Use responses to "why?" questions as branches to causes.
4. Look for causes that appear repeatedly.
5. Reach consensus.
6. Gather data to determine the relative impact of causes.
7. Develop an action plan to address the cause at its root.

Listening System Template

School: Principal: Date: Email:

Types of Data	Parents	Teachers and Administrators	Staff	Students	Patrons	P	I	E	Rationale: Current Practice
Satisfaction Surveys									
What do we currently do with the data?									
Authority to act? (commit resources)									
Who?/When?									
How?									
Focus Groups, Interviews									
What do we currently do with the data?									
Authority to act? (commit resources)									
Who?/When?									
How?									
Website Comments									
What do we currently do with the data?									
Authority to act? (commit resources)									
Who?/When?									
How?									

Proposed = P   Introduced = I   Established = E

Guidelines for Listening Systems: Cyclical, predictable, public (open, transport), user-friendly

Critical Incident

Critical incident is an informal analysis tool that helps teams understand what the most troublesome symptoms in a problematic situation really are. It is possible that the most careful triangulation of data will still fail to reveal patterns that prevent schools and classrooms from moving ahead. Critical-incident analysis is fundamentally a group process to systematically and fairly articulate emerging or persistent problems that influence the quality of our efforts to improve student achievement. It is also a prequel for other tools, such as the Hishakawa Fishbone (cause and effect) or relations diagram.

Critical-incident analysis works like this:

1. Assemble a group of participant stakeholders, making sure that every department or grade level or classification of employee that may be affected by the problem or the challenge is included.

2. Ask each participant to respond in writing to one or two predefined questions with as many specifics as possible. Scaffold your request to elicit an incident that:

Was most difficult to handle or Repeats itself unnecessarily	Costs the most or Wastes the most time or effort
Causes the most problems in completing a *specific* assignment or project or Causes the school embarrassment	Requires the most rework or Inhibits student achievement

3. Select a set of questions that get at the crux of issues that have been resistant to change, that have been slow to improve relative to other district or school efforts, or that keep people from performing at their highest level.

4. Collect the responses and create an affinity chart on which responses are grouped by major categories and presented graphically for discussion.

5. Through consensus or use of a decisionmaking matrix, distill the responses down until you identify the most critical incident and use it as a starting point to identify possible causes and antecedents (using a Hishakawa Fishbone).

Critical-incident material is soft data, not unlike the need for narratives to supplement district or state accountability reports and give the "story behind the numbers" (Reeves, 2004b, pp. 152, 165). It has the capacity to cut through the fog that can cloud a particular challenge and it is an excellent opportunity to model transparency and a safe learning environment for all. It is recommended here as a fast-track tool to identify improvements that are relatively easy to implement, and to ensure that observations and perceptions are part of a comprehensive data system.

APPENDIX

A Data Road Map

A *data plan road map* is designed to reveal areas where improvement has been lacking or growth stagnant, and where efforts have failed to produce results. *Drive carefully!*

1. Intersections

1. _____

2. _____

3. _____

1. _____

2. _____

3. _____

> Identify at least three sets of data you will triangulate with your peers to make visible the invisible in your organization. Connect these intersections with arrows to indicate possible ways to triangulate the data.

1. _____

2. _____

3. _____

2. Data Driving Habits

To Change	To Increase	To Improve	To Create

3. Rearview-Mirror Effect

Headlights: Proactive Strategies Looking Forward

1. _____

   _____ (beginning __/__/200_)

2. _____

   _____ (beginning __/__/200_)

3. _____

   _____ (beginning __/__/200_)

4. _____

   _____ (beginning __/__/200_)

Canaries: Early Warning Signals for Interventions

Classroom	Start Date	School	Start Date	District	Start Date
1.		1.		1.	
2.		2.		2.	
3.		3.		3.	
4.		4.		4.	

4. Traffic Signals and Signs (Feedback Systems)

To Change	To Increase	To Improve	To Create
By __/__/200_	By __/__/200_	By __/__/200_	By __/__/200_

5. Use Your Digital Camera (User-Friendly Embedded Data)

Snapshot Data—Students	Frequency	Snapshot Data—Adults	Frequency

Snapshot Data—Administrative Structures	Frequency	Snapshot Data—Time and Opportunity	Frequency

6. Data in Action: Explicit Changes in DDDM System (Collection, Communication, Calendar)

The Data of Teaching: What Adults Do

To Change	To Increase	To Improve	To Create
By __/__/200_	By __/__/200_	By __/__/200_	By __/__/200_

The Data of Learning: Evidence of Thinking (Bloom's *Taxonomy*)

To Change	To Increase	To Improve	To Create
By __/__/200_	By __/__/200_	By __/__/200_	By __/__/200_

The Data of Improving: Doing What We Do Now, Only Better

To Change	To Increase	To Improve	To Create
By __/__/200_	By __/__/200_	By __/__/200_	By __/__/200_

The Data of Persuading

Trends to Establish	Patterns to Examine	Benchmarks to Achieve	Strengths to Celebrate
By __/__/200_	By __/__/200_	By __/__/200_	By __/__/200_

7. Building Your Superhighway (Leadership)

Strategies to Build Team Thinking	Strategies to Release Authority to Commit Resources	Strategies to Grant Permission to Stop

The Data Road Map

School: _____ School Year: _____

Data Team: _____

	Implementation Timeline		
	Start	Evaluate	Complete

Intersections

❏ Triangulation 1

❏ Triangulation 2

❏ Triangulation 3

Data Driving Habits

❏ To Change

❏ To Increase

❏ To Improve

❏ To Create

Rearview-Mirror Effect

❏ Improve the Headlights

❏ Canaries for the Classroom

❏ Canaries for the School

❏ Canaries for the System

Traffic Signals and Signs

❏ Feedback System Changes

❏ Listening System Changes

Detours and Road Closures

❏ Practices to Subtract

❏ Policies to Subtract

❏ Structures to Subtract

Use Your Digital Camera:
Catch the Scenery

❏ Student Data

❏ Adult Data

Use Your Digital Camera:
Catch the Scenery *(Continued)*

❑ Structure Data

❑ Time and Opportunity Data

Data in Action

❑ Teaching

❑ Learning

❑ Improving

❑ Persuading

Building Your Superhighway
(Leadership)

❑ Team Thinking

❑ Agility in Committing Resources

❑ Permission to Stop

Implementation Timeline *(Continued)*

Start	Evaluate	Complete

Summary: _____

_____

_____

_____

_____

_____

_____

Glossary

ANOVA   *analysis of variance;* a method for dividing the variance observed in experimental data into different parts, each part assignable to a known source, cause, or factor. It is a statistic created to explain statistical differences between representative samples based on central tendency deviations.

AYP   *adequate yearly progress;* term created for Title I schools to monitor improvement gains and extended in the No Child Left Behind Act of 2001 as a measure of improvement gains for all subgroups. Although states develop their own standards, this component serves as a linchpin of accountability in the landmark legislation.

BOE   *board of education;* the governing board for almost 15,000 school districts throughout the United States; referred to as *directors* and *trustees* in some states.

CEUs   *continuing education units.*

CRT   *criterion-referenced test;* a test that measures discrete knowledge and skills.

DDDM   *data-driven decision making.*

EOC assessments   *end-of-course assessments,* also known as *common assessments.*

ES   *elementary school.*

ESA   *English skills acquisition;* levels in acquiring proficiency in English.

ESL   *English as a second language.*

F ratio   part of the ANOVA statistical test. Named after Ronald Fischer, the inventor of the analysis, the F ratio divides the variance between each group by the variance within each group studied (V_b/V_w) to yield a ratio that is used to determine the significance level for the analysis.

FTE   *full-time equivalent;* an acronym usually reserved to discussion of employees or students.

GE   *grade equivalent;* indicates the year and month of school for which a student's score is typical. A GE of 6.2, for example, indicates that the student is achieving at a level typical of students who have completed the second month of grade 6 at the time the test was standardized. Interpret GEs with caution. A student in grade 3 may attain a GE of 6.2—this does not mean that the student is capable of doing sixth-grade work, only that the student is scoring well above average for grade 3.

HS   *high school.*

IQ   *intelligence quotient;* a scaled score with 100 representing the population average in terms of the ability to solve verbal, mathematical, and spatial problems.

ISD   *independent school district.*

KISS   *keep it short and simple;* great advice for just about everything.

KWL   a three-part summarizing reading strategy that has been employed across subjects and ages of learners: (1) what do I Know about a topic?, (2) what do I Want to learn about that topic?, and (3) what have I Learned about the topic?

MS   *middle school.*

NAEP   *National Assessment of Educational Progress;* a comprehensive assessment authorized by Congress to gather samples of student performance on standards in the United States for comparison purposes with students from other nations, track longitudinal trends, and monitor basic skills in core content areas.

NCE   *normal curve equivalent;* equal-interval scores used to compare achievement across subject areas over time. NCEs provide information that is more precise regarding raw score performance than the national percentile score, but absent subscale information, offer little to help in diagnosing student performance or designing interventions.

NCLB   the *No Child Left Behind Act of 2001,* Pub. L. No. 107-110 (2002).

NP   *national percentile;* a scaled score that indicates what percent of participants scored below the individual score reported. A common measure, the NP is often misinterpreted, as the percentile differences are not equal-interval in terms of raw score. NPs compare the achievement of students in a local group with that of students in the nation as a whole.

NRT   *norm-referenced test;* the traditional standardized test that measures students' performance against their peers rather than against standards or criteria.

p value   the value of probability that the results reflected chance differences or were differences between groups that indicated a significance attributed to the independent variables (causes of desired effects, antecedents). p values of less than .05 for given samples indicates that the likelihood that the differences were attributable to chance are less than 5 chances out of 100; hence, a p value or level of significance of .05 or .001 is usually predetermined in most educational research efforts as an acceptable level of certainty.

PDSA   *Plan–Do–Study–Act;* one form of a continuous improvement cycle.

r **value**   the product moment correlation coefficient or Pearson *r* that tells us how similar the rank orders of two different measures are. *r* values range from a perfect positive relationship of $+1.00$ to a perfect negative relationship of -1.00. Both are very unlikely, but could exist in rare circumstances such as the relationship between senior GPA and SAT scores or the negative relationship between grades and behavior referrals. Use of Pearson's *r* is very common, and scattergrams typically depict the outcome of *r* value calculations.

Rdg   *reading.*

SAT   *Scholastic Aptitude Test;* one of two major norm-referenced college entrance exams designed to sort and select students through rankings.

SFETT   *San Fernando Education Technology Team;* an instructional technology effort that has changed work habits dramatically and in doing so, increased graduation, college entrance, and access to employment in a low-income area of Los Angeles.

SIP   *school improvement plan.*

SMART   a proven approach to goal development, ensuring that goals are: specific, measurable, achievable, relevant, and timely. The Leadership and Learning Center adds the letter **B**, as in baseline, to yield B-SMART goals.

SS   *social studies.*

SWOT   *Strengths, Weaknesses, Opportunities, Threats;* an assessment method used to examine organizational environments and organizational health.

USD   *Unified School District;* a term used to connotate a K-12 or pK-12 school system in which elementary and secondary grades are operated by the same organization.

WISC-IV   the fourth iteration of the Wechsler Intelligence Scale for Children, a very popular and well-respected intelligence quotient (IQ) assessment for school-aged children.

Wrtg   *writing.*

References

Ainsworth, L. (2003). *"Unwrapping" the standards.* Englewood, CO: Lead + Learn Press.

Ainsworth, L., & Christinson, J. (2000). *Five easy steps to a balanced math program.* Englewood, CO: Lead + Learn Press.

Ainsworth, L., & Christinson, J. (1997). *Student-generated rubrics: An assessment model to help all students succeed.* Indianapolis, IN: Dale Seymour Publications.

Anderson, B., & Fagerhaug, T. (2000). *Root cause analysis: Simplified tools and techniques.* Milwaukee, WI: ASQ Quality Press.

Berliner, D. (1994). Expertise: The wonder of exemplary performances creating powerful thinking in teachers and students. In J. N. Mangieri & C. C. Block (Eds.), *Creating powerful thinking in teachers and students* (ch. 7). New York: Holt, Rinehart & Winston.

Bernhardt, V. (2000, Winter). New routes open when one type of data crosses another. *Journal of Staff Development, 21*(1), 33–36.

Calhoun, E. F. (1994). *How to use action research in the self-renewing school.* Alexandria, VA: ASCD.

Calkins, L. (1994). *The art of teaching writing.* Portsmouth, NH: Heinemann.

Carr, E., & Ogle, D. (1987). K-W-L Plus: A strategy for comprehension and summarization. *Journal of Reading, 30,* 626–631.

Collins, J. (2001). *Good to great.* New York: HarperCollins.

Costa, A., & Garmston, R. (1994). *Cognitive coaching: A foundation for renaissance schools.* Norwood, MA: Christopher-Gordon Publishers.

Covey, S. (1996). *The seven habits of highly effective people.* New York: Simon & Schuster.

Danielson, C. *Enhancing professional practice: A framework for teaching.* Alexandria, VA: ASCD, 1996.

Darling-Hammond, L. (1997). *The right to learn: A blueprint for creating schools that work.* San Francisco, CA: Jossey-Bass.

Deming, W. E. (2000). *The new economics for industry, government, education* (2d ed.). Cambridge, MA: MIT Press.

DuFour, R. (2003, Fall). "Collaboration lite" puts student achievement on a starvation diet. *Journal of Staff Development, 24*(4), 63–64.

Evans, R. (1996). *The human side of school change: Reform, resistance, and the real-life problems of innovation.* San Francisco, CA: Jossey-Bass.

Fredricks, J. A., Blumenfeld, P. B., & Paris, A. (2004, Spring). School engagement: Potential of the concept, state of the evidence. *Review of Educational Research, 74*(1), 59–109.

Graham, S., Harris, K. R., Fink-Chorzempa, B., & MacArthur, C. (2003, June). Primary grade teachers' instructional adaptations for struggling writers: A national survey. *Journal of Educational Psychology, 279.*

Heacox, D. (2002). *Differentiating instruction in the regular classroom.* Minneapolis, MN: Free Spirit Publishing.

Hord, S. M. (1997). Professional learning communities: What are they and why are they important? *Issues . . . about Change, 6*(1), 1–8.

Intrator, S. (2004, September). The engaged classroom. *Educational Leadership,* 20–26.

Kerlinger, F. N. (1986). *Foundations of behavioral research* (3d ed.). New York: Holt, Rinehart, & Winston.

Killion, J., & Bellamy, G. T. (2000, Winter). On the job: Data analysts focus school improvement efforts. *Journal of Staff Development, 21*(1), 27–31.

Langer, G. M., Colton, A. B., & Goff, L. S. (2003). *Collaborative analysis of student work.* Alexandria, VA: ASCD.

Leadership and Learning Center. (2004a). *Advanced data-driven decision making* (seminar). Englewood, CO: The Leadership and Learning Center.

Leadership and Learning Center. (2004b). *Data teams* (seminar). Englewood, CO: The Leadership and Learning Center.

Leadership and Learning Center. (2004c). *Making standards work* (seminar). Englewood, CO: The Leadership and Learning Center.

Leadership and Learning Center. (2003a). *Effective teaching strategies* (seminar). Englewood, CO: The Leadership and Learning Center.

Leadership and Learning Center. (2003b). *Making differentiated instruction work* (seminar). Englewood, CO: The Leadership and Learning Center.

Leadership and Learning Center. (2002a). *Data-driven decision making* (seminar). Englewood, CO: The Leadership and Learning Center.

Leadership and Learning Center. (2002b). *Writing excellence* (seminar). Englewood, CO: The Leadership and Learning Center.

Lyster, R. (1998). Recasts, repetition and ambiguity in L2 classroom discourse. *Studies in Second Language Acquisition, 20,* 51–81.

Mackey, A., Gass, S., & McDonough, K. (2000). How do learners perceive interactional feedback? *Studies in Second Language Acquisition, 22*, 471–497.

Marzano, R. J., Pickering, D. J., & Pollock, J. E. (2001a). *Classroom instruction that works: Research-based strategies for increasing student achievement.* Alexandria, VA: ASCD.

Marzano, R. J., Pickering, D. J., & Pollock, J. E. (2001b). *A handbook for classroom instruction that works.* Alexandria, VA: ASCD.

Merriam-Webster's Collegiate Dictionary (11th ed.). (2003). Springfield, MA: Merriam-Webster, Inc.

Miami Public Schools. (1999). Miami Dade County public schools district learning technology profile results: A triangulation of data collected through site visits, focus groups/interviews and surveys. Retrieved July 15, 2004, from http://ir.dadeschools.net/TechProfile/results.pdf

National Clearinghouse for Comprehensive School Reform. (2004). *Catalog of school reform models.* Available at http://www.nwrel.org/scpd/catalog/index.shtml

National Staff Development Council [NSDC]. (2001). *NSDC standards for staff development* (revised 2001). Available at http://www.nsdc.org/standards/index.cfm

Northwest Regional Education Laboratory [NREL]. (2001). *Data in a day: Listening to student voices. A self study toolkit.* Portland, OR: Author. [Also available at http://www.nwrel.org/scpd/scc/studentvoices/diad.shtml]

Olson, L. (2004, January 28). States train sights on school districts for interventions. *Education Week, 23*(20), 1, 21.

Popham, W. J. (2004). *Test better, teach better: The instructional role of assessment.* Alexandria, VA: ASCD.

Public Law Number 107-110. (2002). No Child Left Behind Act of 2001.

Quality Counts. (2004). Count me in: Special education in an era of standards. *Education Week, 23*(67), 124–157.

Raymond, M. E. (2003, December 3). *Track the relationship between teachers and their students.* Charlotte (NC) Observer/Hoover Institution.

Reeves, D. B. (2004a). *Accountability for learning.* Alexandria, VA: ASCD.

Reeves, D. B. (2004b). *Accountability in action* (2d ed.). Englewood, CO: Lead + Learn Press.

Reeves, D. B. (2004c). *Assessing educational leaders.* Thousand Oaks, CA: Corwin.

Reeves, D. B. (2004d). *The daily disciplines of leadership.* San Francisco, CA; Jossey-Bass.

Reeves, D. B. (2003e). *Making standards work* (3d ed.). Englewood, CO: Lead + Learn Press.

Reeves, D. B. (2002a). *Holistic accountability.* Thousand Oaks, CA: Corwin.

Report to the Commonwealth of Virginia. (2001). *Results: A triangulation of data collected in focus groups, site visits, and surveys.* Retrieved July 15, 2004 from http://www.pen.k12.va.us/VDOE/Technology/vastudy/vatcst5.pdf

Richardson, J. (2000, October/November). The numbers game: Measure progress by analyzing data. *Tools for Schools, 1*–2.

Sanders, W. L. (1998, December). Value-added assessment: A method for measuring the effects of the system, school and teacher on the rate of student academic progress. *The School Administrator* Web Edition, retrieved August 1, 2004 from http://www.aasa.org/publications/sa/1998_12/sanders.htm

Schlecty, P. (2000). *Shaking up the school house: How to support and sustain educational innovation.* San Francisco: Jossey-Bass.

Schmoker, M. (2001). *The results fieldbook: Practical strategies from dramatically improved schools.* Alexandria, VA: ASCD.

Schmoker, M. (1999). *Results: The key to continuous improvement in education* (2d ed.). Alexandria, VA: ASCD.

Senge, P. (2000). *Schools that learn.* New York: Doubleday.

Shaha, S. H., Lewis, V. K., O'Donnell, T. J., & Brown, D. H. (2004). An approach to verifying program impact on teachers and students. *Journal of Research in Professional Learning, 1,* 1–18.

Shipley, J. (2000). *Orientation to performance excellence* (2d ed.). Seminole, FLA: Jim Shipley & Associates.

Singham, M. (2003, April). The achievement gap: Myths and reality. *Phi Delta Kappan, 84*(8), 586–591.

Steiner, L. (2000). *A review of the research literature on scaling up in education: The problem of scaling-up in education.* Chicago, IL: North Central Regional Educational Laboratory.

Surowiecki, J. (2004). *The wisdom of crowds: Why the many are smarter than the few and how collective wisdom shapes business, economies, societies and nation.* New York: Doubleday.

Viadero, D. (2004, January 21). Achievement-gap study emphasizes better use of data. *Education Week, 23*(19): 9.

Wade, H. H. (2001). *Data inquiry and analysis for educational reform.* ERIC Digest 153-December. Eugene, OR: Clearinghouse on Educational Management, University of Oregon.

Wenglinsky, H. (2002, February 13). How schools matter: The link between teacher classroom practices and student academic performance. *Education Policy Analysis Archives, 10*(12). Retrieved July 3, 2004 from http://epaa.asu.edu/epaa/v10n12/

White, S. (2005). *Show me the proof!* Englewood, CO: Lead + Learn Press.

Index

Do you believe all students can succeed?

Can educators make a difference and produce results?

So much to do and so little time!

Since 1992, school districts and educational organizations seeking to improve student achievement have consulted with The Leadership and Learning Center (formerly Center for Performance Assessment). Educational leaders on five continents have collaboratively created customized solutions based on research and results. If you would like to know more about the services of The Leadership and Learning Center, to learn about success stories in every type of educational setting, to find out about the latest research, or to arrange a presentation by a Center consultant, please visit the Web site at *www.LeadandLearn.com* or contact:

LEAD AND LEARN
Making A Difference…Today

The Leadership and Learning Center

317 Inverness Way South, Suite 150 ▪ Englewood, Colorado 80112

+1.866.399.6019 ▪ Fax 303.504.9417

www.LeadandLearn.com